T0348706

ADVANCE PRAISE FOR *OUTSIDE IN, INSIDE OUT*

"Filled with practical wisdom and real-world examples."
DARREN YAWORSKY, CHIEF FINANCIAL OFFICER, PEOPLE CORPORATION
(A GOLDMAN SACHS COMPANY)

"I can tell you it drives success and has helped us grow our business
in North America."
MICK FITZPATRICK, MANAGING DIRECTOR NORTH AMERICA, MURPHY GROUP

"This book is a must-read for all strategy enthusiasts and novices alike.
Dr. Mortlock's significant experience in strategy is evident."
ROCKY VERMANI, SVP INNOVATION & SUSTAINABILITY, NOVA CHEMICALS

"Brilliantly distills theory and practice."
ALISTER COWAN, BOARD DIRECTOR, THE CHEMOURS COMPANY

"A masterful guide for navigating the complexities of modern business."
MARY MORAN, BOARD DIRECTOR, KUDOS INC.

"An essential read for anyone serious about staying ahead of the curve."
PATRICK LOR, MANAGING PARTNER & VENTURE CAPITALIST,
PANACHE VENTURES

"Discover Dr. Lance Mortlock's comprehensive, easy-to-digest
strategy guide in this exceptional book."
SEBASTIEN GENDRON, CO-FOUNDER & CEO, TRANSPOD INC.

"He has simplified the complexity of strategy development and execution."
PRAMOD JAIN, PRESIDENT & CEO, COMPUTER MODELLING GROUP LTD.

"Sure to become a go-to resource for strategic decision-makers everywhere."
ALICIA QUESNEL, MANAGING PARTNER, BD&P LAW

"Essential for anyone seeking to thrive in today's dynamic marketplace."
RANDY PETTIPAS, CEO, GLOBAL PUBLIC AFFAIRS

"This book will reshape the way you think about
strategy and execution success."
KAM SANDHAR, CHIEF FINANCIAL OFFICER, CENOVUS ENERGY

"A must-read for strategists, planners, and leaders searching
for ways to drive strategic impact and results."
DR. TRISTAN GOODMAN, CEO, EXPLORERS AND PRODUCERS
ASSOCIATION OF CANADA

"Breaks down complex strategic concepts into digestible, actionable steps."
MARK SCHOLZ, CEO, CANADIAN ASSOCIATION OF ENERGY CONTRACTORS

"This strategy book offers a vital approach to aid organizations
in reshaping the future."
KENDALL DILLING, CEO, PATHWAYS ALLIANCE

"The perfect approach to balancing the many competing needs
of successful strategies."
HUGUES JACQUEMIN, CEO, NORTHERN GRAPHITE

"Brilliantly written and immensely practical."
CLAUDIA D'ORAZIO, EVP HUMAN RESOURCES &
INFORMATION TECHNOLOGY, CENTERRA GOLD

"Provides actionable insights backed by one of
the most practical strategists I know."
ANNE MARIE TOUTANT, BOARD DIRECTOR, IAM GOLD

"Cuts through the noise with precision, practicality, and purpose."
CATHERINE MCLEOD-SELTZER, INDEPENDENT CHAIR,
KINROSS GOLD CORPORATION

"This book made me want to drop everything and
reassess how I am running my company."
AMANDA HALL, CEO & FOUNDER, SUMMIT NANOTECH

"Helps managers and leaders enhance their most important skill:
To think and act strategically."

GARY HART, PRESIDENT & CEO, ALTALINK
(A BERKSHIRE HATHAWAY COMPANY)

"A must-read for anyone looking to build strategic-thinking capacity."

SCOTT BALFOUR, PRESIDENT & CEO, EMERA INC.

"Its integrated insights are not just valuable—they're indispensable."

MARK POWESKA, PRESIDENT & CEO, ENMAX

"Provides a roadmap for turning strategic vision into reality."

DAVID LEBETER, PRESIDENT & CEO, HYDRO ONE LTD.

"A book leaders focused on reshaping their strategy and driving
transformative change cannot wait to buy."

GREG TWINNEY, CEO, GENERAL FUSION

"An indispensable resource for leaders at all levels."

MARK LITTLE, BOARD DIRECTOR, GENERAL FUSION

"A strategy masterpiece that demystifies the complexities
of strategic planning."

JASON RAKOCHY, CHIEF OPERATING OFFICER, EAVOR TECHNOLOGIES INC.

"It's not just a book; it's a beacon of clarity and inspiration."

GURSH BAL, CO-CEO & CO-FOUNDER, ZENO RENEWABLES

"Uses real-world examples of strategy to help leaders
elevate their game to the next level."

CHRIS LOPEZ, BOARD DIRECTOR, ALGONQUIN POWER & UTILITIES CORP.

"Cuts through the noise and provides clear, actionable guidance."

ROD GRAHAM, BOARD DIRECTOR, CALGARY MUNICIPAL LAND CORPORATION

To my wife, Elisabeth, and our daughters,
Penelope and Olivianne

DR. LANCE MORTLOCK

OUTSIDE

IN

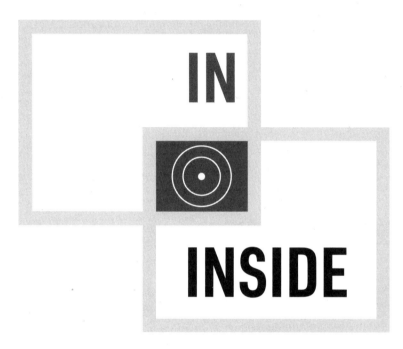

INSIDE

OUT

**UNLEASHING THE POWER OF BUSINESS STRATEGY
IN TIMES OF MARKET UNCERTAINTY**

Published by ECW Press
665 Gerrard Street East
Toronto, Ontario, Canada M4M 1Y2
416-694-3348 / info@ecwpress.com

Editor for the Press: Jennifer Smith
Copy editor: Jen Albert
Author photo: Mathieson & Hewitt Photographers
Cover design: Jess Albert

Note: These advance praise quotes reflect the personal endorsement of Dr. Lance Mortlock as an individual author, and not as a Partner of the Ernst & Young Canada firm he is employed by and represents.

LIBRARY AND ARCHIVES CANADA CATALOGUING IN PUBLICATION

Title: Outside in, inside out : unleashing the power of business strategy in times of market uncertainty / Dr. Lance Mortlock.

Names: Mortlock, Lance, author.

Description: Includes bibliographical references and index.

Identifiers: Canadiana (print) 20240498011 | Canadiana (ebook) 2024049802X

ISBN 978-1-77041-820-2 (hardcover)
ISBN 978-1-77852-382-3 (PDF)
ISBN 978-1-77852-381-6 (ePub)

Subjects: LCSH: Strategic planning. | LCSH: Leadership.

Classification: LCC HD30.28 .M67 2025 | DDC 658.4/012—dc23

This book is funded in part by the Government of Canada. *Ce livre est financé en partie par le gouvernement du Canada.*

PRINTED AND BOUND IN CANADA   PRINTING: FRIESENS   5   4   3   2   1

Purchase the print edition and receive the ebook free. For details, go to ecwpress.com/ebook.

CONTENTS

KEY CONVERGENCE 2: STRATEGIC CHOICES

PART 3: PREPARE FOR EXECUTION

PART 4: STRATEGY EXECUTION

TABLE OF FIGURES

INTRODUCTION

"Strategy is a plan, ploy, pattern, position and perspective."
—HENRY MINTZBERG, ACADEMIC & AUTHOR

BALANCING BOTH SIDES OF THE STRATEGY EQUATION

In the winter of 2021, I began working with a UK-based engineering and construction company that wanted to grow by expanding its reach into the United States. The US is a vast market with lots of lucrative opportunities for a firm that specializes in infrastructure for the energy, transportation, and natural resources sectors. But for that reason, there is also the potential for failure without a comprehensive strategic plan. I knew that the firm had previously embarked on an investment program in another jurisdiction that did not meet the long-term goals of the business, forcing it to withdraw from the market. That experience weighed heavily on the minds of senior executives. They couldn't afford a similar experience in the US.

There are many dozens of strategic options available to executives and, to add to the confusion, many of them contradict each other. In an increasingly complex and uncertain business environment, choosing the wrong one can be catastrophic. The approach I outline in this book is relatively straightforward, but that doesn't mean it's easy or that it doesn't require discipline.

Throughout my 25 years as a strategic advisor, I have seen many leaders fall into the trap of relying on only one-half of my approach, the *inside out*. They focus on what is easiest and most familiar, what they can best control—their internal performance, metrics, investment portfolio, and capabilities—and beyond that rely on gut and intuition, which is a big mistake. They fail to do the difficult work of combining inside-out with *outside-in* thinking. In the case of this engineering firm, I was working with leaders who understood what I was saying and agreed to work with me on balancing both sides of the equation to ensure they had a comprehensive understanding of both their strengths as a company and the realities of the US marketplace.

It wasn't just about determining where to enter the US market—for example, identifying areas that offered pipeline and infrastructure construction opportunities—but also the art of how to make that happen. To understand that we first took into consideration all of the firm's internal capabilities, including any risks relating to a growth strategy of this kind (inside out).

Next, we conducted a market assessment of the US (outside in) to evaluate the current trends and extent of opportunities there as well as the specific locations to focus on. This included insights into the potential customer base as well as the overall competitive landscape and determined a potential mergers-and-acquisitions approach, including potential joint venture opportunities.

This firm was willing to carefully evaluate the barriers of entry to the US, something not all clients are ready to do. The firm's evaluation included the following:

- Understanding what entering a mature market means in terms of entrenched players and geographic disbursement of contracts in the construction space
- Considering the specific resources necessary for the move to be successful
- Balancing reputational factors. We learned that clients most often award construction contracts to companies with a solid reputation for successfully completing large and complex projects
- Analyzing existing relationships and the role they play, which could make forming joint ventures challenging

Our next step in the outside-in analysis was using a scientific customer segmentation approach to truly comprehend the market. We created a customer "heatmap" to understand those customers critical to success if the firm wanted to enter the US market. We used three criteria:

- Planned projects and required capital
- The required services customers would expect
- Geographic location

Once potential customers had been identified, we drew up detailed profiles that reflected suitable acquisition or joint venture targets. We refined the data to reflect all other critical factors such as size, sector, and location. What made this strategic planning exercise unique was the rigour and discipline that my approach applied to the process. Nothing was subjective, which was critical for management given the magnitude of the decision and the cost of failure. Yet many firms grow impatient at one stage or another of this process. Traditional companies so often operate in silos, with different departments owning different puzzle pieces and no one willing, or able, to think about the complete picture with the pieces all slotted together.

By contrast, the leaders of this UK firm put the enterprise first, cutting across organizational boundaries and leveraging the four-part outside-in, inside-out blueprint I outline in this book. We combined many aspects of strategy development into an integrated, holistic approach that helped the company understand all of its strengths and weaknesses as well as the realities of the US marketplace it hoped to enter. In the end, management decided to execute its strategy by doing a full-on acquisition of an existing firm rather than a joint venture and, as of this writing, are busy integrating it into the legacy business.

HOW HAS STRATEGY EVOLVED?

Over the last 75 years, strategy has evolved in response to changes in the business environment, technological advances, globalization, and evolving social norms. Before 1960, strategy originated from a need to defeat enemies; for most of human history, it was primarily associated with the military. Strategic management did not formally exist in business until the 1960s.[1] The previous consensus on business management was that consistency was the critical condition for firm performance, and the only lines of thinking were management and policy.

In 1965, with the publication of his book *Corporate Strategy*, Igor Ansoff, a Russian-American mathematician and business manager, defined the term *strategy* for business and developed the Ansoff Matrix, a framework to plan strategies for growth. This inspired several other academic and business professionals to build their own frameworks, such as the LSAG model, which was the inspiration for the SWOT model of today. Around the same time, Harvard Business School professor Alfred Chandler pioneered strategy implementation through the "structure follows strategy" model instead of focusing on strategy formulation. Meanwhile, very large corporations emerged as dominant players in the economy. This led to the development of a corporate strategy which focused on the overall direction and scope of the organization. For example, General Electric and DuPont pioneered strategic planning to align their businesses with long-term goals.

The 1970s were about growth, diversification, and portfolio analysis. The Profit Impact of Marketing Strategies (PIMS) study, initially developed by senior managers at General Electric, showed a link between increased market share and profits, leading to creative growth strategies (horizontal integration, vertical integration, diversification, franchising, mergers and acquisitions, joint ventures, and organic growth).[2] The strategists in the 1970s also started to apply financial portfolio analysis to a company's operating divisions, treating each as a semi-independent profit centre. Several techniques were developed to analyze these corporate portfolios, including the famous BCG Matrix and Porter's Five Forces.

Decentralization was the focus of the 1980s. Strategic management theory led to elaborate management planning. It became the mainstream management theory when the 1970s models began to be criticized for centralizing all matters to head office staff, causing a decline in the ability to adapt to changing circumstances on site. This gave rise to Japanese-style business management, such as total quality management (TQM),[3] which is process-oriented, gradual in nature, long term, and people-focused. It emphasizes quality control and customer satisfaction.

By the late 20th century, there was a noticeable acceleration in the pace of societal change. In past generations, periods of change were always punctuated by stability, allowing society to assimilate and deal with change before the next disruption arrived. The shift to relentless modifications created both conflict and opportunity for strategists. There was a significant rise in innovative technologies, such as the World Wide Web, mobile phones, SMS messages, 3D graphics, lithium-ion batteries, and gene therapy and cloning, disrupting established industries and creating enormous opportunities for companies that leveraged them. The business strategy was reframed as an ongoing, never-ending, integrated process requiring continuous reassessment and reformation. The strategy must be partially deliberate and partially unplanned but always ready to adapt. Several strategists also began to use scenario planning techniques to deal with change.

In the 21st century, artificial intelligence (AI) is changing everything. AI is revolutionizing business strategies across various industries by automating tasks, enhancing customer experiences, and enabling data-driven decision-making. AI technologies like robotic process automation and natural language processing streamline workflows by handling repetitive tasks, allowing leaders to reduce operational costs and allocate human resources to more strategic roles. AI-powered chatbots and virtual assistants provide personalized customer support, while recommendation engines enhance customer experiences by suggesting relevant products or services. And AI enables businesses to make informed decisions through data analysis and predictive analytics, anticipating market trends and customer preferences. Its ability to foster innovation leads to new applications and solutions, such as personalized marketing and supply chain optimization, helping companies unlock new strategic revenue streams. Embracing AI as part of the strategy development process is essential for businesses to remain competitive in a rapidly evolving landscape, making AI not just a buzzword but a transformative force essential for future success.

WHY IS STRATEGY SO IMPORTANT?

Despite numerous books, articles, and, dare I say, consulting firms focused on strategy, according to a 2015 report by Cândido and Santos in the eminent *Journal of Management & Organization*, the success rate of strategy execution could be better. The failure percentages found in scientific studies range from as low as 7 percent to as high as 90 percent, with an average of about 50 percent.[4]

However, well-conceived strategy provides stability in crises, something customers, employees, and investors can depend on. Today's business environment is increasingly complex and dynamic, as technology, the geopolitical climate, and consumer demand have intersected for radical disruption in many industries. Operating in this uncertain and rapidly changing environment has made developing a successful strategy more pressing. Leaders unwilling to spend the time, treasury, and talent required to build an effective strategy are essentially sailors without a compass, entirely at the mercy of choppy seas.

A healthy strategy provides the business with a purpose, a clear set of values, and a distinct direction, or North Star, that can be communicated to the organization. As I wrote in an article in *CEOWORLD Magazine*, it helps define success and provides a roadmap for the organization to achieve it.[5] With clear goals, a company can develop action plans, measure performance, efficiently deploy resources, make quick and effective decisions, adapt to changing circumstances, and sustain success.

WHAT ARE THE COMMON PITFALLS OF STRATEGY?

In my experience, businesses can run into trouble in several ways, resulting in ineffective or unsuccessful strategies. Common pitfalls of strategy include the following:

- *Poor execution*: "Without a strategy, execution is aimless. Without execution, strategy is useless," said engineer and entrepreneur Morris Chang. A brilliant strategy may put you on the competitive map, but only solid execution keeps you there. Unfortunately, most companies struggle with implementation. They over-rely on structural changes, such as reorganization, to execute their strategies. Though structural change has its place, it produces only short-term gains.[6]
- *Lack of quantitative analysis*: In the modern business environment, making decisions based on gut instinct or intuition is no longer viable. Sufficient qualitative and, especially, quantitative analysis is required for effective strategic decision-making.
- *Creating strategy in a vacuum without the proper engagement*: To be effective, a strategy must consider the external environment. At the current rate of change, practices like trend analysis and scenario planning are essential to ensure your strategy is resilient in the face of uncertainty.

- *Confusing strategy and operational effectiveness*: Operational effectiveness means performing the same activities *better* than rivals. Companies can reap enormous benefits from operational effectiveness, as Japanese companies demonstrated in the 1970s and '80s through TQM and continuous improvement. However, these best practices are easily emulated and drive competitive convergence instead of a sustainable competitive advantage.
- *Not making the right strategic trade-offs*: The essence of strategy is choosing what *not* to do. A strategic position is only sustainable if trade-offs exist because some activities are incompatible. Trying to straddle different positions or be all things to all people leads to massive inefficiencies.[7]
- *Confusing practical and "blue-sky" strategy*: Blue sky refers to a creative thinking approach that removes all limitations and explores all options regardless of how unfeasible they may seem. It can be a useful exercise, but it can be easy to get lost in this line of thinking when developing a strategy. Final decisions on strategic objectives and initiatives must be rooted in practical thinking.
- *Not aligning on the timeframe*: Correctly timing strategic moves can determine success or failure. A good strategy must be long-term but not so long-term that it misses shorter-term opportunities. The sweet spot can vary among industries (for example, tech strategy will have a much shorter time horizon than real estate), but a general guideline is to refresh the corporate strategy every three to five years. However, companies must always be ready to adapt to unforeseen circumstances.
- *Not engaging or communicating with employees*: In most companies, strategies are subjected to rigorous quality tests from above, that is, by top management. Yet, the view from below— from the point of view of those working lower down in the organization—is equally important and too often neglected.[8]

Outside In, Inside Out addresses these common challenges and pitfalls. It brings a novel framework that supports a more integrated, engaged, and aligned strategy. One that properly balances outside-in with inside-out analysis and strategy development with execution.

A NEW STRATEGY DEVELOPMENT AND EXECUTION FRAMEWORK

For an article published by EY, "The DNA of the Chief Strategy Officer: Don't Wait for the Perfect Move before Making Your First Move," I created a framework to help executives in the development and execution of their strategy.[9] The chart shown in Figure 1 is an iteration of the original version conceived in my work with EY and is the culmination of 25-plus years as a strategist, delivering various components of the approach to clients worldwide and seeing the need to have something that puts it all together in an integrated way.

Strategy is complex and multifaceted. It involves different aspects of an organization working together seamlessly like a well-oiled machine. Past business books and thinking do not adequately address the integration that is essential to a successful strategy. The framework I propose emphasizes the interconnections between the various components of strategy development and execution, acting as a glue and weaving different perspectives cohesively.

Outside In, Inside Out interprets this framework, taking the thinking deeper beyond the EY article. It provides a how-to guide, including vital considerations, methods, frameworks, activities, insights, and case examples from around the world. Strategy is not easy, but my objective with this book is to develop more skilled leaders, strategists, planners, advisors, consultants, analysts, and board members. I want to help simplify concepts and increase consistency and integration of strategy in organizations. Done right, it's powerful stuff.

The framework is broken down into six simple sections: The four-part structure of the book corresponds to the four quadrants shown in Figure 1, where each bullet point relates to a specific chapter. There are also two stand-alone chapters (1 and 11) that introduce key convergences, critical points of fusion where several components of the process come together in relation to both strategy development (the left side of Figure 1, covered in Parts 1 and 2) and strategy execution (the right side of the diagram, covered in Parts 3 and 4). These key convergence points are at the crux of, and fundamental to, the integrative aspect of the outside-in, inside-out approach.

The framework's first key convergence, strategic planning (Chapter 1), is the essential starting point because both the strategy development and preparation-for-execution sections underpin the entire process.

Next, Part 1 covers the outside in (Chapters 2–5), providing an external lens for strategy development. What is happening in the marketplace, within

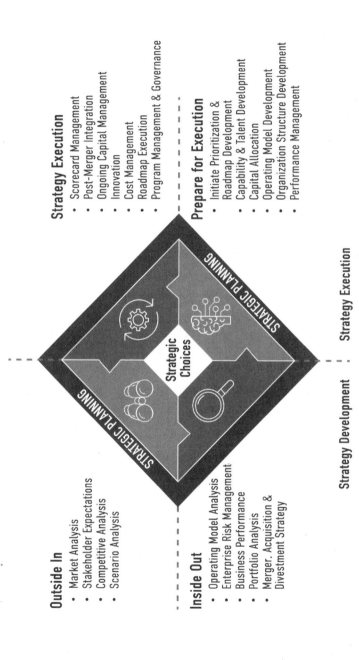

Strategy Execution

- Scorecard Management
- Post-Merger Integration
- Ongoing Capital Management
- Innovation
- Cost Management
- Roadmap Execution
- Program Management & Governance

Prepare for Execution

- Initiate Prioritization & Roadmap Development
- Capability & Talent Development
- Capital Allocation
- Operating Model Development
- Organization Structure Development
- Performance Management

Outside In

- Market Analysis
- Stakeholder Expectations
- Competitive Analysis
- Scenario Analysis

Inside Out

- Operating Model Analysis
- Enterprise Risk Management
- Business Performance
- Portfolio Analysis
- Merger, Acquisition & Divestment Strategy

Strategic Choices

STRATEGIC PLANNING

STRATEGIC PLANNING

Strategy Execution

Strategy Development

Figure 1: Strategy development & execution framework

9

your industry, and to your competitors? Through research, businesses can assess market conditions to better understand critical signals, trends, risks, and uncertainties. It's about looking outside the four walls of the organization.

Part 2 focuses on the inside out (Chapters 6–10). This is all about what is happening internally, within the organization. Performance assessments provide metrics on the business's results, how the organization's systems are performing to produce products and services, and its risk management, mergers and acquisitions (M&A) strategy, and overall growth. Inside out focuses on understanding where a company stands from a current state perspective.

What's essential and novel about this framework is the advantage of bringing these outside-in and inside-out sections together in a fusion of analysis and perspectives to inform a set of strategic choices. Chapter 11 is the second stand-alone chapter and explains this key convergence. This fourth section is where the rubber hits the road: investment choices are made; growth decisions, either organic or inorganic, are decided; and structural choices are agreed upon.

Once strategic choices are made, it's time for the organization to move to the right side of the framework, the execution component of the strategy equation. Part 3 lays the groundwork for execution in Chapters 12–16. Here, leaders must ensure the firm has the right initiatives prioritized, appropriate talent, enough capital, and an operating model and performance management system to drive success.

Lastly, the organization can execute the strategy (Part 4, Chapters 17–21). Strategy implementation needs to be monitored through scorecards as acquisitions get integrated and capital managed. Products and services are subject to continuous innovation as part of the ongoing strategy execution.

Strategy is neither linear nor straightforward; it takes numerous twists and turns, and many of this framework's components overlap. The lines between strategy development and execution can be blurred, so in some cases, I have combined components. For example, business performance, performance management, and scorecard management are integrated into Chapter 8 and straddle various sections of the model, the same with capital allocation and ongoing capital management in Chapter 14.

In this book, I will guide you through the various components of strategy development and execution shown in Figure 1. And importantly, how they fit together and are integrated will be explained. Ultimately, you'll better understand how to make your strategy future-ready in a complex and uncertain world.

KEY CONVERGENCE 1

STRATEGIC PLANNING

CHAPTER 1
STRATEGIC PLANNING

"Strategy without process is little more than a wish list."
—ROBERT FILEK, PARTNER AT ACCENTURE

THE FUTURE OF TRAVEL IS DIGITAL

US airlines carried 195 million more passengers in 2022 than in 2021, up 30 percent year-over-year. For the full year of 2022, January through December, US airlines carried 853 million passengers, up from 658 million in 2021 and 388 million in 2020.[10] I think it's fair to say that things have returned to normal post-COVID as people travel more now than ever.

I have worked with various North American airport authorities, and it's a fascinating business. Operating critical infrastructure that allows millions of people to travel safely worldwide means that everything must run well. I worked on a project with a major international airport to help design the strategic planning process end-to-end, from the upfront thinking on strategy to planning initiatives for execution, or "strategy execution," as we called it.

Early on, we realized the importance of designing the strategic planning process in a way that considered all the possible options to enhance efficiency, including numerous digital technology trends such as automated trash collection, biometrics, sensors on luggage carts to identify their locations, biogas shuttle buses, Facebook chatbots, cybersecurity, using Internet of Things (IoT) technologies for guest wayfinding, parking guidance systems, and traffic monitoring. Furthermore, other technology trends around customer engagement—like augmented and virtual reality for wayfinding, lounge/terminal entertainment, loyalty programs, digital signage, and payment apps—had to be factored in as well. It was all about the future possibilities to transform the customer experience. Given that Statista's Digital Market Outlook estimates that the global revenue of travel apps is expected to rise by 17 percent in 2023 over the previous year, amounting to nearly a whopping US$400 million, all this digital focus was not surprising.[11]

It was also crucial in the strategic planning stage to consider passenger trends, such as global travel volume growth. The International Air Transport Association (IATA) expects passenger volumes to double to 8.2 billion by 2037, representing a 3.5 percent compound annual growth in total passenger traffic.[12] It was also vital to understand younger travellers, who engage in technology when travelling in different ways (they use it more often, are quick to adopt new technologies, like augmented reality, expect information on demand, and generally tend to use contactless options for transactions throughout airports); have other travel priorities (they expect more engagement through their mobile applications, such as shopping promotions, everywhere, including in airports); and use various communication media. These are all fundamental factors when considering the airport experience; personalized travel is becoming more critical. Cargo trends, including blockchain tracking, warehouse automation, and unmanned freight drones, were necessary considerations for a significant logistics hub.

The strategic planning process we developed leveraged concepts from American psychologist Joy Guilford, which include expanded thinking outside the box of what we already know, de-emphasizing convergent thinking (focusing on a route to one familiar solution) in favour of divergent thinking (finding new, unexpected ideas by exploring many potential avenues, often using free-association thinking).[13]

It was also essential to develop a process that cascaded down into the organization. The research and planning team plays a role in identifying market trends, risks, and uncertainties, but management makes choices. Once those choices were made, the airport needed a process to ensure initiatives were identified and employees executed them. This annual cycle was created with enough flexibility to enable break-in work but enough structure to ensure people understood the parameters of what they needed to do, both when and with whom.

What I liked about what we did with the airport was that the upfront outside-in analysis was future-focused and a little uncomfortable. It challenged the status quo and helped leaders consider what they could, and should, be doing. The end-to-end process we developed was also simple, easy to understand, integrated, and considered the timing of critical milestones like board meetings. It also explained how the strategic plan translated to more detailed planning efforts like the annual business plan, budget, forecast, and performance management process.

Since we finished our work, this North American airport has seen record passenger numbers through its terminals in 2023. It is poised for liftoff growth in the coming years.

It can be said that, done right, the strategic planning process needs to underpin various strategy-related development and execution activities. It acts as the glue that holds everything together, aligned, and integrated. Drawing from examples as diverse as Starbucks, start-up eyewear company Warby Parker, and the US military, this chapter outlines a progressive, integrative step-by-step approach to strategic planning for a risky and uncertain future.

◆ ◆ ◆

WHAT IS STRATEGIC PLANNING?

According to the Business Development Bank of Canada (BDC), every company needs a strategic plan to know where it's headed, prepare for change, and build a strong, aligned team. A strategic plan defines who you are as a business and lists concrete actions to achieve your goals. When the unexpected occurs, a strategic plan helps your business survive and find new opportunities while staying true to your values and mission.[14]

From a context perspective, strategic planning underpins both the development and execution of strategy. It is a key convergence point that involves the strategic planning process and the strategic plan itself, which together aid in integrating the various components of the strategy. The importance of strategic planning cuts across organizational size and industry. The strategy, strategic plan, and business plan work in tandem, with the big-picture strategy broken into discrete tactical plans that people throughout the organization can understand.

Strategic planning defines the organization's overarching direction, setting a clear mandate that outlines what the organization wants to be and how to achieve it. The plan establishes a course of action that balances the organization's immediate needs with the longer-term outlook. It requires setting the strategic direction, scenario testing, examining capital and resource allocation, integrating the long-range business plan, and setting targets. Catherine Cote at Harvard Business School says, "Strategic planning is the ongoing organizational process of using available knowledge to document a business's intended direction. This process prioritizes efforts, effectively allocates resources, aligns shareholders and employees, and ensures the organizational goals are backed by data and sound reasoning."[15]

Benchmarking experts at Gartner, Inc., a technological research and consulting firm, define strategic planning as how the enterprise will realize its strategic ambitions in the mid-term. Too often, strategic plans are created and then forgotten until the next planning cycle begins. A well-crafted integrated strategic plan turns an enterprise strategy into a clear roadmap of initiatives, actions, and investments required to execute the strategy and meet business goals.[16] Strategic initiatives are the "how" of the business planning process—the set of projects and activities an organization will implement to reach its desired goals. Performance drivers are measurable factors that link the strategy and the critical performance metrics. Without translating the strategic direction and integrated business plan into a coherent set of strategic initiatives, organizations can end up with a proliferation of well-intentioned but ultimately ineffective and resource-intensive projects that don't reflect their purpose or objectives.

CASE STUDY
Strategic planning driving transformational success at Starbucks

One great example of a business that developed a solid strategic plan is the barista master Starbucks. In the early 2000s, Starbucks was experiencing a slowdown in growth and faced increased competition from small local coffee shops and larger chain stores. In response, the company developed a comprehensive strategic plan focused on bringing together several key areas.[17]

First, Starbucks recognized the need to differentiate itself from competitors by offering a more upscale experience. If customers were going to be paying $5.95 for a Pumpkin Spice Frappuccino, it needed to be good. To achieve this, they began remodelling stores to create a more sophisticated ambience. They introduced new menu options, such as premium teas and food items.

Second, Starbucks identified the need to expand its customer base beyond its traditional core of affluent urban consumers. To accomplish this, they launched a series of initiatives to attract new customers, such as introducing drive-thru locations and offering pre-packaged coffee for purchase in grocery stores.

Third, Starbucks recognized the importance of international expansion as a growth opportunity. The company opened stores in new global markets, such as China and India, adapting its menu and design to local preferences.

Starbucks poured vast sums of money into technology, marketing, and employee training to implement this strategic plan. Furthermore, as Starbucks chairman Howard Schultz once said, "You have to have 100% belief in your core reason for being."[18] It was successful; Starbucks saw a significant increase in sales and profits in the following years. Starbucks had revenue of $36.53 billion in the 12 months ending March 31, 2024, with 7.45 percent growth year-over-year.[19] This example demonstrates the importance of developing a comprehensive strategic plan with actionable strategic initiatives to address critical business areas and of investing in the necessary resources.

HOW TO APPROACH STRATEGIC PLANNING

Integrated planning process and levels

It might seem obvious, but integrated planning, by its very nature, helps to enhance integration across an organization. While communication and participation within planning processes in general are perceived to have an integrative effect, the authors of a 2009 article in the *Journal of Management Studies*, from Aston University in Birmingham, argue that these effects are unlikely to arise simply from bringing people together.[20] They claim that integration is everything and explain how strategic planning can deliver strategic integration within organizations. Planning occurs at different levels with increasing detail, much like a pyramid. Figure 2 depicts how the overarching business strategy cascades to the strategic and business plans and influences the performance management cycles throughout the enterprise. Tight integration and flexibility at the different levels are vital in this process.

It starts with the business strategy that sets the direction for the company, including how the organization will stand out in the marketplace and the specific areas that will drive the strategy's focus. The business strategy informs the strategic plan, which might be revisited only once every few years. The strategic plan articulates the details, including strategic targets that are financial and operational. Business plans, sometimes called operating plans, flow from the strategic plan and are the basis for defining business unit performance targets and initiatives. These business plans, which in most organizations are created annually, are financially brought to life through the annual budget, which supports the implementation of the strategy and represents the money that can be spent.

Performance management drives the performance cycle of action, change, and results (performance loop), and the forecast helps assess performance in delivering against the business plan and budget. Done well, integrated planning maintains alignment from the business strategy to the performance management cycle.

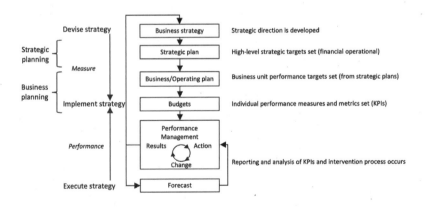

Figure 2: Integrated planning process

CASE STUDY
Managing complexity with integrated planning in the United States military

The United States military is a highly effective and efficient fighting machine that can strategically plan and execute a mission in any corner of the planet. You might ask, are business and military strategic planning techniques at all similar? To address this question, I spent time with General David Petraeus, now retired, who commanded coalition forces in Iraq and was the former director of the Central Intelligence Agency.

The general explains how, in dealing with uncertainty, the US military develops plans at multiple levels, each nested within the other. There is a clear separation between running current operations and planning future ones, but the role of the planning team is to coordinate and leverage expertise from the working groups in an integrated way. Petraeus adds, "Tactical have to be nested within the operational and the operations within the strategic, with constant efforts to keep everything synched and aligned."

A well-developed strategic plan in business also includes tightly integrated components of the business management cycle, including the strategy and long-term plan, the annual plan, business reporting and analysis from the front lines, budgets, and the forecast. Integrating these subsystems makes each component work in concert with the others to tell a consistent story.[21]

Success at different levels of planning reflects management's appreciation that attention to the business strategy and strategic plan is different from the budget and forecast. The budget and forecast must be rigorously focused on current conditions while the business strategy and strategic plan focus on future options and flexibility. Combining both as part of the integrated planning process drives impact.

Overall, integrated planning at different levels helps ensure that an organization's activities align with its overall strategy, goals, and objectives. It also helps to identify potential risks and opportunities and ensures that resources are allocated efficiently to achieve the desired outcomes.

Lower down the organization's food chain, strategic planning makes the strategy relevant to management, preparing their minds for necessary adaptations during the implementation stage. "Strategy, conceived as a shared framework in the minds of all strategists, is a strong glue that can align the organization around a chief purpose."[22]

Strategic growth options through planning horizons

Defining the horizon is critical when thinking about the strategic plan. Categorizing the goals into three different revenue horizons helps ensure businesses consistently balance the focus between the needs of today (Horizon 1), the future state of the business (Horizon 3), and the steps required to get there (Horizon 2). The definitions of the three horizons are as follows:

- *Horizon 1: Maintain and defend core business*: The most immediate revenue-making activity will be Horizon 1. It can be mapped by identifying a company's most significant assets. If you were a retailer, this would include the daily goals of selling, marketing, and serving your product/customers. Your goals in Horizon 1 will improve margins and existing processes, lower costs, and keep the cash coming in.
- *Horizon 2: Nurture emerging business*: There may be an initial cost associated with Horizon 2 activities. However, these investments should provide fairly reliable returns based on their extension of the current proven business model. Examples could include launching new product lines and expanding your business geographically or into new markets. It can be considered the bridge between Horizon 1 and Horizon 3.
- *Horizon 3: Create genuinely new business*: These innovative ideas, leading to new products and services to replace obsolete existing ones, may be unproven and potentially unprofitable for a significant period. This would encompass research projects, pilot programs, or new revenue lines requiring a significant upfront investment.

Mistakes can be disastrous. In 2009, Motorola tried to create a new business: marketing luxury cell phones. However, due to a strategic planning failure, investing in this kind of technology and market caused Motorola to lose millions. With a focus on Horizon 1, and only aspects of Horizon 2, their phones' interface was seen as clunky compared to its rivals. They failed to embrace Horizon 3 and the 3G technology that was innovative at the time, and their smartphones dithered between Linux- and Windows-based operating systems.

A merger was also the cause of a strategic planning failure at eBay. In 2005, eBay merged with Skype, thinking it would enhance and defend its core business. But the values and systems of the two firms needed to be better integrated. In 2009, when eBay reversed the merger, it had already experienced significant decreases in stock value.

As a final example, in 2011, the telecommunications giant Cisco was merging its Umi consumer TelePresence system with its business TelePresence operations and announced it was jettisoning several new products, including a flip video camera and Eos media. Some analysts believed that closing the doors on the Flip Video camera was a mistake, and that from a Horizon 1 perspective Cisco should have defended and maintained the business, or at the very least the technology should have been retained for broader application. The lack of strategic planning leadership cost more than 6,500 employees their jobs and hurt the company's financial performance.[23]

Taking your eye off the big picture to focus on just one of the three horizons can jeopardize, or at least severely hurt, your enterprise overall. As a key convergence point, integrated strategic planning considers all aspects of your business, bringing them together and balancing priorities and resources to ensure better decision-making and increase the likelihood of better performance outcomes.

CASE STUDY
Seeing new business models with strategic planning at Warby Parker

In terms of creating a new business, a company that developed a robust strategic plan is New York-based Warby Parker. This start-up eyewear company, founded in 2010, planned to disrupt the traditional eyewear industry by offering stylish and affordable glasses, using technology to provide a seamless customer experience.

Through outside-in analysis, Warby Parker recognized that the conventional eyewear industry relied heavily on a complex supply chain that added high costs to the final product. To offer more affordable glasses, they designed their operations from the inside out to offer a direct-to-consumer model that cut out the intermediaries and allowed the company to provide glasses at a fraction of the cost of traditional brands. The company started as an online-only retailer. Seeing the importance of providing an omnichannel experience for customers, they began opening brick-and-mortar stores called Guideshops where customers could try on glasses and receive styling advice from Warby Parker's trained employees. The company also developed a program that allowed customers to try on glasses at home before purchasing.

Warby Parker's leaders also looked into the future and recognized that social responsibility was becoming increasingly meaningful to consumers. So the company developed a strategy emphasizing its commitment to sustainability and giving back. It adopted environmentally friendly practices in its supply chain and production processes and established a program that provided free glasses to people in need for every pair of glasses purchased.

Finally, Warby Parker provided stellar customer service using technology to create a seamless experience. The company invested heavily in customer service training for its employees. It developed a technology platform that allowed customers to easily purchase glasses, track their orders, and receive personalized recommendations.

By creating a comprehensive, integrated strategic plan that focused on seeing the disruptive new business models—omnichannel retail, social responsibility, and technology—Warby Parker was able to carve out a niche in the highly competitive eyewear industry and become a successful, highly-regarded brand.[24] The company now boasts 26 million active customers, 3,000 total employees, and 190 storefronts.[25]

The annual business planning cycle

University of Toronto's Roger Martin claimed that while all executives know that strategy is essential, almost all find it frightening because it forces them to confront a future at which they can only guess. Worse, choosing a strategy entails making decisions that explicitly cut off other possibilities and options. An executive may fear that getting those decisions wrong will wreck their career.

The natural reaction is to make the challenge less daunting by turning it into a problem that can be solved with tried and tested tools. That nearly always means spending weeks or even months on an annual process that is disconnected from any rigorous outside-in or inside-out analysis, preparing a comprehensive plan for how the company will invest in existing and new assets and capabilities to achieve a target—an increased market share for existing products or services or a share in some new ones—but essentially focusing on the status quo. By the end of the annual process, everyone feels much less frightened.

That may be an excellent way to cope with the fear of the unknown, but fear and discomfort are essential to strategy-making. The objective of integrated strategic planning is not just to eliminate risk but to increase the odds of success. A good strategy results from a simple fit-for-purpose process of thinking through what it would take to achieve your goals, then assessing whether it's realistic to try.[26] At that point, the annual planning calendar can be put to good use to help make the strategic vision a reality, but that regular planning cycle should not be the tail that wags the big dog of strategy formulation and execution.

In any organization, various stakeholders must develop and execute the strategic plan. Communicating the complexities of the different integrated elements to management at all levels is critical. The planning calendar, created with care and balance (careful not to overdo it), effectively shows everyone how the different parts come together.

An annual planning calendar involves activities that help an organization align its resource and priorities with its overall strategic vision, such as budgeting, forecasting, and performance management. Furthermore, it includes important dates, such as the start of the fiscal year, key planning milestones, and deadlines for submitting budgets, forecasts, and other planning documents. The annual planning calendar is essential for the following reasons:

- *Sets direction*: Helps an organization set its direction for the upcoming year. This process allows the organization to review its current strategies, identify areas for improvement, and develop new goals and objectives to help achieve its long-term vision.
- *Provides focus*: Ensures that everyone in the organization is focused on the same goals and objectives. By setting priorities and aligning resources, the organization can ensure that all activities are aligned with its overall strategic direction.
- *Supports decision-making*: Provides vital information necessary for informed decision-making. For example, budget forecasts can help allocate resources, while performance plans can help managers identify improvement areas.

- *Ensures accountability*: By setting clear goals and objectives and monitoring progress throughout the year, managers can ensure that employees meet their targets and that resources are used effectively.
- *Provides structure*: A clear structure and timeline for the planning process ensure that all necessary steps are taken promptly and help avoid last-minute rushes or oversights.
- *Improves communication*: An integrated planning process ensures all the teams involved in the planning are on the same page and everyone understands their roles and responsibilities. Researchers have found that visualization should not just be seen as an attractive way to communicate strategic planning process outcomes and monitor their progress but as a powerful tool that can enable strategizing as a joint managerial practice.[27]
- *Helps manage resources*: By identifying key milestones and deadlines, managers can allocate resources to ensure everyone has what they need to complete their tasks on time.
- *Facilitates continuous improvement*: Helps organizations continually review and refine their planning process. With each planning cycle, managers can identify areas for improvement and make changes to the process to make it more effective.

In summary, the annual planning calendar is a necessary process that helps organizations align their resources and activities with their strategic goals and objectives, providing direction, focus, and accountability for achieving desired outcomes.

◆ ◆ ◆

CONSIDERATIONS

According to an article in *Chief Executive* magazine, failure rates of strategic plans are astronomical; research indicates that only 20 percent of strategic plans succeed.[28] An organization's leadership must be thoughtful about its strategic planning process to ensure that it is an enabler, not a barrier, to success. The method also has to allow for flexibility through the year so a firm can quickly change direction based on market context. Effective strategic planning processes should consider the following:

- *Challenge the status quo*: We live in highly uncertain times, and to succeed, as I said along with my colleague Dr. Mauricio Zelaya in a *Chief Executive* magazine article, we need bolder strategic plans.[29] Business leaders should challenge the organization and define ways to take it to a new level of performance beyond the current state. The strategic plan should constantly stimulate dialogue and sometimes action. Great strategists—and great business leaders—have to learn the "art of questioning."

- *Integrate the internal and external*: Integrating external research (outside in) and current state internal assessment (inside out) is vital. Different areas of internal responsibility, like enterprise risk management, corporate development, HR, and portfolio management, must be integrated into a coherent story with the external context, such as customer needs, future scenarios, and market trends. There is a critical role for the strategic plan to help cut across organizational silos internally and externally, serving as a key point of convergence for the entire enterprise.

- *Consider disruptive forces*: Articulate the external disruptions that the organization needs to be mindful of and help it face the current facts squarely, whatever they are. These could be supply-chain, digital, or broader geopolitical disruptions like war or an election, which could have game-changing impacts on a business.

- *Be future-focused*: The short-term reality for organizations is paying attention to immediate conditions, the "now," through current state analysis. Still, the strategic plan must also consider longer-term, future-focused aspects, including the "next." Success comes from a mix of both as part of the strategic plan. Multiple time horizons should be considered.

- *Balance the qualitative and quantitative*: Include sufficient qualitative and quantitative analyses within the strategic plan. It's important not to overanalyze, but certain aspects must be grounded in facts, figures, and financials. A firm must have the right balance of detail with supporting financials, but also be able to tell an engaging story.

- *Balance structure and flexibility*: A strategic plan must be structured but also provide room for agility because markets, as well as the execution of the strategy, are seldom linear. Things change all the time and need room for break-in strategic initiatives. One study by researchers at the University of Mississippi found that firms with planning flexibility tended to be more innovative, driving better performance.[30]
- *Be okay with ambiguity*: You don't need all the answers. Good strategic plans should make the leadership team uncomfortable by articulating risk and uncertainty, since change is constant. It's important to be able to wallow in the ambiguity.
- *Include execution*: Developing a fantastic strategic planning process is only half the challenge. The other half—translating the strategy into results through action and execution—can be even more challenging, especially when the new strategy involves moving outside the core.
- *Manage the stakeholders*: The strategic planning cycle and process need to be aligned and integrated with the board while recognizing that the CEO owns the strategy and should develop it with input from the board. Involving the board just enough through the process is vital to success—nose in, fingers out, as Jim Brown said in his book *The Imperfect Board Member: Discovering the Seven Disciplines of Governance Excellence*.[31]
- *Allow for frequent collaboration and communication*: Offer ways to bring different teams together to chart a cohesive plan for the future. With support from the chief strategy officer (CSO), the strategic planning team plays a vital role as a facilitator of decision-making across levels and functions.[32]
- *Integrate risk management*: Effective strategic plans integrate risks through working with the chief risk officer. Avoid the temptation to run the strategic planning process without enterprise risk management involved every step of the way.

PART 1

OUTSIDE IN

CHAPTER 2
MARKET ANALYSIS

"Monitoring market indicators is like being a doctor who regularly checks a patient's vital signs. It helps you detect early warning signals of potential problems and opportunities so you can make informed decisions before it's too late."

—SUZE ORMAN, FINANCIAL EXPERT & TV PERSONALITY

THE RED DRAGON DISRUPTS GLOBAL MANUFACTURING

A kitchen makes a house a home. Across North America, demand for quartz countertops for kitchens and bathrooms has increased dramatically in recent years. Given this growing demand and one of my North American client's existing quartz mines, certain key individuals in the company felt constructing a multimillion-dollar manufacturing plant was an exciting investment that should be pursued; others were unsure.

The company required information on the countertop market's attractiveness to make what would be a game-changing decision that could turn out well or prove disastrous. So, the team and I set about completing an in-depth analysis of whether the growth in demand for quartz countertops was strong enough to justify a huge investment to become a quartz slab manufacturer. The focus was to assess and identify insights into market conditions, recent and expected changes in supply and demand, competition (including the threat of low-cost products entering the market), pricing forecasts and scenario analysis, and alternative uses for raw quartz.

As the work started, the research included information-gathering conversations with numerous fabricators (potential customers), competitors, raw-quartz suppliers, and equipment manufacturers. The team wanted to get a complete understanding of the market dynamics from all angles.

Through the detailed assessment, we initially found that demand for quartz in the US and Canada would grow from 52.7 million square feet in 2012 to 96.2 million square feet in 2022. However, supply was expected to grow much faster over the same period. This finding was crucial because it meant that quartz prices were at serious risk of plummeting. While at the time prices seemed strong and were expected to increase for a couple of years, the team found that if Chinese-made products overcame perceived quality differences and penetrated the market, prices were expected to drop. It was also found that competition was fierce through effective marketing from established suppliers, and Chinese imports acted as the low-cost challenger.

The research concluded that fabricators were not bound to supply agreements, and quality and selection were often not differentiators—all brands had them—so price and availability were what primarily influenced demand for quartz products. Furthermore, Chinese products cost about a third of local products, and many manufacturers believed the market is already saturated.

In the end, while not popular with management, the outside-in market study recommended that the company refrain from investing in a new manufacturing plant, which the CEO agreed to. I recall meeting the CEO almost 10 years later at an EY-hosted cocktail party in Toronto. She remembered me immediately, and as we got reintroduced, she said that I was "the guy who saved her and her family putting $50 million at risk during unfavourable market conditions."

As we fast forward to 2024, it's clear that the red dragon has not been contained. The total production value of China's manufacturing industry has ranked first globally for 11 consecutive years.[33] In my client's marketplace, there is an overabundance of product and Chinese firms now offer cheaper high-quality alternatives, so prices have come under tremendous pressure.

This quartz mining and manufacturing example demonstrates the power of making decisions based on facts and data rather than gut and intuition. This chapter outlines the first element of outside-in analysis, to align a strategic plan with the most effective market analysis approaches (the Ansoff Matrix, PESTEL analysis, and more) for Industry 4.0, the Fourth Industrial Revolution.

◆ ◆ ◆

WHAT IS MARKET ANALYSIS?

In a rapidly changing world, it can be tempting to rely on gut feeling or intuition to make a quick decision in a critical moment rather than committing the necessary time and energy to gather and analyze data from an unbiased perspective. But I've found that solely gathering opinions and information from within an organization is ineffective; there is a need for new ideas and perspectives, or else groupthink may end up winning out. Market analysis addresses these issues by analyzing unbiased outside-in information and data.

CASE STUDY
Market study challenges at retail giant Target led to expansion failure

It's hard to believe that retailing powerhouse Target skipped market analysis when it launched its brand in Canada. The company's leaders banked on name recognition to drive customer traffic. After buying the leases of a defunct discount chain in Canada in 2013, Target quickly opened 124 Target stores within 10 months. The conglomerate spent millions on social media, radio, TV, and billboard marketing but didn't take the time to zero in on the specific Canadian consumer segment.

Customers in Canada knew the brand, but when they went into stores, they saw different products with higher prices than they'd seen in US stores, and distribution issues meant shelves were often empty. Target made the same mistakes as many retailers coming to Canada do, thinking that it is just like the US and neglecting to acknowledge that a tiny population in a massive country can create huge supply chain issues and costs.

In less than two years, Target closed its Canadian stores and declared the launch a failure.[34] It was estimated that about 17,000 employees lost their jobs and Target posted $5.4 billion in pretax losses for the quarter.[35] The lesson: do your market analysis. The time and cost of doing proper outside-in research is worth the investment every time.[36]

The world is awash in data. In fact, according to the latest estimates, 328 million terabytes of data are created each day.[37] The information required for an in-depth market analysis is out there, ready for the gathering. External market data allows us to test a set of hypotheses associated with a belief, and then push each premise to confirm or debunk the idea. The primary purpose of a market study is to use this outside-in research to enable unbiased, fact-based decision-making to resolve an organization's most complex strategic issues. A market penetration strategy can be created based on research, to describe a clear action plan that specifies how a company will reach customers and achieve a competitive advantage.

This data is analyzed to understand the current state of the market, identify potential opportunities, and anticipate challenges. The findings of an external market analysis are usually used to develop a marketing plan, establish pricing strategies, optimize product positioning, and identify potential areas for expansion. The study can also help companies identify potential partners, suppliers, and other stakeholders.

When integrating market studies and external market analysis into the strategy, I've discovered it's essential that people perceive this valuable information to be useful so it will be fully leveraged; in other words, highlighting the crucial insights from the outside-in market analysis helps ensure the market information gets used by the organization and not discarded. Overall, an external market analysis is vital for businesses to stay competitive and adapt to the constantly changing market environment.

HOW TO APPROACH MARKET ANALYSIS

Market analysis efficiency enabled by technology

In my experience, market studies typically start with defining the outside market to be analyzed. This includes determining the market study's scope and identifying potential focus areas. For example, which products, services, geographies, industries, and competitors interest you? Market studies can be extensive and conducted over many months, so clarity on the scope is essential to achieving the eventual objectives.

Once the scope is clear, detailed research can be performed. This is where primary and secondary research—both used in various fields, including business, social sciences, and market research—is essential.

Primary research involves collecting new and original data directly from the source or through surveys, experiments, observations, interviews, or focus groups. It answers specific research questions and gathers data relevant to a research project. Secondary research, on the other hand, involves analyzing existing data already collected by other sources—books, articles, reports, databases—from government agencies, research organizations, or academic journals.

Primary research is more time-consuming and expensive than secondary research, but it provides more accurate and specific information. Gathering primary data directly from stakeholders, like customers, is explored further in Chapter 3. Combining both methods results in the most effective and comprehensive strategy.

Following the completion of the research stage, the final step is to compile the market study and deliver the report. This is where the magic happens: after verifying all the content, including data sources, the material is packaged into a final report and delivered.

There are new tools companies can use to facilitate the process. Natural language processing (NLP) is an exciting area of artificial intelligence in which computers are taught how to speak, write, listen to, and interpret human language. Many investment firms are already beginning to use NLP to analyze external market data, including annual reports and news articles.[38]

Another exciting and related technology-enabled tool I've come to appreciate is sentiment analysis, a crucial skill for online reputation management (ORM), as it allows you to understand how your customers, competitors, and influencers feel about your brand, products, or services. It helps you monitor and measure your online mentions, reviews, ratings, social media posts, and other market feedback sources. You can automate and scale the process of extracting, analyzing, and responding to online feedback using NLP tools. Sentiment analysis can also help you by using NLP techniques to classify the polarity, emotion, and intention of text or speech. Popular and reputable tools include Google Cloud Natural Language API, IBM Watson Natural Language Understanding, and MonkeyLearn.[39]

Supporting strategy with market analysis insights

An outside-in market study can provide helpful data on which to base decisions and inform the strategy as it moves through the steps of strategy development.

I've found that market studies help provide industry-specific data on market trends, detailed market insights, and more specific information about products, services, and business models to help the company capture new market opportunities and make informed decisions about where to compete. Businesses can make informed decisions within the context of their own industry by staying up-to-date with the latest market dynamics. For example, uncovering industry segments that are more attractive and areas of high competition that you might want to avoid.

Market studies also help evaluate the external competitive positioning of the company's offerings and strategic assessment of where they stand relative to others. An external market analysis can help companies identify the strengths and weaknesses of their competitors. This information can be used to develop competitive strategies, including specific pricing models to maximize revenue and profitability. Chapter 4 explores competitive analysis in more detail.

Market studies can be performed on customers to better understand new customer needs, preferences, and willingness to pay. This supports a current- and target-state portfolio assessment by identifying where product gaps exist and what the future-state product portfolio should look like. By understanding customer needs, businesses can tailor their products and services to meet changing customer preferences and develop marketing strategies that resonate with their target audience. Again, more to come in Chapter 3 on stakeholder analysis.

CASE STUDY
Overlooking changing customer needs at Kodak collapses company

One unfortunate example of not addressing changing consumer preferences with market research is Kodak and its problems in acknowledging the advent of digital photography.

Kodak peaked in 1996 when the company had over two-thirds of global market share. Kodak's revenues reached nearly $16 billion; its stock exceeded $90 per share; and the company was worth over $31 billion. The Kodak brand was the fifth most valuable brand in the world. However, just a few years later, by the early 2000s, Kodak faced financial troubles, losing its market share to competitors like Canon and Sony. In 2012, decades of value had vanished, and the company filed for bankruptcy, unable to adapt to the changing industry landscape.

The sad thing is that Kodak did the necessary research, but it chose to save money instead of listening to what the outside-in market research revealed. Surprisingly, back in the 1980s, the company looked at factors such as the costs and flexibility of digital photography, and the study was right on point. Digital photography was indeed poised to become the next big thing. Kodak even developed a digital camera but shelved the project after realizing the camera would undermine film sales and its existing products.

So why did the company remain static? The problem was the foundation of Kodak's business model: traditional film photography. Due to heavy investment in paper and chemicals, the company felt it was unwise to pursue the market research results (and the imminent reality of digital photography). The lesson learned is that companies must be prepared for their market research insights to give answers they may not like. Businesses need to keep in mind that the purpose of their research is to serve their customers and provide consumer experiences, all while keeping pace with evolving consumer tastes and technologies. Otherwise, there is no point in conducting market research in the first place.[40]

Another use of market studies can be around alliances, partnerships, and acquisitions. They can provide data to help assess growth opportunities involving these different types of relationships. Shortlists are created once acquisition targets have been evaluated in terms of strengths, weaknesses, and degree of strategic and cultural fit. Chapter 10 provides more detail on strategy related to mergers, acquisitions, and divestments.

From a talent perspective, market studies can be performed on the labour market. This can be interesting in cases where a surge in labour is required for a large capital project. Understanding the potential labour market pool can offer valuable insights into where talent can be sourced, and market studies can help uncover different sources of labour, skills, and capabilities and highlight potential gaps that must be managed.

Finally, market analysis can help pinpoint potential risks and challenges, such as regulatory changes, economic shifts, or changes in consumer behaviour. This information can be used to develop contingency plans and risk management strategies to help companies mitigate these risks. It serves as a key input into the enterprise risk management approach, explained in Chapter 7.

In summary, more than 25 years as a strategic advisor have taught me that market research provides an in-depth understanding of internal and external factors impacting an organization in different areas, informing strategic choices and strategy development.

Ansoff's timeless matrix

The Ansoff Matrix, or Product-Market Expansion Grid, is a strategic planning tool that helps businesses analyze market growth strategies. Developed by Igor Ansoff in 1957, it can be used to decide how to grow before creating a market penetration strategy.

Specifically, the matrix describes four alternatives for expanding an organization in existing or new markets with existing or new products. The level of risk for the organization will vary depending on the quadrant where the organization places itself. The four alternatives are as follows:

- *Market Development*: Using existing products to enter new markets requires minimal product or service development. Targeting different customer segments, industrial buyers, and new areas, including foreign markets, can develop a market.
- *Market Penetration*: Finding new products for existing markets can be accomplished by decreasing prices, increasing promotion, enhancing the supply chain (i.e., distribution), acquiring a competitor, or minor product enhancements.
- *Diversification*: In this quadrant, the organization creates new products to enter new markets. Although it's a high-risk undertaking—the expense makes failure costly—consumers are always waiting for shiny new offerings, and competitors will be eager to create them. There are two types of diversification: 1) Related, where the organization enters an industry with similarities so that potential synergies can be accomplished. 2) Unrelated, where the organization decides to enter an entirely

new industry with no similarities, so there is greater uncertainty and risk.

- *Product Development*: New products can be developed by investing in research and development, acquiring new products or the right to produce them, or forming an alliance or partnership with another company.

CASE STUDY
Coca-Cola and new product launch missteps

Coke's prominence in the soft drink industry is well established. It's managed to sustain a kind of iconic cool and its consistently effective marketing campaigns have contributed to its loyal following. But despite its reputation for being "the Real Thing," even Coke isn't immune to making a misstep.[41]

When sales began to fall off in the 1970s and the first part of the 1980s, the company thought the taste was the cause of the decline.[42] The company's leaders leveraged Ansoff's Matrix to analyze and fix the situation, focusing on product development and creating a related product called "New Coke," a beverage sweeter than the original version of Coke and Pepsi. Taste tests indicated that success was on the horizon; outside-in market research showed that more people preferred the taste of New Coke to the original Coke and Pepsi.

However, as celebrated brand consultant Walter Landor once said, "Products are created in the factory, but brands are created in the mind." The new product's introduction had many flaws. Market researchers did not factor in the emotional impact Coke, with its specific design, had on people. They also did not explain to taste test subjects that they would eventually have to choose between drinking the original Coke and the New Coke. The disaster occurred when the company withdrew the original Coke from shelves to sell only New Coke. Rather than boosting sales, this move proved a colossal flop. Consumers missed their familiar beverage and were put off by a differently designed Coke announced as "New."

Even restoring the original Coke to sell alongside New Coke could not fix the issue. In time, New Coke disappeared. The marketing and sales team made a costly error and failed to factor in consumers' emotional connection to the brand's products.[43] Although Coca-Cola never shared how much exactly they lost, the *New York Times* claimed $30 million was spent on unwanted concentrate and $4 million on market testing.[44]

The Ansoff Matrix is a helpful tool for businesses because it provides a framework for analyzing markets and selecting growth strategies. It helps companies identify growth opportunities, align their resources and capabilities with their objectives, and give a clear understanding of growth options. As we can see from the Coke case study, this tool is not a silver bullet on its own. However, as one layer of analytics in a comprehensive, integrated strategic plan—and used in conjunction with other outside-in market study techniques—it provides a structured approach to evaluating growth strategies, which helps businesses minimize risk, encourage creative thinking about their options, and produce a visual tool that is easily shared and understood by different stakeholders.

PESTEL analysis

The world uncertainty index remained elevated in 2023,[45] and the best tool to cope with uncertainty is the PESTEL analysis. Invented over 50 years ago by Francis Aguilar, in part to help understand external uncertainty, it has proven timeless in its utility. It's one of the most effective methods I've used to structure research for external market trends and indicators.

A PESTEL analysis is a framework used in strategic planning and market analysis to evaluate the external factors that may impact an organization's performance. An acronym that stands for political, economic, sociocultural, technological, environmental, and legal, the PESTEL analysis helps businesses understand the macroenvironmental factors that affect their industry and the opportunities and threats they may face. By evaluating each aspect, companies can identify the risks and opportunities associated with each element and develop strategies to mitigate risks and capitalize on opportunities.

Here are the steps involved in performing a PESTEL analysis, a process that has helped me on different engagements:

1. *Define the objective*: The first step in performing a PESTEL analysis is to identify the specific business area that the analysis will focus on. This might be a new product or service, a market expansion, or a change in industry regulations, for example.

2. *Identify relevant factors*: Once the objective is defined, the next step is identifying the relevant factors for each PESTEL category. This involves gathering information on the political, economic, sociocultural, technological, environmental, and legal factors that may impact the objective.

3. *Evaluate each factor*: Once the relevant factors have been identified, the next step is to evaluate each one to determine its potential impact on the objective. This involves analyzing the trends, opportunities, and threats associated with each factor and assessing their potential impact on the business.

4. *Prioritize the factors*: Once each element has been evaluated, the next step is to prioritize them based on their potential impact on the objective. This involves identifying and focusing on the most significant factors in the analysis.

5. *Develop strategies*: The final step is to develop strategies to mitigate risks and capitalize on opportunities. This involves identifying actions that the business can take to address the most significant risk factors and achieve its overall strategic objective.

Looking to the future and the continuing proliferation of data, I think it's also important to consider ways to apply more advanced technology to perform PESTEL-type analysis. For example, CognitiveScale uses machine learning to analyze and predict market trends by analyzing data from various sources such as social media, news articles, and financial reports. The company uses NLP to extract insights from unstructured data and machine learning algorithms to identify patterns and trends. This helps businesses make informed decisions about their products and services.[46]

Overall, a PESTEL analysis provides a structured framework for evaluating the external factors that may impact a business. By analyzing each aspect and developing strategies to address them, companies can better understand their environment and make informed decisions to improve their performance.

Understanding potential through market sizing techniques

Market sizing estimates the potential revenue or profit size of an existing or new product or service. It involves researching and analyzing the relevant market data to determine the total demand, the share of competitors, and the potential revenue that can be generated from the market. It helps businesses understand the size and growth potential of the market they are operating in or considering entering. My experience has found that some of the reasons why market sizing is essential include the following:

- *Identifying market opportunities*: Market sizing helps businesses determine the size of the potential market and its revenue. This information is critical for identifying opportunities and developing appropriate strategies to reach the target audience.
- *Determining market share*: Market sizing provides businesses with information on the market share of competitors. This information is essential for determining the industry's competitive landscape and understanding the business's position relative to its competitors.
- *Evaluating market potential*: Market sizing provides businesses with a realistic estimate of the size and growth potential of the market. This information is essential for evaluating the viability of a new product or service, assessing the potential for expansion into new markets, and determining the potential return on investment.
- *Informing business decisions*: Market sizing gives businesses the necessary data to make informed decisions about investment, product development, marketing strategies, and pricing.

Figure 3 shows a consolidated market sizing approach that combines three types of market sizing techniques into a pool of estimates.

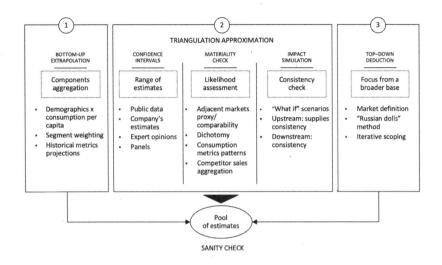

Figure 3: Market sizing approach

◆ ◆ ◆

CONSIDERATIONS

Exceptional strategy development processes are built on a solid foundation of outside-in facts combined with a deep understanding of the market, not simply gut and intuition. Key considerations when performing market analysis include the following:

- *Know your hypotheses*: Consider and document what you want to test externally before starting a market study. An ambiguous hypothesis or focus area can lead to missed deadlines, unhelpful information, unclear direction, and cost overruns if a belief is vague or open to change every time new data is found. It will also produce incomplete results if an idea is too narrow.
- *Obtain primary data when possible*: While often more challenging to quantify, taking the time to talk to the end users, customers, or critical stakeholders can uncover important considerations and dramatically change the conclusions. Also, consider ways to leverage NLP to gather secondary data efficiently through automated processes. With technology you can cover more ground.

- *Understand the quality of your data sources*: Not all data sources are created equal. For secondary research, be skeptical of any data source that isn't recent, and check that the institute that developed the data is credible and can provide references. Primary research can be especially tricky, as this is often a gathering of people's opinions. When conducting primary research, use a sufficiently large sample size so that you're not basing your assertions on the views of one or two individuals, but rather a broad perspective from multiple people.

- *Understand how the findings of the market study will be used, and make sure the report produced is easy to understand*: Without a clear understanding of the decision that will be made based on the market study, the report's findings may not answer the right question. Taking the time to test the direction of the information with the audience throughout its creation can help prevent this and ensure focus. Ultimately the market study should be planned upfront to assess a specific question you're trying to answer.

- *Consider all focus areas*: The most obvious place to research doesn't always tell the complete story. Keep an open mind early on. Use frameworks such as Porter's Five Forces to ensure there are no blind spots in your research and a wide net is used before zeroing in on the key insights.

- *Quantify the critical findings of all areas*: While direct calculations may not be possible, there are always ways to extrapolate and estimate values, which can provide beneficial results and insights when completed with the correct logic. Decision-making based on facts and logic is always easier to justify, explain to others, and achieve buy-in with.

- *Be directional, not precise*: Market studies are not meant to provide exact predictions but to give direction and context. It's better to be generally correct than precisely wrong.

- *Know when to stop your analysis*: Market studies have a nasty habit of becoming bloated and can be multi-month or even year-long exercises. It is important to remember that more is not always better. By being explicit about the hypotheses that require testing and understanding the depth of accuracy needed, it is much easier to recognize when the goal has been reached. At this point, cut off the analysis—even if that means discarding research that still needs to be completed.

- *Understand the organizational barriers to using external market data*: In a paper published in *Organizational Science*, researchers gathered data from 152 firms spanning multiple industries. The paper's key findings are that firms' attitudes toward external knowledge can be influenced by their perceptions of the value of external expertise, the risks associated with external knowledge, and the appropriateness of the sources.[47]

CHAPTER 3
STAKEHOLDER EXPECTATIONS

"The customer is not always right, but they are always the customer.
They hold the keys to our success."
—MAXINE CLARK, FOUNDER OF BUILD-A-BEAR WORKSHOP

THE VOICE OF THE CUSTOMER IS THE ONLY SOURCE OF TRUTH

Over the past 10 years, heavy industries like energy, mining, power, utilities, chemicals, and construction have evolved globally from sectors that society thought of as essential to day-to-day life, to today, where some governments and the not-for-profit sector, especially environmental organizations, consider heavy industries to be an existential threat to humanity. However, despite market and societal headwinds, the use of energy, rare metals and minerals, plastics, and cement, to name a few, is not going away any time soon. We continue to drive our cars, fly to sunny destinations, live in well-built houses, and purchase vast quantities of everyday products that depend on these industries. ·

Heavy industry needs strong advocacy, and trade associations exist to help protect the interests of the membership base, ensuring fact-based and balanced dialogues occur. One such industry trade association, representing various companies in a highly scrutinized sector, was seeking to understand its effectiveness. Times were tough. Facing a dramatically changing industry, consolidation in the member base, significant technological challenges, regulatory requirements, and political and societal opposition, the association needed support to meet the present and future challenges of the industry.

With help from me and my team, the association decided to interview and engage internal and external stakeholders, large and small, to understand whether it was serving the members in the right way, representing their interests, and focusing on the essential strategies.

Quantitative and qualitative outside-in information was captured anonymously so that open, frank, and direct feedback was received. We also looked at aspects of inside-out strategy: structure, governance, and performance. The overall intent was to receive honest feedback to drive change in a more informed, fact-based, and measured way.

The team combined all the findings into key observations and insights. Some comments proved valuable but were hard for our client to swallow. Still, as we explained, the feedback may be damning, but it needed to be uncovered. These views might not have been shared if the association had not engaged its external stakeholders meaningfully and provided the starting point for change.

The association shifted gears entirely once the devastating but frank feedback was gathered. It developed a set of strategic recommendations to bring to its governing body that proposed changes needed to resolve the criticisms. The association leveraged examples from similar industry associations from other countries and pondered what would drive success. The association knew that to be an effective organization, it needed to consider four dimensions: leadership, strategy, structure, and foundational elements.

Some significant risks were also revealed through the stakeholder engagement process. Doing nothing would result in losing more members, sending the association into the abyss. When developing a strategy, getting caught up in your own medicine and thinking you can do no wrong is easy. The Dunning–Kruger effect is a cognitive bias whereby people with low ability or experience in a particular task or area of knowledge tend to overestimate their expertise. We were conscious of this. It's clear that engaging your customers or broader stakeholders in getting feedback is the only source of truth about your actions.

Today, a few years after we presented the assessment, the industry remains a tricky and highly scrutinized sector, requiring the best thinking, innovation, and engagement. But the association has a refreshed leadership team and a new strategy and continues to look for ways to represent the industry more effectively.

As this example illustrates, perceptions of success vary from stakeholder to stakeholder, making it a complex business area to measure. This chapter explores this complexity with several best practices for managing stakeholder expectations, using as an example truck manufacturing company Caterpillar's innovative use of artificial intelligence (AI).

◆ ◆ ◆

WHAT IS STAKEHOLDER EXPECTATIONS?

The concept "the customer is king" was pioneered by three highly successful retailers in the 1900s: Harry Gordon Selfridge, John Wanamaker, and Marshall Field. Naturally, customers' expectations and behaviour have a huge influence on the success of your business, but customers are not the only stakeholders to take into account. Managing stakeholder expectations means ensuring that *all* stakeholders' needs, interests, and concerns are identified, understood, and appropriately addressed. Stakeholders include not only customers, but also employees, shareholders, suppliers, partners, regulators, and other individuals or groups affected by, or interested in, the company's operations or performance.

The global authority on project management, the Project Management Institute, explains how everything you do or don't do sets an expectation for future behaviour. Stakeholders, especially customers, must be consistently and frequently managed to ensure a successful outcome. Establishing the rules governing successful and unsuccessful results and managing those rules give the project team the guidelines to set and manage stakeholder expectations.[48]

CASE STUDY
Local community engagement at Arsenal Football Club

Arsenal Football Club (or The Gunners, as I know them), a leading soccer team in London, England, has several stakeholders with varied relationships with each other and the team: the London Borough of Islington, local residents, supporters, and supporters with disabilities, to name a few. On one level, coordinating the Stadium Management Plan between the club and its supporters highlights Arsenal as operating at the forefront of an excellent football game experience.[49] However, the team also takes great care to manage and cultivate multiple stakeholder connections, within Emirates Stadium and beyond.

First, the organization uses the Mendelow power/interest matrix to demonstrate how the team could manage these diverse groups. The matrix serves a valuable purpose, identifying the different power and interest levels of each stakeholder group and helping management to develop specific strategies to enhance participation or engagement of each different group.

For example, outside-in initiatives prioritized by the club include weekly football sessions with adults with learning disabilities and mental health challenges and youngsters who are deaf or visually impaired. The extent of this outreach is impressive: over the 2022–23 season, Arsenal in the Community (the delivery team for this program) delivered 7,193 sessions across their host borough and neighbouring areas and engaged more than 5,000 participants each week, all with a focus on happiness and health, active lifestyle choices, and community connection.[50,51,52]

The club's motto has long been *Victoria concordia crescit*, Latin for "Victory through harmony." It describes the team's effective stakeholder management very well.

I cannot highlight enough the importance of managing stakeholder expectations as part of the outside-in analysis. Doing so can help build stakeholder trust and support, which can be critical to the business's success. It can also help to minimize conflicts, ensure compliance with regulations and standards, and enhance a company's reputation and brand. Successfully navigating stakeholder expectations, in my experience, comes down to two key elements: defining a project's success and failure, and then setting and managing expectations. I've found that staying connected fuels business resilience and have written on the subject several times. Engaging with stakeholders helps companies stay abreast of external threats, changing customer needs, and emerging technology trends.[53]

HOW TO APPROACH STAKEHOLDER EXPECTATIONS

Managing the triple constraint

The triple constraint refers to the three most significant restrictions on any project: scope, schedule, and cost. The triple constraint is sometimes referred to as the project management triangle or the iron triangle. Defining success and failure in the eyes of the stakeholder has traditionally meant evaluating a project against this triangle. Unfortunately, success is perceptual, and perceptions vary from stakeholder to stakeholder. This makes it hard to judge whether the project succeeded.

Through my own work, I've determined that the triple constraint model does have some benefits and helps teams evaluate success related to schedule, scope, and cost. The model also stipulates that cost is a function of scope and schedule, or that cost, schedule, and scope are connected so that if one changes, another must also change in a defined and predictable way. The significant disadvantage to the triple constraint model is that delivering projects on time and within budget and scope may address only some of a client's expectations.

In addition to schedule, cost, and scope, it's important to understand quality expectations and customer satisfaction. In a paper in the *Journal of Consumer Psychology*, the authors discuss the differences between service quality and customer satisfaction. They argue that service quality is a multidimensional construct that includes the technical and functional aspects of service delivery. On the other hand, customer satisfaction is a global evaluation of the overall service experience.[54] Both must be managed carefully as part of a broader stakeholder expectation effort.

I've learned that success in terms of stakeholder expectation management is likely all these things combined: carefully balancing the needs from a schedule, cost, scope, quality, and satisfaction perspective.

Voice of the customer through the loyalty grid

According to a study by the management company Qualtrics, 80 percent of companies believe they deliver superior customer service. However, only 8 percent of customers agree.[55] These are alarming results. *Voice of the Customer* (VoC) is a term that describes a customer's feedback about their experiences with, and expectations for, products or services. It focuses on customer needs, expectations, and understandings. When defining a project's success or failure, VoC can help identify expectations not previously captured in the triple constraint model (cost, schedule, scope).

Research shows that understanding the customer is critical to the product development life cycle. Professor Robert Cooper at Penn State University explains that successful companies developing new products strongly focus on the customer (leveraging the VoC), use a disciplined approach to product development, and have a supportive organizational culture.[56]

I also think we can learn a lot from VoC to support product development. Researchers at the University of Utah and MIT propose a methodology for capturing customer needs called quality function deployment (QFD), a total-quality-management process using the VoC to guide product development. The researchers' paper also discusses how QFD can prioritize customer needs and preferences.[57]

My experience on projects has shown that one of the ways to understand how VoC identifies a project's perceived success or failure is through the customer loyalty grid, as illustrated in Figure 4. Listening to the VoC is essential; delivering only what is required to fulfill the contract results in customer indifference, not satisfaction, delight, or loyalty.

	Expected	Unexpected
Stated	**Satisfaction** What your customer actually tells you is vital to them.	**Delight** What your customer hopes, desires and asks for but does not expect you to provide it.
Unstated	**Indifference** Includes customer needs and wants that are basic to fulfilling the agreement between you and the customer.	**Loyalty** Providing benefits above and beyond what the customer is even aware of. Builds long term commitment.

Figure 4: Customer loyalty grid

VoC analysis helps businesses collect valuable customer insights and transform them into data that can be implemented to serve customers better by providing in-depth knowledge of their perspectives and expectations. The better a company understands its customers, the more it can increase loyalty and retention—which increases revenue—as well as attract new customers.

However, maybe the customer is only sometimes king. Anthony Ulwick, the CEO and founder of Strategyn and author of *What Customers Want: Using Outcome-Driven Innovation to Create Breakthrough Products and Services*, found through 12 years of watching organizations that most market research and product development needs to be corrected. He said that the problem is that companies ask customers what they want and then take that information to make changes that don't satisfy customers.[58] He thinks customers should not be trusted to develop solutions because they are not informed enough to help with innovation.

Meeting customer demands to the letter also tends to result in "me-too" products (such as customers asking for missing features that other manufacturers already offer). In the mid-1980s, for example, market studies conducted by US automakers Ford, Chrysler, and GM revealed that customers wanted cup holders in their vehicles, a feature Japanese manufacturers had provided for years. But when American companies finally added the frequently requested cup holders, none gained an advantage; customers merely said, "It's about time." A VoC-based analysis might have overcome the challenges posed by Ulwick.

Cordis Corporation is a medical device manufacturer in Florida. In 1993, the company's annual sales were $223 million and its stock was valued at around $20 a share. Cordis conducted outcome-based voice-of-the-customer interviews with cardiologists, nurses, and other laboratory personnel. The discussions focused not on what features these professionals would like to see in an angioplasty balloon, but on the results they wanted to achieve in their jobs—before, during, and after the surgery. Cordis used the interview data to get at the heart of a new product strategy that addressed critical, unsatisfied needs in new market segments. The data also led Cordis to conclude that some of its products then in development were likely to fail, so it suspended further costly work on them. As a result, Cordis's revenues nearly doubled within two years, reaching $443 million by June 1995.[59]

In summary, defining project success and failure by the ability to meet cost, schedule, and scope criteria, while necessary, may not be enough to achieve client satisfaction. Additional data points gleaned from voice-of-the-customer approaches and the customer loyalty grid enable us to paint a more fulsome outside-in picture of how the client defines success.

CASE STUDY
Managing nuclear-sized project needs at EDF Energy

When many stakeholders have complex needs, a systems-based approach can help. Utility powerhouse EDF Energy is the largest producer of low-carbon electricity in the United Kingdom. From turbines to electric cars and heating, it is committed to supporting the reduction of carbon emissions to net zero.

Many projects that EDF Energy executes require informing, and engaging with, stakeholders (customers, employees, and shareholders). Two of EDF's past nuclear power generation projects had an understandably high media profile: Hinkley Point C and Sizewell C. Both projects represented long-term construction development, so EDF needed an efficient way to manage both stakeholder and public engagement before its submission for planning permission.

EDF employed an easy-to-use, purpose-built system that included data on the literally thousands of diverse stakeholders. This outside-in system helped the organization map stakeholders, coordinate communications, and track and manage stakeholder issues. Furthermore, EDF was able to group stakeholders into what it called "smart categories" relevant to their needs for information and interest levels, allowing the firm to precisely target its communication strategies.[60]

As explained by the International Atomic Energy Agency (IAEA), a leading world authority that oversees nuclear safety, engaging with a wide range of stakeholders is a vital part of nuclear power development. The IAEA states that involving stakeholders in decision-making can enhance awareness, understanding, and confidence in the application of nuclear science and technology and improve communication among the key stakeholders involved.[61]

Leveraging technology to understand stakeholder expectations better

Similar to the examples shared in the market and competitive analysis in Chapters 2 and 4, using technology to understand stakeholder expectations is an exciting and powerful way to develop strategies. For example, two analytics experts at Caterpillar's truck manufacturing company have written about using deep learning and natural language processing (NLP) to model customers' perceptions based on their multimodal data, such as social media texts and audio recordings. The authors argue that analyzing textual reviews can provide deeper insights than exploring customer experiences and satisfaction.[62]

Communications: the key to managing stakeholder expectations

Through trial and error, I've come to appreciate that communication is the most important aspect of setting and managing stakeholder expectations. In my experience, you need to consider the following principles when communicating with stakeholders for this purpose:

- *Establish a regular, transparent means of communication*: Depending on what group you are engaging with, this could be weekly status reports or meetings where information such as action items, progress to date, upcoming activities, and decision points are discussed. Or it could mean focus groups, where sharing new information and receiving feedback is vital to the engagement process. For example, at leading digital health and wellness company Kilo Health, Ilona Bernotaite and the leadership team have implemented the "Ask CEO-CHRO-CFO Anything" program. Employees receive a Calendly link to book a 15-minute chit-chat with any senior leader. This approach encourages transparency, demonstrates an open-door policy, and allows leaders to directly address employees' comments, questions, and concerns.[63] The point is to ensure that stakeholders receive reliable, accurate, and recurrent information and provide them with a platform to raise issues.
- *Overcommunicate*: When managing stakeholder expectations, it is important not to assume anything. Ensure essential messages are communicated frequently in different mediums (for example, in person as well as email) and documented and revisited to confirm understanding. Don't fixate on avoiding the delivery of bad news. Instead, if you anticipate something going haywire, be sure to raise it as a point of discussion in status meetings and reports. In the case of hydrocarbon pipeline development that typically involves construction over vast distances, North American giant TC Energy communicates with landowners along the route regularly to avoid protests and costly construction delays.[64]
- *Proactively plan for problems and potential conflicts*: When projects are new, allocate time for undiscovered work and develop a contingency plan. Agree beforehand with the stakeholders in question on how you will collectively manage conflict and document the approach. Establishing this understanding removes

ambiguity around addressing concerns should something go wrong during the project. For example, when a fault with a product is discovered by the manufacturer, transparent communication upfront is essential to protecting any brand impact or safety consequences. When Apple released the iPhone 4 in 2010, users flagged a significant drop in signal strength when holding the phone in a specific way. The issue was the antenna design, which caused signal attenuation. Instead of denying the problem, Apple acknowledged it publicly, CEO Steve Jobs held a press conference, and Apple offered a free bumper case to every iPhone 4 user, turning a negative into a positive.[65]

CASE STUDY
Reaching new heights with stakeholder management at the Burj Khalifa, UAE

Having worked in the Middle East, I've always been astounded by the scale and pace of infrastructure development as the desert is transformed into impressive modern cities. One example of such development is the construction of the Burj Khalifa skyscraper in Dubai. At 828 metres high (more than 160 storeys), the Burj Khalifa project was a colossal undertaking, estimated to cost $1.5 billion. It was a collaboration between the government of Dubai, developer Emaar Properties, and various contractors and suppliers.[66]

From the outset, the project team recognized the importance of managing stakeholder expectations. The project required international outside-in collaboration with more than 30 organizations from around the globe, and at its peak employed over 12,000 workers and contractors representing more than 100 nationalities. Furthermore, given the size and scale of the development, logistics and planning were essential to success, as were world-class communications. Consequently, the project team regularly met with stakeholders, including government officials, investors, and neighbouring property owners, to inform them of the project's progress and address any concerns.

To manage expectations around the project's timeline, the team set realistic deadlines and communicated regularly with stakeholders about any changes or delays. When the completion date was pushed back from 2008 to 2010, the project team worked with stakeholders to ensure that they understood the reasons for the delay and that it would maintain the quality and safety of the project. As for the cost, members of the project team worked closely with the developer

to ensure the project was completed within budget and without unnecessary cost overruns, while regularly updating stakeholders on the project's financial status.
The project team also worked closely with members of local communities to minimize the impact of construction on their daily lives by implementing measures to reduce noise and dust levels.

In conclusion, remember what can happen in terms of project failure when stakeholders' expectations aren't fully understood and addressed. The consequences can be disastrous.

◆ ◆ ◆

CONSIDERATIONS

Engaging with stakeholders is critical to getting outside-in input in the strategy development process, and managing their expectations is essential to the success of any project or initiative. As Steve Jobs said, "Get closer than ever to your customer. So close, in fact, that you tell them what they need well before they realize it themselves."[67] Engaging stakeholders successfully is essential to the business system and to organizing your operating model and service delivery approach. It starts by exploring your environment and understanding who your stakeholders are and what they want, but it also includes world-class communications.

- *Assess the environment*: Identifying all relevant stakeholders and their interests, needs, expectations, and priorities is essential. To help assess the stakeholder environment, ask these questions: Where does the power lie? Where do points of conflicting agenda exists between stakeholders? In the cast of characters, whose actions will have the most significant impact? Are there any hidden agendas or goals that are not openly articulated? What are the goals of the stakeholders who hold the power?
- *Leverage technology*: Where possible, consider ways to gather insights on critical stakeholders using AI and NLP to accelerate data capture and analysis. In complex stakeholder environments,

using technology can be particularly powerful to uncover useful information.

- *Prioritize your stakeholders*: While considering multiple and sometimes conflicting expectations, you must also decide which stakeholders to focus on and in what sequence. Businesses don't have limitless capacity to manage all stakeholders.

- *Consider the culture of stakeholders*: In the context of project management when stakeholders do not share a common culture, project management must adapt its style and processes to cope with these differences. Three significant aspects of cultural differences can affect a project: communication style, negotiation tactics, and decision-making processes.

- *Set realistic goals*: When setting goals or targets, it's essential to ensure they are achievable and realistic given the resources available, including budgets, people, and technology. Unrealistic goals can lead to disappointment and frustration among stakeholders. Under promise and over deliver.

- *Balance competing interests*: Stakeholders may have different and sometimes competing interests to your own. It's essential to strike a balance among these interests and to communicate openly about how decisions are being made.

- *Identify champions*: Supportive stakeholders are vital to a project's success and can help build momentum and bring others on board, so building strong, trusting relationships with interested parties from the start is critical.

- *Be flexible to changing expectations*: When managing stakeholders, it's essential to be flexible and adaptable. Plans may change due to unforeseen circumstances and different needs, and it's crucial to adjust schedules and communicate changes to stakeholders.

- *Be responsible*: It's essential to be responsible to stakeholders for the project's outcomes. This includes taking responsibility for mistakes or failures and addressing concerns or issues when they arise.

- *Communicate regularly with stakeholders*: It's also essential to keep stakeholders informed about the status of the project or operation, changes in timelines or budgets, and any risks or issues that arise. Understand and leverage your different communication channels.

CHAPTER 4
COMPETITOR ANALYSIS

*"The ability to learn faster than your competitors may be
the only sustainable competitive advantage."*
—ARIE DE GEUS, FORMER SHELL EXECUTIVE & SCENARIO PLANNER

UNCOVERING AN UNLIKELY SOURCE OF INSPIRATION

Mining and energy companies build and operate facilities and infrastructure in some of North America's most remote regions, within a land mass of 24 million kilometres squared. Ensuring workers in these regions are housed, safe, and fed is critical to keep industry and economies moving. It's an essential service. Servicing the remote camps that accommodate these workers are specialized catering companies, and it's a highly competitive sector. According to IBISWorld, the US had 85,851 caterer businesses as of 2023, an increase of 4 percent from 2022, leaving little room for organic growth.[68] In addition, the large price swings that affect various natural resource commodities impact company spending in this area.

In the context of volatile commodity prices for their clients, one of North America's largest catering companies providing essential housing and living services in places not supported by traditional municipal infrastructure struggled to sustain their own share price performance. To increase shareholder value, the company set ambitious targets to grow its Industrial Services division from a revenue and a margin perspective.

Management needed a detailed market assessment for each of its business units, outlining the size of each geographical area it operates in and the key risks and opportunities. They sought a "where to play, how to win" strategy that would allow them to reach their revenue and profit targets, including internal improvements that could be made and specific organic and inorganic growth opportunities.

We embarked on the research and development of a detailed market assessment report, which consisted of studying core and adjacent markets through supply and demand analysis. The team examined the competition, focusing on strengths, weaknesses, critical financial data, services delivered, suppliers, strategic relationships, customers, geographic market presence, significant investors, strategies, and overall value proposition. It was comprehensive and came at a time when the organization needed to climb out of a big hole.

The critical analysis of the competition led the organization's leaders to develop a strategy to reach their revenue and profit aspirations. It helped them with the strategic differentiators and outcomes, growth enablers, and critical actions needed to win and thrive in the marketplace. Research data was meticulously analyzed through various, sometimes stressful, high-stakes engagement sessions with the firms' leaders. Not only was the competition assessed to inform the organization's strategies, but they were also evaluated as potential takeover targets. Furthermore, the outside-in analysis of the competition and other market drivers helped the company zero in on four key differentiators: market responsiveness through a data-driven and fact-based approach; market dominance through strategic investment in expansion, geographies, and new services; internal process and production efficiencies; and new technology.

The organization's leaders also looked outside their industry and immediate competition for ideas that would help them overcome historical challenges. Each company that was part of this wide-ranging competitive analysis offered unique insights into how they serve their customers and maintain dominant status in their respective markets. For example, Air Canada has a tiered, standardized service offering that provides customer flexibility while supporting economies of scale. Coffee giant Tim Hortons focuses on centralizing back-office services, leading to cost reduction and consistency of delivery. Costco prides itself on inventory management to reduce shrinkage and sourcing locally to lower capital costs. Finally, US-based cruise line operator Royal Caribbean Group focuses on digital innovations, such as an integrated phone app that manages your user experience (pre-cruise planning and onboard convenience), to increase revenue streams beyond beds and food and, by engaging customers digitally, they increase the ability to collect valuable data.[69] These examples helped my client understand more about analogous sectors so they could apply the lessons learned.

In the highly competitive market of camps and catering, an ongoing and detailed understanding of the market, including direct and indirect or unconventional competitors, feeds success. My client, the North American organization, took a structured and strategic approach to thinking outside its company walls and embraced the opportunity to learn from others. As the CEO said, "We co-developed and eventually owned the resulting strategy." The company continues to prosper, has completed several acquisitions, and is well-positioned for a brighter future.

The story of this camps and catering company illustrates how crucial competitor analysis is for incumbent organizations and new market entrants to understand the landscape in which they operate from the outside in. This chapter provides a step-by-step game plan to guide readers toward successful structured competitor analyses, with examples that include Nike, BMW, and Mercedes.

◆ ◆ ◆

WHAT IS COMPETITIVE ANALYSIS?

Steve Jobs once famously quoted (or misquoted) Pablo Picasso when he said, "Good artists copy; great artists steal." Competitor analysis is critical for incumbent organizations and new market entrants alike, who must understand their competition to gain and retain market share. When an organization decides "where to play," robust competitor analysis will help determine if there is a significant opportunity to exploit the market. Gaining market share in an already saturated market is much more difficult, so competitor analysis is also crucial for incumbent organizations fighting to stay relevant and grow their market share. This can only be done by improving their value proposition over their competitors.

A subset of outside-in analysis and conducting a market study (Chapter 2), competitor analysis is a specific step in evaluating the market that looks at a company's direct and indirect competitors, a deep dive into their strengths and weaknesses, including strategies, strategic relationships, product lines, branding, marketing and sales plans, target markets, market share, financials, and value proposition.

Competitor analysis is about putting yourself inside your competitors' heads. According to McKinsey, a strategy and management consulting firm, it is just as common to see companies overestimate the risk and speed of competitive responses as it is to see them ignore the threat. The most vivid example is when considering a price change relative to a direct competitor. Will it follow? Understanding its economics will give you part of the answer to whether it could or should follow suit. You may have the better margin to afford a cut and have deeper pockets to sustain a price war. Or your brand may have higher loyalty, allowing you to increase prices with lower volume risk. But more than rational game theory is needed to make decisions because behavioural biases may thwart rationalism. A competitor may not match a price cut due to pressure to meet short-term targets, difficulty aligning internally, or dismissiveness about the risk. They may react strongly if an improved market share influences their managers' incentives.[70]

CASE STUDY
Competitor analysis at clothing company Gap, Inc.

Outside-in analysis can be used as input in an organization's "where to play, how to win" strategy to inform decisions about entering new markets or to develop strategies to gain and retain market share for existing players.

The American clothing and accessories retailer Gap, Inc. faced a net sales decline of 2 percent in 2018, and that pattern continued for several years. The company prepared to shut down 230 flagship stores over the next two years as it tried to restructure its business. Gap's competitors include Zara, H&M, Forever 21, and Uniqlo.

To regain its focus on democratizing fashion and making shopping fun, Gap embarked on a detailed competitor analysis that examined strengths and weaknesses in each competitor's brand, supply chain, sustainability, product range, global presence, identity, design, and marketing.[71] It was comprehensive, and the company managed to turn things around, now boasting annual revenues of over $16 billion, with a presence in over 40 countries worldwide. Furthermore, CEO Richard Dickson announced net income for the year ended February 3, 2024, of $185 million or

$0.80 per share, compared to a loss of $273 million or -$0.75 in the previous year. Operating income reached $214 million in the fourth quarter of 2023 compared to a loss of $30 million a year before. Dickson said that results exceeded expectations.[72]

My deep familiarity with this topic has helped me appreciate that getting it right is critical to success. According to Christopher Tompkins, the co-founder, head strategist, and CEO of The Go! Agency, a full-service digital marketing firm, there are three reasons a competitive analysis is essential. It helps establish benchmarks, a process of building points of reference to competitors against which you can measure your growth. Secondly, you can use these benchmarks to identify and fill crucial gaps in your business and, thirdly, they help you determine your "why?" When a potential customer is considering your product and a similar product, the "why?" of your brand will often be the determining factor in closing that sale.[73]

In summary, effective strategy formulation and implementation should have competitive analysis as the cornerstone. It helps executives improve their company's offering and performance as well as understand and predict strategic moves by competitors. A warning, though: It's complicated and time-consuming, requiring significant organizational resources, creativity, imagination, and insight. This complexity can lead to flawed competitive analysis, which in turn can mean ineffective, if not disastrous, strategies.

HOW TO APPROACH COMPETITIVE ANALYSIS

A structured approach to competitive analysis

A competitive analysis will help you see your unique advantages and any potential barriers to growth. This will help energize your marketing and business strategies. It also keeps your business proactive instead of reactive. Many entrepreneurs operate on preconceived ideas about their competitors and the market landscape. Those ideas may need to be made more accurate or at least updated.

1. *Identify your competitors*: This sounds straightforward, but there are different kinds of competitors to consider. Direct competitors are businesses that offer similar products and services and target the same customers in the geographic area that your company serves. Secondary/indirect competitors offer different products and services and target a more diverse clientele in the same general category. For example, a winery and a brewery are secondary competitors because they both sell alcohol. Substitute competitors are businesses that offer different products and services but target the same customers in your geographic area.

2. *Gather information about your competitors*: Once you've identified them, evaluate them in terms of the "four Ps" of the marketing mix, a concept developed by marketing professor Edmund Jerome McCarthy:[74]

    - Product: Compare their products to yours, ideally by purchasing and trying them out. How is the quality? What features do you like or dislike?
    - Pricing: How are their products and services priced? Do their prices vary for different channel partners and customers? What is their discount policy? Can you estimate their cost structure?
    - Place: What is their geographic reach or service area compared to your business?
    - Promotion: What marketing tactics are they using to interact and engage with customers? What is their presence on social media? Data might be incomplete but gather as much as possible until you exhaust your channels.

3. *Analyze your competitors' strengths and weaknesses*: During a workshop session with your team, it's essential that you can easily compare the performance of your competitors with your own. Start by ranking your competitors in the above criteria on a scale from 1 to 10. Next, prepare a written evaluation of each competitor's respective strengths and weaknesses. For example, are

they popular because of their location? Visibility? Quality of their staff? Are their prices too high? Does their product lack a crucial feature demanded by customers? Summarize everything that would make a consumer choose (or not choose) each competitor.

4. *Determine your competitive advantage*: With all the information at your fingertips, it's time to determine what the results mean for your business strategy. "What are we good at relative to the competition and where do we want to focus?" says Business Development Bank of Canada senior business advisor Mallika Kazim. "It's a little bit of a 'who do you want to be when you grow up?' kind of question."[75] Analyzing the competitive landscape will help pinpoint your competitive advantage. It could be a distinctive strength that appeals to your target market and something you can build your brand image and message around. Or, if you see a weakness in the competition, you could lower your prices and launch new promotions to take advantage of the opportunity.

CASE STUDY
Innovation and competitive analysis at shoe dogs Nike

Nike is one of the world's largest suppliers of athletic shoes and apparel, holding a whopping 38.23 percent of total market share in 2022. Even as competitors grow, Nike remains the most influential player in the industry.[76] Nike's "Just Do It" philosophy allows it to focus on staying ahead of its competition, dedicating entire teams to this effort.

According to *Business Chronicler*, Nike's competitive strategy focuses on innovation, brand-building, and expanding its direct-to-consumer channels. Its primary means of developing new products and technologies is research through the secretive Nike Sport Research Lab (NSRL).[77]

Located in Beaverton, Oregon, the NSRL is owned by Nike and used to develop new products and technologies. According to *Forbes*, the lab applies an analytical framework to articulate a problem effectively, define a solution, conduct an outside-in competitive analysis, and create a go-to-market strategy.[78]

Through its innovative approaches, Nike has maintained its digital prowess and a robust product pipeline, increased speed-to-market capabilities, improved offerings, and sustained a targeted focus on women, all of which drive growth and margin expansion over the competition.[79] As founder Phil Knight once said, "Play by the rules, but be ferocious."[80] Nike's results are nothing short of breathtaking, with global revenues of $51.21 billion in 2023, an increase of over $4.5 billion compared to the previous financial year.[81]

Leveraging technology to support competitive analysis

AI has revolutionized the competitive intelligence process. I've used it to identify market opportunities and threats more accurately than humans could. This is because AI analyzes information faster than humans and can better evaluate data points. In terms of potential scope, according to the Marketing Institute, AI can be applied in three ways:

- *Forecasting*: Combining available data with machine learning algorithms to develop competitive intelligence forecasts and predictions based on past events.
- *Pattern and trend recognition*: Sifting through massive amounts of data and finding competitive patterns and trends.
- *Market profiling*: Creating profiles on competitors and products that can be used for competitive advantage.[82]

An example of an organization gathering competitor information using more advanced techniques is the healthcare services company IQVIA. This biopharmaceutical company has leveraged an asset intelligence tool, as well as data science experts, to provide AI-augmented insights on competitors, enabling faster and more informed decisions.[83]

Competitive positioning framework

Visualizing where you stand compared to the rest in your market is essential to competitive analysis. Once you've gathered data on your competitors and analyzed their strengths and weaknesses, a competitive positioning framework, as shown in Figure 5, is used to compare the position of your products or services relative to theirs. I've come to appreciate that visualization is always helpful in strategic dialogues amongst decision-makers. The power is in the conversation, and frameworks can help with that. The framework illustrated can plot where external competitors are from a positioning perspective, helping to identify them and assess their offerings and current strategy relative to yours.

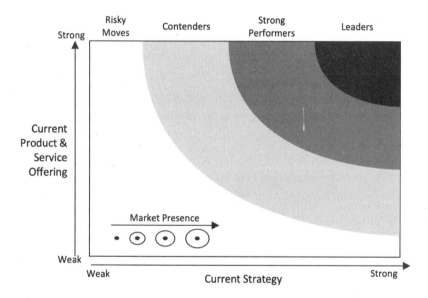

Figure 5: Competitive positioning framework

More specifically, businesses can identify areas where they have a competitive advantage by analyzing their current offerings and strategies against their competitors, including product features, pricing, and customer service. Knowing where they excel can help businesses better focus resources and efforts to maintain and strengthen their advantage. And analyzing the offerings and strategies of competitors can also help businesses identify areas where their business is at a disadvantage in terms of product quality, pricing, marketing, and other factors, allowing them to address problem areas, close gaps, make improvement investments, and improve competitiveness.

Based on the analysis of a company's offerings and strategy vis-à-vis the competition, businesses can build differentiation strategies, such as improving customer service or offering a more comprehensive range of product features, which can help them stand out and attract and retain customers.

By building a competitive positioning framework, businesses can better understand their competitive environment, allowing them to evaluate their current offerings and strategies, weigh the pros and cons of different options, and choose to invest in those most likely to succeed. That way, they are better able to stay ahead of the curve and maintain a competitive edge in their market.

· Competitor grouping to simplify analysis

Through extensive project work, I've determined that it makes sense to combine competitors into groups to drive the analysis further, especially when there are loads of them. Positioning maps are an effective tool for visualizing the outputs and crunching large amounts of data. The most common characteristics include price, quality, market share, brand, cost, company size, R&D capability, sales channels, and geographic market presence. Grouping can be based on relevant market factors and strategies. For example, the automobile industry has several strategic groups, including luxury cars, sports cars, economy cars, and family cars. BMW and Mercedes-Benz are examples of the luxury car strategic group, while Toyota and Honda are in the economy car strategic group.

Groupings also help identify strategic competitors and benchmark their performance so that blind spots, unserved segments, or more favourable strategic groups can be easily noticed. This framework can also help find alternative paths to success based on other groups' actions. Once the criteria have been selected, defining each variable's scale and then positioning companies on the map is the secret to success. For example, in the cellular phone market, Apple and Samsung belong to a high-end strategic group, while budget-friendly brands like Xiaomi and OnePlus form a different group. Knowing these groups in a fulsome way allows your company to better understand how and where to compete— high-end vs. budget. Furthermore, grouping smartphones based on, say, price (low to high) and features (basic to advanced) reveals where each brand stands in consumers' minds and, therefore, how to compete.

Another example is fast-food restaurant chains in the food service industry. These chains differentiate themselves from other strategic groups such as fine dining, cafés, and family restaurants based on low prices, quick service, and selection of food offerings. Del Taco is a case in point, offering variety, fast service, fresh, and low-priced food at 600 locations across the US.[84] Whether it's mobile phones or fast food, each company can tailor their strategies, identify unique growth opportunities, and optimize their competitive positioning by understanding the different groups and their own placement on the competitive positioning framework in relation to them.

Once the groups are established, you can decide on the best action. Will you stay in the current group and defend the hill? Or will you move to another group with more favourable conditions? Did you see an opportunity to create a new strategic group and leave altogether? The choice is yours.

Acquisition assessment framework

Neutralizing the competition through acquisition is one way of squashing a threat. A company acquisition assessment framework is a tool I've often used to evaluate the potential purchase of another company. It helps assess the strategic fit of the target company and identify potential risks and opportunities associated with the investment. The framework typically includes an analysis of the target company's financial performance, market position, customer base, and other vital factors that may impact the acquisition's success. Using an acquisition assessment framework, companies can make more informed decisions about whether or not to pursue an acquisition strategy (see Chapter 10) and how to structure the deal.

A target company acquisition assessment framework is helpful in the following ways:

- *Evaluating strategic fit*: The framework can help the acquirer evaluate the strategic fit of the target company, including assessing how the target company's business model, products or services, customers, and geographic footprint align with the acquirer's overall strategy and objectives.
- *Assessing financial performance*: It can help the acquirer assess the target company's financial performance, including its revenue, profitability, cash flow, and other key financial metrics, which can help the acquirer determine the potential financial impact of the acquisition and whether it is financially viable.

- *Evaluating operational capabilities*: The framework can help the acquirer evaluate the target company's operational capabilities, including its supply chain, production processes, distribution channels, and other vital operational factors. This can help the acquirer determine whether the target company has the resources and capabilities to support the acquirer's overall strategy and objectives.

- *Assessing management team*: The framework can help the acquirer assess the target company's management team, including their skills, experience, and track record. This can help determine whether the management team can lead the target company post-acquisition and whether they fit the acquirer's culture and values.

A target company acquisition assessment framework is helpful because it provides a disciplined approach to evaluating potential acquisition targets. While it can't eliminate acquisition risks,[85] considering a range of factors and criteria can help the acquirer make savvy decisions about pursuing an acquisition and how to structure the deal to magnify the potential benefits and minimize the risks.

◆ ◆ ◆

CONSIDERATIONS

As former chair and CEO of General Electric Jack Welch once said, "An organization's ability to learn, and translate that learning into action rapidly, is the ultimate competitive advantage."[86] It's essential that you never stop learning from the competition. Competitive analysis is critical to understanding the outside-in landscape and making informed decisions about your business strategy, including potential acquisitions.

Some key considerations to keep in mind when conducting a competitor analysis are as follows:

- *Identify your competitors*: This should be comprehensive and include direct competitors who offer similar products or services, indirect competitors who offer products or services that are not the same but can satisfy the same customer need, and substitute competitors that offer different solutions or products that could replace the need for your product or service.

- *Analyze their strengths and weaknesses*: Evaluate your competitors' product offerings, pricing strategies, financials (EBITA, share price, sales, debt, revenue), acquisitions, market share, marketing tactics, distribution channels, and anything else that contributes to their competitive advantage or disadvantage. Be honest about your assessment. Where possible, drive automation efficiency by leveraging technology like NLP, so that you can assess more information faster.

- *Consider your blind spots*: Researchers have found that decision-makers typically have specific "blind spots" when considering competitors' contingent decisions, including overconfidence, tunnel vision, limited resources, information overload, and trying to avoid copycat behaviour. These blind spots may explain persistent, commonly observed phenomena such as industry overcapacity, new business entry failures, and acquisition premiums.[87]

- *Assess geographic coverage*: Consider the geographic areas the competitors operate in and where they have the most significant footprint. If your business has a perceived product or service advantage, entry into a new geographic market could provide a significant growth opportunity.

- *Evaluate their marketing strategies*: You should evaluate your competitors' marketing strategies, including their branding and advertising campaigns, social media presence, pricing strategy, and other tactics they use to reach customers to gain insights into their brand positioning, messaging, and target audience.

- *Consider external factors*: External factors such as economic conditions, regulatory changes, and technological advancements can impact your competitors' performance and strategy. Understand the relative impact of these external factors on your competitors.

- *Monitor their actions*: Keeping track of what your competitors are doing and noting any changes in your competitors' strategy or market position can help you stay ahead of the curve and adapt your strategy to remain competitive. For example, make note of new product or service offerings launched by the competitors and any strategic acquisitions, divestments, partnerships, and alliances.

CHAPTER 5
SCENARIO ANALYSIS

"The problem with the future is that it is different. If you are unable to think differently, the future will always arrive as a surprise."
—WOODY WADE, AUTHOR & FACILITATOR

PLANNING FOR MULTIPLE FUTURES ENERGIZES RESILIENCE

In the context of trying to reach net zero carbon emissions, the world is in the midst of a massive energy transition, upending traditional patterns of electricity generation, distribution, and usage. According to EY, disruption in the global power-system markets and the traditional utility business model is driven by the three Ds: decarbonization, decentralization, and digitalization.[88] But no one knows with any certainty how exactly the drive to net zero will play out or how quickly it will occur.

As aggressive decarbonization and net-zero targets are escalating, and electrification is accelerating, utilities and grid operators must keep pace to meet the growing needs of electricity system stakeholders. Innovation and digital transformation are both an answer to the challenges of the energy transition and a driver of new business models and solutions. Energy generation, distribution, and transmission are becoming more progressive in the competitive space.

For example, declining costs in solar lead to a more distributed grid. Estimates predict that new solar and battery storage projects will make up 60 percent of new generating capacity worldwide by 2025. These advances will require utility grids to accommodate the resulting increases in two-way energy flows. As technology and customer needs evolve, utilities must invest in digital technologies to improve their asset performance and operations. The US Inflation Reduction Act allocated nearly $3 billion toward developing and improving transmission systems, including modification of control systems and facilities. And interestingly, customers are now actively engaging with the grid—seeking low-cost and flexible ways to participate in the energy transition. EY research found that 86 percent of consumers are interested in generating their electricity at home.[89]

Given all this change, uncertainty, and disruption, one of North America's significant electricity transmission and distribution providers identified the need to build a stress-tested strategy against multiple potential futures. The organization wanted to find ways to remain agile, better anticipate outside-in market trends, challenge critical assumptions, and improve risk management and performance through monitoring signals. By doing this, the organization hoped to better predict which scenarios were playing out and use that information to make decisions. Since the speed of energy transition, electric vehicle adoption, and future regulation were unknown, management decided to engage my help in leveraging scenario planning to help plan for risk, uncertainty, and opportunity.

The problem statement was clear: How will electrification trends and uncertainties be monitored to identify the most likely scenario and inform investment decisions in the strategic and business planning cycles?

The team and I identified four scenarios based on the degree of stakeholder involvement and pace of innovation:

1. Consumer supremacy (low stakeholder involvement/fast pace of innovation) sees rapid growth in electrification due to technological advancements, customer choice, and free market dynamics.
2. With limited regulatory involvement, "hydrocarbon heavy" (low stakeholder involvement/slow pace of innovation) sees a resurgence in fossil fuel consumers making consumption decisions primarily based on costs.
3. Electric evolution (high stakeholder involvement/fast pace of innovation) is characterized by global coordination to decarbonize through the energy transition, electrification, regulatory oversight, and political intervention.

4. Volatile geopolitical relations and "bad actors" lead to stagnation (high stakeholder involvement/slow pace of innovation), which is characterized by a stagnated, but highly regulated, economy and failed energy transition efforts.

The scenarios were leveraged by this utility giant to stress test the strategy, allowing for updates, better preparation, risk mitigation, and different decisions on where to invest. Scenarios helped management build a resilient business based on a better appreciation of possible and probable futures and enhanced flexibility. The senior vice president for strategy and growth was particularly pleased with how we "challenged and engaged the strategy function, leadership team, and board" using scenarios. The organization remains a dominant North American transmission and distribution company, providing safe and reliable electricity to millions of customers.

Using further real-world examples such as credit card powerhouse Amex and others, this chapter explains the benefits of scenario analysis and how to integrate it into a flexible and effective strategic planning process.

◆ ◆ ◆

WHAT IS SCENARIO ANALYSIS?

To help interpret the future, scenario analysis is a vital part of the outside-in analysis. When companies heavily depend on certain external factors (e.g., the value of a currency, price of oil, and political environments), analyzing different scenarios is essential to build strategic flexibility. Scenario analysis supports agility when adapting to changing external settings. It is not about predicting the future (that's forecasting)[90] but anticipating a range of possible futures. By challenging the assumptions underpinning the baseline view, scenarios allow executives to peer around the corner at alternatives. Identifying risks and opportunities in various possible futures supports making good decisions when facing uncertainty.

According to Philip Walsh, a business professor at Toronto Metropolitan University, a better understanding of the performance of firms and strategic implications within a changed environment can be achieved using the combination of a PESTEL analysis, internal resource analysis, and use of scenarios.[91]

I firmly believe scenario planning is indispensable to building a robust, bottom-up strategy. In fact, scenarios must be part of a more extensive strategy system.[92] The external signposts and potential outcomes developed during the scenario planning process help clarify an organization's uncertainties and inform the strategic opportunities which drive strategy implementation.

I've also found that the benefits are plentiful. Based on an extensive academic and practitioner literature review, I wrote a research paper on the eight practical applications and associated benefits of scenario planning, which include the following:[93]

- *Strategy validation and testing*: Stress testing the viability of current strategies allows you to create more robust and future-proof ones. Scenario planning helps review strategy on an iterative basis.
- *Complex decision-making*: Scenario planning can help with a specific strategic issue and to assess and decide on opportunities considering multiple market drivers. It also helps uncover the worst-case scenario and associated actions.
- *Educational learning*: Helps understand the causal relationships between variables in the system, drives anticipatory learning capability, identifies the impacts on internal capabilities, and encourages collaboration and team learning.
- *Nimbleness*: Creates an organization capable of reacting and responding as drivers in the market change. Scenario planning also builds enhanced strategic flexibility and agility, preventing a rigid business plan that cannot evolve and adapt.
- *Assessing uncertainty*: Helps businesses monitor strategy execution by assessing environmental changes over time, understanding what they mean to the organization, and better anticipating the future.
- *Risk management*: Produces a complete and more rigorous strategic plan that considers appropriate risks and threats and defines mitigation strategies for each risk in advance.
- *Innovation*: Scenario planning helps frame future aspirations and creates a context for contingencies. It also helps develop

innovative responses to strategic imperatives and challenges. It considers emerging technologies that might not be fully developed but are coming.

- *Options analysis*: Scenario planning ensures more than one strategic option is considered and charts different paths an organization can follow based on the external reality. Furthermore, scenario planning helps consider how allocating resources to a new course of action would play out.

HOW TO APPROACH SCENARIO ANALYSIS

Without repeating the detailed approach outlined in my last book, *Disaster Proof: Scenario Planning for a Post-Pandemic Future*, this section provides an abridged version on how to successfully build and leverage scenarios.[94] The process, represented in Figure 6, involves eight steps.

1. Identify stakeholders and define the scope

In the first step of the scenario development process, the project scope is defined. The goal is to clarify the strategic problem stakeholders want to address using scenarios. What's the core problem? What world or company problem are you trying to solve? I've learned that the key is for stakeholders to agree on a focal question that frames the scenario planning by setting the time horizon, formulating additional boundaries, and drawing up the project structure.

In my experience, it's also vital to determine who needs to be involved and to agree upon the scope and timeframe of the scenario planning process. Establish a straightforward question about your business's future and set the time horizon and level of planning, which will be dependent on factors like the rate of change within your sector, local and international politics (such as elections), product life cycles, and the behaviour of competitors, to name a few.

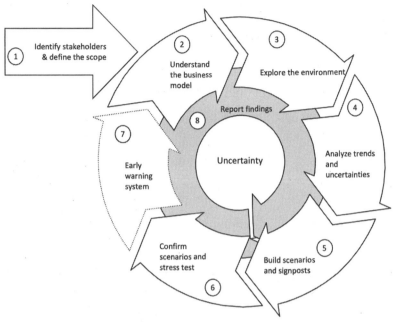

Figure 6: Scenario planning process

CASE STUDY
Developing scenarios at CPA Canada helps see into the future

Engaging a comprehensive set of external stakeholders helps identify a diversity of perspectives, ideas, risks and opportunities to inform and enrich the scenario planning process. For example, CPA Canada (the association for professional accountants) used scenario planning to help better understand what the accounting profession would look like by 2030.

CPA Canada assembled an impressive group of 40 business leaders, prominent thinkers, and stakeholders nationwide. In a series of impactful roundtable discussions, the participants—CPAs and non-CPAs from finance, industry, technology, government, and academia—defined the scope and asked themselves: What will the profession look like in 2030 and beyond? Trust me, it's an important question. Having worked at Big Four accounting giant EY, I've seen how important it is to think about and prepare for an uncertain future.

To answer that core problem or question, CPA Canada had to ask a bigger one: What will the world be like in a decade or two? Their response comprised four "scenarios" encompassing disparate future visions. In some, the international community bands together; in others, it fractures apart. Some scenarios envision technological change as a force for good; others see it as a threat.

"Of course, it's impossible to predict the future," says Tashia Batstone, CPA Canada's senior vice president of external relations and business development at the time. "The coming years will likely contain elements of all the scenarios rather than just one. They're not what we think or hope the future will be, but simply what's plausible. The value of the scenarios is that they frame the discussion. They encourage CPAs to think differently, from the outside-in, and consider the challenges and opportunities we may face in the future."[95]

2. Understand the business model

In the second step, the business model of the organization is analyzed. The business model canvas, invented by Alexander Osterwalder, a Swiss business theorist and entrepreneur, is a template that depicts how a business operates,[96] including how it creates, delivers, and captures value with its goods and services.

The canvas is a visual chart that describes elements such as the organization's value proposition, essential resources, key partners, customer relationships, customer segments, cost model, channels, revenue streams, infrastructure, customers, and finances. I've found that the business model canvas simplifies the visualization of how all the company's components connect to create value and helps identify which elements are vulnerable to changing external circumstances and would benefit from scenario analysis.

Considerations when developing and understanding the business model canvas include the following:

- *Customer segments*: Identify and define the target customer groups. Who are they? What are their needs and preferences? This step helps understand the audience.
- *Value propositions*: Clearly articulate the value the organization's product or service provides to customers. What problem does it

solve? How does it meet their needs? The value proposition is the heart of your business.

- *Channels*: Determine how the business reaches the customers. What distribution channels are used? Is it through direct sales, online platforms, partnerships, or other methods?

- *Customer relationships*: Describe the type of relationships the organization has with customers. Is it personal assistance, self-service, automated, or community-based?

- *Revenue streams*: Define how the business generates revenue. Consider pricing models, sales volume, and payment methods. What are the main sources of income?

- *Key activities*: List the critical tasks the business must perform to deliver value to customers. These activities could include production, marketing, distribution, or customer support.

- *Key resources*: Identify the essential resources the business needs to operate effectively. These can be physical (e.g., equipment, facilities), intellectual (e.g., patents, software), or human (e.g., skilled employees).

- *Key partnerships*: Define strategic alliances or partnerships that enhance the business. What collaborations provide access to resources, expertise, or new markets?

3. Explore the environment

The third step explores the external environment to understand the sources of outside-in disruption and the uncertainty surrounding them. The goal is identifying developments that could drive future change and significantly impact the focal question. The external environment is explored from a macro-environment perspective. Using well-known strategy tools and frameworks, such as Porter's Five Forces and the PESTEL analysis, all potential external sources of change outside the organization are systematically uncovered and discussed. There are several important considerations I typically keep in mind:

- *Scan the macro and micro business environment*: Use the PESTEL analysis to identify forces of change—including political, economic, social, technological, environmental, and legal trends and uncertainties—that could have an enormous impact on the organization's business model. Use research methods such as expert interviews, brainstorming sessions, desktop research, and surveys to generate a long list of potential forces.

- *Scan the business environment specifically*: Use Porter's Five Forces framework to identify forces of change that might affect the company. This analysis is focused on the behaviour of suppliers, buyers, and competitors and the appearance of substitutes and new entrants. Using additional research methods, generate a long list of potential forces.

- *Create a master list*: Create the list by deleting all the issues and external developments that fall outside the scope (timeframe, boundaries, and focal questions).

4. Analyze trends and uncertainties

The world is increasingly uncertain due to the disruption caused by new digital technologies, deregulation, new business models, and the threat of new competitive entrants. This unstable competitive environment increases the level of uncertainty for senior executives and strategic planning teams who bear responsibility for a firm's strategic development. Specific challenges include the future direction, scope, and strategy required to deliver on corporate objectives. This, in turn, places increased scrutiny on the strategic planning tools used to undertake a rational and comprehensive analysis of the competition. While scenario planning is an established constituent of the strategist's toolbox, the increasing dynamism and uncertainty in many markets have made it essential.[97]

In the fourth step, the list of external developments is analyzed. In my experience, the goal is to arrive at a small number of critical uncertainties that are the driving forces of change in the external environment. Key uncertainties have the potential to swing the future in a particular direction.

There are three steps used to determine critical uncertainties. First, external developments with low impact on the focal question are removed. Second, external effects are grouped, and a cross-impact analysis is carried out. Finally, a distinction is made between critical trends (with a predictable impact) and critical uncertainties (whose influence should be explored in a set of scenarios).

5. Build scenarios and signposts

In the fifth step, the scenario framework is set, and detailed scenarios and signposts are developed. Part of this exercise is to create in-depth written descriptions of each of the four most critical scenarios and to identify the key signposts that will indicate you are going down any one of those four potential paths. Signposts are like an early warning system to alert you that a significant potential change you've identified in your business environment (a scenario) is indeed coming.

My involvement in scenario projects has helped me understand that a reliable way to create divergent scenarios is first to picture key uncertainties on axes that frame the poles of what seems possible within the set timescale. A scenario frame, or matrix, forces the scenario writer to think more broadly about the future, describing alternative courses of action. Key steps involved in building scenarios include the following:

- *Build scenario frame*: Create divergent scenarios by picturing key uncertainties on two-by-two axes that frame the poles of what seems possible within the set timescale, creating a quadrant of four potential scenarios. Select the essential two critical uncertainties to create a scenario frame. Define their extreme positions. The two critical uncertainties selected should have a low interdependence on each other.
- *Translate available trends to the scenario frame and identify signposts*: Use trend clusters (similar trends that relate to each other) to translate trends to each of the four quadrants of the scenario frame created in the step above. Not all trend clusters will be as relevant per quadrant. Using all previously identified trend clusters helps to build a picture, from which a fuller description will be created for each scenario, a comprehensive written description of each possible future that is challenging, plausible, consistent, relevant, divergent, and balanced. Based on the scenario frame developed, for each of the four scenarios you've focused on, identify the signposts that measure whether a particular scenario is playing out. For example, one of the quadrants or scenario frames could describe a particular political

party getting elected and being anti-industry. The signpost could be the election of that political party.

- *Develop detailed stories*: Describe several root causes for each of the four scenarios. Root causes are the main reasons why the world might head in the direction of the scenario. To structure the scenario stories, describe the implications in different layers of meaning. A narrative can be written for each scenario based on the defined root causes and trend results. For example, we expect a new government to be elected in a specific scenario, with implications regarding the regulation of the industry in question. This means new and different business impacts dealing with this regulation, which must all be described in a realistic, comprehensive way to fully understand the potential consequences for the business.

- *Illustrate scenarios*: Visually illustrate the scenarios with pictures to stimulate action and ideas. Scenarios should be accessible and understandable to the people within the organization. Possible illustration methodologies include cartoons or mock newspapers with headlines suggesting future events or video documentaries describing potential events.

CASE STUDY
Collaborative scenarios at Fast Future, APEX, and Future Travel Experience

Post-COVID-19, Fast Future (a research and consulting firm), APEX (Airline Passenger Experience Association), and Future Travel Experience (an events and media company) formed a team to look at the airline industry's future using scenarios. The outside-in external research study they performed effectively involved broad stakeholder engagement using a 16-question survey completed by 269 industry professionals from 47 countries, alongside additional research and expert interviews. The participants of a subsequent webinar, which drew over 900 participants, were also polled on some of the questions.

Initial results identified that the recovery of commercial aviation would depend on numerous factors. Using what Fast Future CEO Rohit Talwar refers to as "the driving force model of scenario development," the research team built scenarios using a matrix based on two fundamental axes: economic recovery and industry collaboration. This matrix was the basis of the study's four scenarios.

The first, Survival of the Safest, envisioned a deep recession and fragmented industry response. In this scenario, the report suggested passengers' reluctance to fly would be heightened by confusing protocols that differed by country, airline, and airport.

The second scenario, Love in a Cold Climate, predicted what air travel could look like if there was an economic recession but a coordinated industry response. While financial hardship would mean fewer leisure travellers, the report argued that business travellers and those with disposable incomes would be more likely to feel safe when flying, spurring growth in demand.

Meanwhile, Hope and Glory imagined a solid economic recovery but a fragmented industry response. In this scenario, the study predicted that the air transport ecosystem would rely on passengers to take responsibility for testing, vaccination, and certification, meaning that air travel demand would return. Still, revenue would lag due to intense competition.

The fourth scenario, Sealed and Secure, imagined economic recovery alongside a cross-sectoral approach. This was a scenario where the industry tightened and enhanced the travel experience.[98]

When building scenarios and signposts, I've found it's also essential to understand how they link together. There are signals in the world—for example, interest rates, election polling, or airline travel statistics—indicating that a particular scenario is playing out. Signals or signposts, which are simply pointers that a specific trend is happening, are usually economic, sociopolitical, competitive, and technological in nature.

6. Confirm scenarios and stress test

In the sixth step, the scenarios and signposts developed are presented, discussed, and settled upon with the key workshop stakeholders. Strategic choices and options are also identified. The strategic choices are the explicit and implicit choices the organization has made in developing its strategy, drawn from a set of strategic options available. They will then be both ranked and rated in the four scenarios to assess their fit with the external environment. The goal is to create a comprehensive framework to test the strategic options (stress test the strategy). A precise evaluation framework ensures that strategic options align with the company's tolerance for risk.

American Express (Amex) began a scenario planning exercise in 2018. When stress testing the strategy against the scenarios, the organization leveraged scenario planning to help prepare for the worst outcome: downturns. The CFO, Jeff Campbell, explained how having a playbook based on downturn scenarios greatly assisted in managing the organization when, instead of a recession, an even worse-case scenario actually played out: the COVID-19 pandemic. The team created economic scenarios and held senior management meetings, saying, "OK, we're faced with these facts; how do we want to respond?" They didn't leave home without it. They went through a second exercise again in 2022, modelled on the first, to develop a new playbook for how they might run the company through a sustained inflationary period like the 1970s.[99] Much of what they planned for has actually played out in real life.

7. Early warning system (optional)

In the seventh step, an external early warning monitoring system is developed to keep tabs on changes in the external environment and assess the probability of the scenarios. This step is about using the signposts in a proactive way to help monitor the external world and manage the business implications. Performance management is explored more broadly, beyond scenario related signposts in Chapter 8, but essentially this monitoring system can be a dashboard tracking mechanism, including triggers from the external environment that indicate that one or more of the alternative scenarios are unfolding. Regular testing of scenarios improves their effectiveness. The early warning system offers a structured approach to obtain expert input on key change indicators and helps report the current assessment of the scenarios and assess the implications on the organization's strategic options.

Key considerations my work with clients has uncovered include the following:

- *Examine the monitoring needs and requirements*: Monitoring the external environment is critical to managing uncertainty. Monitoring needs often include information on scenario probability, development of critical uncertainties, and perspectives of internal and external experts.

- *Identify the key change indicators*: Identify events, developments or opinions that inhibit or enable changes in the external environment and indicate changes in the critical uncertainties. Select a balanced set of indicators that are representative, valid, and significant and can be measured to estimate the overall development of the critical uncertainties.
- *Identify an expert panel*: Identify a panel of subject matter experts. They can consist of internal experts within the company as well as external experts.

8. Report findings

The final step is to produce a report that provides key findings and recommendations from the scenario-planning exercise, including an overview of the analysis performed and the key stakeholders consulted. To produce this report, ensure you do the following:

1. *Develop a draft report*: After the workshops with key stakeholders, prepare a draft report with detailed scenarios and signposts and an overview of the scenario planning analysis, including the methodology used and stakeholders consulted.
2. *Discuss the draft report with key stakeholders*: During this session, walk stakeholders through the information and answer questions as required.
3. *Update and finalize the report*: Once final discussions and clarifications have occurred, issue a report to management to feed possible scenarios into the strategic planning process.

◆ ◆ ◆

CONSIDERATIONS

Identifying and exploring different possible, plausible, and probable future scenarios helps to develop a flexible strategy that can be responsive to a range of possible outcomes and is vital in an uncertain world. It's about preparing for the future from the outside in.

Here are some key considerations when engaging in scenario planning:

- *Identify key uncertainties*: Start by identifying the uncertain factors that could significantly impact the future, driving change for the business. These could include technology, political developments, economic conditions, social trends, and legal and environmental changes.
- *Develop plausible scenarios*: Once you have identified the critical uncertainties, develop a range of likely scenarios (worst case and best case) that explore how these factors could interact and evolve. These scenarios should be internally consistent and represent various possible outcomes based on existing data and trends. Be careful to avoid developing scenarios that are practically impossible, as you'll lose engagement of stakeholders expected to use the scenarios.
- *Assess likelihood and impact*: Evaluate each scenario based on its probability and potential impact on your organization, including risks and opportunities. This will help you prioritize which scenarios to focus on and develop strategies for, and which ones to spend less time on. It's important to be careful not to quickly ignore and disregard certain scenarios, even if the probability of the scenario happening is low.
- *Consider multiple perspectives*: Include numerous perspectives and stakeholder viewpoints when developing scenarios. Stretched thinking through diversity is key. This will help you comprehensively understand each scenario's potential risks and opportunities.
- *Be agile and flexible*: Scenario planning is about developing a flexible and responsive strategy that can adapt to various possible outcomes. It's not meant to be linear. As such, it is essential to remain agile and flexible and be prepared to adjust your strategy as new information and developments arise. It's also important to identify strategies that remain the same regardless of the scenario that might play out.

- *Anticipate future possibilities*: Scenario analysis anticipates a range of possible futures. Other methodologies can be appropriate but have limitations. For example, contingency planning deals with one uncertainty at a time. In contrast, sensitivity analysis examines the impact of changing one variable while keeping all others constant.

- *Remember that volatility is the leading driver in creating and destroying value*: Research shows that managers prefer to focus mainly on strategy execution, whereas external effects have an equally significant impact on the strategy. Scenario analysis allows a company to take into account external forces and have a better understanding of external volatility.

- *Develop signposts as early warning signals*: It's essential to develop early warning signposts to help assess whether a particular scenario may be emerging and playing out. It is analogous to weather forecasting, studying atmospheric conditions to predict what the weather will potentially be like in seven days.

- *Monitor and update regularly*: Finally, it is essential to periodically monitor and update your scenarios and strategy in response to changing conditions and new information. This keeps them fresh and relevant and will help ensure that your organization remains well prepared and can effectively respond to various possible outcomes.

PART 2

INSIDE OUT

CHAPTER 6
OPERATING MODEL ANALYSIS

"The same products, services, or technologies can fail or succeed depending on the business model you choose. Exploring the possibilities is critical to finding a successful business model."
—ALEXANDER OSTERWALDER, AUTHOR & ENTREPRENEUR

UNEARTHING LEASING OPPORTUNITIES IN NORTH AMERICA'S HYDROVACING BUSINESS

According to Mordor Intelligence, the construction market in North America is projected to reach US$2.46 trillion in 2024, with an anticipated increase to US$3.11 trillion by 2029. This growth is expected at a compound annual growth rate of 4.82 percent during the forecast period (2024–2029). Given the extensive scale of construction, substantial excavation and soil removal are necessary, particularly in densely developed areas.[100]

Hydrovac trucks are highly specialized vehicles designed for precise and non-destructive excavation and digging, combining high-pressure water and a powerful vacuum system to break up and eliminate soil. These suction trucks prove valuable in situations where traditional excavation methods may be challenging or risky. They safely locate and expose underground utilities such as pipes, cables, and conduits and are used to create trenches without jeopardizing existing infrastructure, all while reducing the risk of damage and minimizing environmental impact.

Adding to its existing manufacturing and services business, one of the largest hydrovac companies in North America aimed to double its business by exploring the opportunity to lease hydrovacs, renting the equipment to customers instead of selling assets on a short- or long-term basis. The company's leaders recognized the leasing opportunity as crucial to future growth for five reasons:

1. A growing share of customers were self-performers.
2. The commoditization of hydrovacs across the industry.
3. The company's favourable position to grow in this market.
4. The predictability that long-term customer leasing agreements could bring to the business.
5. The potential positive impact on profit and share price.

Before a decision could be made, though, company leadership engaged me and my team to perform a strategic assessment of the operating model for leasing. The analysis needed to consider target customers, technical requirements, support requirements, legal agreements, and financial returns, leaving no stone unturned.

To conduct the analysis, we initially researched industry norms related to leasing, identifying strategic and competitive variables that drive success from the inside out. We then defined the new leasing proposition, performed a detailed assessment to identify strengths and weaknesses, and provided final recommendations on whether to proceed or not.

The operating model analysis concluded that the company should target specific customer segments for leasing purposes, and a profitable opportunity was unearthed. However, achieving this valuable goal would require new rent-purchase options, warranty improvements, enhanced crew training, and new pricing methods. Not to mention balancing the company's finite resources between its traditional growth avenues and this new growth opportunity.

Furthermore, it was found that the new leasing services team would need to collaborate closely with the manufacturing team and the existing (or possibly a new) sales and marketing team, creating new structural connection points within the organization. The analysis also found that to be successful, the company would need new technology, performance metrics, business processes, sales approaches, agreement structures, and an integrated communications plan.

This example underscores the importance of inside-out operating model analysis using detailed assessment capabilities. Assessing something as critical as a new line of business, like leasing, requires carefully evaluating risks, opportunities, and constraints within a business operating model so that a new target state can be designed.

The target-state design positioned the hydrovac company to successfully launch its new line of business. The key executive involved in the project acknowledged, "We would not have been able to complete this highly important assessment and growth strategy work within the required timeframes without the help of you and your team."

This chapter highlights the process of assessing an operating model from the inside out by examining essential criteria, emphasizing the importance of reducing complexity, and showcasing the power of critical thinking and analysis in establishing a baseline for a future operating model.

◆ ◆ ◆

WHAT IS OPERATING MODEL ANALYSIS?

My work as a strategic advisor has helped me understand that an operating model represents how a company plans to execute its strategy and deliver value to customers and other stakeholders from the inside out. It includes the characteristics, tasks, activities, processes, and capabilities that the company follows and can be visualized using charts, graphics, tables, and maps. Whereas a business model outlines how a company captures and offers value through its products and services, value proposition, and customer segments,[101] an operating model serves as a blueprint for implementing the business model.

An essential part of strategy development is assessing an organization's current internal state, which can be effectively done through an operating model analysis. An operating model bridges the "why" of strategy with the "how" of day-to-day operations; a thorough examination of an organization's operating model strongly indicates where a company realizes its strategy.

In my experience working with various organizations globally, I have observed that an operating model comprises eight elements, each of which will be addressed in the analysis:

1. Strategy and design principles
2. Service delivery
3. Governance and risk management

4. Stakeholder relations
5. Risk management
6. Organization design
7. People and culture
8. Processes, information technology, and performance management

A valuable operating model drives efficiency. McKinsey claims that companies must increase revenues, lower costs, and delight customers, and to do that, they should consider how to continuously reinvent the operating model to stay competitive. Organizations know where they want to go; they want to be more agile, quicker to react, and more effective. They want to deliver excellent customer experiences, use new technologies to cut costs, improve quality and transparency, and build value.

But while most companies are trying to get better, they tend to fall short. That's because they adopt one-off initiatives in separate units that don't have a significant enterprise-wide impact; or they adopt the improvement-method-of-the-day, which almost invariably yields disappointing results; or they create programs that provide temporary gains but aren't sustainable.

For companies to build value and provide compelling customer experiences at lower costs, McKinsey has found that businesses must commit to a next-generation operating model. This new way of running an organization combines digital technologies and operations capabilities in an integrated, well-sequenced way to achieve step-change improvements in revenue, customer experience, and cost.[102]

HOW TO APPROACH OPERATING MODEL ANALYSIS

Creating a baseline through a current state assessment approach

A current state assessment leveraging a performance scale can be used as part of the operating model analysis to indicate where an organization stands from an inside-out perspective in the present moment. The organization's current state can also be compared to its target state and an industry benchmark, thereby identifying gaps and areas to improve.

Here are the critical steps involved in a typical approach to performing this assessment:

1. *Initiate and scope*: Clearly define the scope of the assessment, including the business processes, systems, and stakeholders that will be included (see the next section for more on which components of the model to consider). It's also imperative to establish the objectives of the evaluation, identifying areas for cost savings, driving effectiveness, improving operational efficiency, becoming more digitally enabled and/or enhancing customer experience.

2. *Assess current state*: Interview vital organizational stakeholders to understand the company's operating model, including gathering data on the organization's operating model components. Process mining is a technique that can help here by collecting data through analyzing event logs and extracting process-related data. Process mining tools like Celonis, UiPath, Fluxicon, and Appian. These tools can help identify bottlenecks, inefficiencies, and other issues in business processes and evaluate the performance of business processes to find areas for improvement.[103] Once the data is gathered, you can evaluate the current state of the operating model, assessing its maturity (using a five-point scale) across various components, which involves comparing the current state against industry best practices and benchmarks.

3. *Design future state*: Based on the evaluation, identify the areas of the operating model that need improvement, prioritizing opportunities based on their impact on the business, change capacity, feasibility, and cost. Next, design the operating model that solves the critical problems and develop a roadmap for improvement, including specific initiatives, projects, timelines, milestones, and resource requirements. Researchers coined the term *business model roadmapping* as an approach to defining the transition path from a current to a desired operating model.[104] (See Chapter 15 for more details on operating model development.)

4. *Implement and monitor*: Implement the roadmap for improvement and monitor progress against the objectives

established at the beginning of the assessment. This involves regularly tracking and reporting on critical metrics and adjusting the roadmap when necessary and assessing value realization.

Unpacking maturity assessment components

Once the scale for assessment is agreed upon, the next step is deciding which of the operating model's different components need to be assessed. These components represent various aspects of how work gets done. Following are the typical features of a business operating model that I've used in this type of analysis. While not all components need to be assessed in detail, they can be important in different ways depending on the context of the specific business. It's vital to use experience and judgment to decide on which components to deep dive on and those that require only a high-level assessment.

- *Strategy and design principles*: The organization's mission, vision, and goals, as well as the strategies and tactics used to achieve them. The design principles define how the organization should operate and provide rigour, consistency, and structure to guide the design process.
- *Service delivery*: Defines critical service areas, high-level activities, and core competencies; defines functional activities and describes changes required to move to a future state.
- *Process*: The set of activities an organization uses to create value, including the design, implementation, and management of these processes. Provides an integrated view of how an organization's work is done. Models are the starting point for any efforts to improve performance, and they use standard tools and techniques to ensure integration and alignment across functions.
- *Organization design, people, and culture*: Defines organizational structure, responsibility, accountability, culture, values, required skills and leadership style, and how people will be managed.
- *Information technology*: The systems and tools used to support an organization's processes and achieve its goals, including hardware,

software, and data management. How effectively an organization uses industry-leading technology can be critical to success. Hot topics right now include service orientation, networked ecosystems, digitization, innovation, and customer orientation.[105]

- *Governance and risk management*: This covers the policies and procedures that ensure an organization's activities are aligned with its objectives and values; the oversight and decision-making structures that guide an organization; the infrastructure that supports the ongoing management of business processes, including the roles, responsibilities and assignment of who makes what decisions associated with business processes; and provides a framework that balances stakeholder interests and risk mitigation.

- *Performance management*: A comprehensive set of key performance indicators (KPIs) for an organization's business processes that align them with its strategic objectives and allow it to measure performance against the organization's past, industry peers, and strategic goals.

- *Stakeholder relations and engagement*: Documents key stakeholder groups, critical needs, and relative influence and describes the connection points needed between teams and stakeholder management.

In addition to the maturity assessment on all of the components described above, management consulting firm Bain & Company claims that to ensure success when assessing an organization's operating model it needs to be evaluated against a higher set of design principles. For example, increased centralization of corporate services to drive lower cost and increased efficiency, or a focus on greater connectivity to customers in how work gets done. A carefully drafted set of design principles helps align the leadership team around objective criteria for designing the operating model, allowing senior leaders to objectively evaluate operating model options based on agreed-upon principles.[106]

In my experience, KPIs are another vital component that must be considered. These are quantifiable measurements to gauge a company's long-term performance that help determine a company's strategic, financial, and operational achievements, especially compared to other businesses within the same sector.

Electric vehicle maker Tesla is a first-rate example of the importance of a performance management system as part of an operating model. During the Q4 2021 earnings release, Tesla produced a record 305,840 vehicles and delivered 308,650 vehicles. From a KPI perspective, production is a big deal for the company because it has consistently been criticized for being bad at ramping up. Increased manufacturing scale means driving market share and profits up for Tesla. On another measure, Tesla's automotive gross margin expanded in the same quarter to 30.6 percent, up from 19.2 percent the previous year. Gross margin is one of Tesla's best profitability measures because it isolates its vehicle production costs. Tesla grew its gross margin in Q4 even as sales of lower-priced models outpaced its higher-margin models.[107] These KPIs and others help Tesla understand where the company sits in relation to competitors in an intensely competitive, rapidly changing industry, and keep it on track toward its future-state goals.

Overall, the operating model components are like an interconnected and interdependent web. I've learned that changing one part can impact others, so assessing and optimizing the entire operating model is essential. By doing this, organizations can ensure that their strategies, processes, people, technology, and governance are aligned and optimized to achieve their objectives.

Complexity reduction as part of the operating model analysis

Global data creation is projected to swell to more than 180 zettabytes by 2025, up from 64.2 zettabytes in 2020. This is one example of how businesses are becoming more complex than ever.[108] Having executed numerous projects in this space, I've found that complexity reduction can be an essential part of a business operating model analysis because it can help organizations streamline their operations, reduce costs, filter key information for decision-making, and improve efficiency.

Complexity reduction can involve organizations reviewing their business processes to identify steps that can be eliminated, automated, or simplified, reducing the time and resources required to complete tasks and improve efficiency. Organizations can also review their product and service offerings to identify those that could be more profitable or better align with their long-term strategic objectives or rationalize their offerings to focus on their best and most strategic products and services.

Taming complexity can be a source of competitive advantage. At Netflix, for example, the company's famous "Reference Guide on Our Freedom &

Responsibility Culture" stipulates that it is the duty of managers to eliminate unnecessary rules. This principle enables the company to continue developing new products and processes while avoiding a continual increase in complexity.[109]

Operating model analysis can also help firms simplify organizational design by reviewing their structure and roles to identify areas of duplication or overlap. By redesigning an organization, leaders can eliminate unnecessary layers of management, reduce bureaucracy, and improve decision-making. And organizations can review their governance structures to identify sources of waste and consider areas of opportunity for centralization.

I've found that deciding whether to centralize or decentralize core capabilities is a necessary operating model decision. When thinking about digital capabilities in a global company, for example, some might argue that they should be put in just one central hub, pointing to examples like Booking.com, the $15 billion global leader in travel accommodations, which co-locates over 1,700 developers in one location to optimize the tens of thousands of A/B tests that keep them in the lead. But others could argue that digital needs to be local, given the nature of retail, and each country needs its digital team to adapt to the local conditions. They can justify their arguments with examples from Amazon, which has prospered in the US but struggled in countries like the Netherlands, where the company doesn't have warehouses.[110]

CASE STUDY
Keeping things simple at Standard Chartered Bank, UK

Hybrid working models can drive efficiency. Standard Chartered Bank is a global financial services company headquartered in London, UK, that operates over 1,200 branches across 60 markets and employs around 83,000 people. About 90 percent of the bank's profits come from Asia, Africa, and the Middle East.

When the pandemic occurred in 2020, the bank's management team saw it as a catalyst for reimagining its operation and reducing complexity from the inside out. They looked at where and how employees choose to work. While many companies reduced their offices, Standard Chartered Bank took a more measured approach. It decided that a hybrid working model was the best way to maximize efficiency, promote employee well-being, and attract more talent.

Standard Chartered Bank built a new portal on ServiceNow HR Service Delivery, connecting backend processes such as document and data management while building dynamic workflows to support employee journeys.[111]

In summary, operating model analysis can identify areas to streamline operations and reduce costs by reducing a business's complexity. In my opinion, centralization is one of many critical decisions that need to be made to reduce complexity as part of an operating model. This can result in a more efficient and effective organization better positioned to achieve its strategic objectives. Chapter 19 further explores methods related to cost management.

External benchmarking tools for headcount analysis

Finally, although challenging, headcount analysis is a must-do in any operating model review and forms part of the organization component described earlier. Including benchmarking in this assessment can be used to help a company's leaders understand how their workforce compares to their peers in size, structure, and cost. This information can help organizations plan their workforce needs more effectively and identify areas where they may need more staff. Headcount benchmarking can also help identify cost-optimization opportunities by identifying areas where they may be overspending on labour.

◆ ◆ ◆

CONSIDERATIONS

Understanding inside-out operating model deficiencies and opportunities is fundamental to executing successful strategies. It brings the strategy to life.

Here are some key considerations to keep in mind when performing a business operating model assessment and analysis:

- *Understand the scope and objectives*: Clearly define the scope and objectives of the assessment, including the key questions you want to answer, the stakeholders involved, and the timeline and budget for the project. For example, is the assessment enterprise wide or a specific business unit or function?

- *Gather data*: Collect relevant data on the organization's strategy, risks, processes, technology, organization, talent, governance, and other vital areas of information. This may involve interviews with key stakeholders, observations of work practices, measuring cycle times, analysis of documents and data, and benchmarking against peers and industry standards.

- *Analyze the data*: Use a structured approach to analyze the data and identify key findings, trends, and insights. This may involve using tools such as process mapping, value stream mapping, gap analysis, and SWOT analysis to identify areas that are working well and areas for improvement. For example, where are multiple steps involved in a process or activity, or approvals that can be eliminated and streamlined. Techniques like Lean and Six Sigma can be used.

- *Develop recommendations*: Based on the analysis, develop proposals that address the essential findings and support the organization's strategic objectives. These recommendations should be practical, actionable, and prioritized based on their potential impact and feasibility. You cannot do it all, so focus on what will move the needle the most, based on capacity constraints.

- *Engage internal stakeholders*: Share the findings and recommendations with key stakeholders, including senior management, board members, and employees to get alignment and buy-in. Solicit feedback and engage stakeholders in developing a plan for implementing the recommendations.

- *Implement and monitor*: Develop a plan for implementing the recommendations, including timelines, resources, and metrics for success. Make sure change management and communications is considered in the implementation plan. Monitor progress and adjust the plan to ensure the organization achieves its strategic objectives.

- *Continuously improve*: Business operating model assessment and analysis are ongoing, particularly when the external context changes. Organizations should regularly review and update their operating model to ensure it remains aligned with their strategic objectives and evolving market conditions.

CHAPTER 7
ENTERPRISE RISK MANAGEMENT

"In a world that's changing really quickly, the only strategy that is guaranteed to fail is not taking risks."

—MARK ZUCKERBERG, FOUNDER OF FACEBOOK (META)

MANAGING A RISKY REFINING BUSINESS

North America is an essential global oil hub. The US and Canada are home to over 90,000 miles of crude oil and petroleum product pipelines and over 140 refineries that can process around 20 million barrels of oil daily.[112]

Oil refineries are typically large, sprawling industrial complexes with extensive piping running throughout, carrying streams of fluids between large chemical processing units, such as distillation columns. Common hazards are fires or explosions resulting from the presence of flammable liquids and gases and risk of burns, asphyxiation, diseases like cancer, or system corrosion due to use of toxic chemicals.

As part of the strategic planning process, one of North America's largest refineries was preparing for an upcoming board meeting. It has operated uninterruptedly and with excellent safety and operational reliability for many years, providing crude oil products to millions of customers across North America. However, management was keen to align on crucial risks. To do so, they needed to understand, and rank by priority, the risks that should be monitored and managed based on current internal and external assessments. There was also a need to explain how risk management connected with the broader strategic planning process.

The project team and I were tasked with defining the enterprise risk universe and identifying, assessing, and prioritizing risks before filing a report. We identified business risks across several dimensions of the operating model through interviews and workshops and determined how strategies and plans affect the risk profile and how the expressed tolerance for risk influences the risk profile and response.

Our research found a cocktail of risks, including geopolitical challenges affecting trade, unpredictable regulatory changes, market volatility, supply and demand shocks, increasing market concentration, digital disruptions and cyber security in general, oil and gas consumer brand challenges, crude supply and refined product contract management uncertainty, environmental impacts, and safety concerns. Furthermore, the team engaged management to consider the potential impacts, current activities, and gaps related to managing those risks. This was vital because there is no sense in identifying risks if you're not going to do something about them.

The exercise concluded with a high-stakes two-day workshop with the key leaders where they came to understand the critical importance of integrating risk with strategic planning. An effective enterprise risk management (ERM) program provides a window into the universe of risks that can impact an agency's ability to deliver its mission—a mission often articulated in a strategic plan. As a result, the strategic planning process is an ideal place to find and, in some cases, respond to, a surprisingly overlooked type of enterprise risk. Integrating ERM and strategic planning from the inside out can strengthen future plans while helping focus limited resources on the risks that matter most.[113]

The workshop helped to bring the most critical risks to the table to discuss what was missing and what else management should be concerned about as well as to agree on the prioritization of those risks. You cannot manage and mitigate everything. The management team selected the top threats to monitor and created action plans for complex turnarounds and making the necessary capital available. They started by identifying who was responsible for the various risks and initiating a process for management board oversight.

This example highlights the importance of understanding your critical risks as part of the ERM process. Using further examples from the US banking system, including Morgan Stanley, this chapter outlines the steps to establishing an effective and timely ERM process and the consequences of getting it wrong.

◆ ◆ ◆

WHAT IS ENTERPRISE RISK MANAGEMENT (ERM)?

ERM is designed to identify potential events that, if they occur, would have a negative impact on a company and to follow-up by creating a plan to manage risk. It provides a proven framework within corporate governance for risk management. The concept of ERM has been around for as long as I can remember; it was formalized primarily as a result of initiatives by the Committee of Sponsoring Organizations (COSO).[114]

COSO defines ERM as "the culture, capabilities, and practices, integrated with strategy-setting and performance, that organizations rely on to manage risk in creating, preserving, and realizing value," and emphasizes that organizations are most successful when they consider culture, strategy, and business objectives in risk management.[115]

Another expert organization, the Project Management Institute (PMI), claims that the risk management process should attempt to answer three questions for the project manager and their team:[116]

1. What are the risks and opportunities for this project?
2. What are the suitable risks and opportunities we can manage?
3. What will we do to proactively manage those risks and opportunities?

I've found that the challenge with risk management is that most companies' ERM programs operate with a compliance and informational focus, resulting in a highly detailed catalogue of wide-ranging risks within the organization, ranging from nominal to potentially catastrophic. ERM programs are often run independently without being integrated into an organization's strategy-setting (Chapter 1) and performance management processes (Chapter 8), usually resulting in mismanaged risks. Case in point, a Harvard Law School paper I published with colleague Chris Palmer cited analysis that found that some 55 percent of board members identified risk management as often struggling to keep pace with changes in strategy, uncovering an opportunity to focus on greater strategy integration."[17]

To be successful, a firm must think about governance and culture together when considering ERM as a basis for all other components. Governance sets the entity's tone, reinforcing the importance of ERM and establishing oversight responsibilities, and culture is reflected in decision-making. For ERM to be done well, it should be integrated into an organization's strategic plan by setting strategy and business objectives. With an understanding of the business context, an organization can gain insight into internal and external factors and their effect on risk, setting its risk appetite in conjunction with its strategy. The business objectives allow the strategy to be implemented, shaping the entity's day-to-day operations and priorities.

CASE STUDY
Enterprise risk management at Nationwide Insurance, UK

A study of the UK's Nationwide Insurance company found that a carefully designed ERM program—one in which all material and corporate risks are viewed and managed within a single framework—can be a source of long-term competitive advantage and value through its effects at both a macro, or company-wide, level and a micro, or business unit, level.

At the macro level, ERM enables senior management to identify, measure, and limit to acceptable levels the net exposures faced by the firm, from the inside out. By managing such exposures mainly to cushion downside outcomes and protect the firm's credit rating, ERM ensures the company can maintain its access to capital and other resources necessary to implement its strategy and business plan.

At the micro level, ERM adds value by ensuring that all material risks are "owned" and operating managers and employees carefully evaluate risk-return trade-offs throughout the firm. To this end, business unit managers at Nationwide must provide information about significant risks associated with all new capital projects—information that senior management can then use to evaluate the marginal impact of the projects on the firm's total risk. To encourage operating managers to focus on the risk-return trade-offs in their businesses, Nationwide's periodic performance evaluations of its business units attempt to reflect their contributions to total risk by assigning risk-adjusted levels of "imputed" capital, on which project managers are expected to earn adequate returns.[118] With assets in 2023 of £298.6 billion,[119] leading enterprise risk management remains essential to ongoing stability and success at Nationwide Insurance.

Risk management is critical to any business and organization. I've learned that it creates and protects value and is integral to all organizational processes. Explicitly addressing uncertainty is part of inside-out decision-making and is systematic, structured, and timely. ERM is tailored to consider human and cultural factors based on the best available information. Done correctly, it's transparent and inclusive, dynamic, iterative (by constantly adjusting and updating), responsive to change, and facilitates continual improvement of the organization.

HOW TO APPROACH ENTERPRISE RISK MANAGEMENT

Enterprise risk management framework

According to a report by Quantivate, 57 percent of senior-level executives rank risk and compliance as one of the top two risk categories they feel least prepared to address. Only 36 percent of organizations have a formal ERM program.[120]

Given these challenges, getting an ERM framework right is critical. The framework I recommend contains four steps and their associated activities:

1. Identifying and analyzing risk, which provides for recognizing, understanding, and describing current risks
2. Assessing and prioritizing risk, comparing risks to various criteria and determining a firm's tolerance for risk
3. Taking actions focused on managing and controlling risk (likelihood or consequence)
4. Monitoring and reviewing, determining the status of actions and controls executed to identify changes from expectations

1. Identifying and analyzing risk

This first step involves identifying the key risks and then summarizing each one. One way to identify corporate risk is to analyze business processes and perform a SWOT analysis to gauge the company's performance regarding strengths, weaknesses, opportunities, and threats. Another way is to survey for risks at every level of the organization after analyzing workflows and processes. You can also identify common risks by reviewing past incidents and near-misses or by using simulations, scenario role-playing, flowcharts, and risk mapping.

The clarity of the description is critical. After identifying risks, they must be explained in such a way that allows them to be understood by all who read them (even if they're being read out of context). Consider describing risks in terms of the root cause of the risk, the event that might occur if the risk plays out, and the consequence of the event. A risk event is an uncertain event or set of circumstances that, if they occur, would affect objectives—an unplanned variation from objectives, either positive or negative, which arises as the result of risks occurring.

CASE STUDY
Compliance & risk management failures at US banks lead to massive fines

Significant fines against big banks are unfortunate reminders that ongoing failures to correct long-standing compliance and risk management deficiencies will have consequences. The Office of the Comptroller of the Currency (OCC) issued significant fines against three major banks for compliance and risk management failures.

On October 7, 2020, the OCC walloped Citibank with a $400 million penalty for long-standing deficiencies involving the bank's enterprise-wide risk management, compliance, data governance, and internal controls—shortcomings that its parent company, Citigroup, is also being held accountable for by the Federal Reserve.

On October 8, 2020, the OCC hit Morgan Stanley with a $60 million fine for risk management problems resulting from a 2016 data breach, which involved failures by the bank to decommission two data centres properly. In dismantling these centres, the OCC concluded, the bank employed inadequate risk management measures.

On October 14, 2020, the OCC assessed an $85 million civil penalty against USAA Federal Savings Bank, which serves US military members. The charges stem from the bank's failure to implement and maintain adequate compliance risk management controls and an information technology risk governance program.[121]

All three examples highlight the importance of proper inside-out risk management with integrated ERM oversight, management, and control.

2. Assessing and prioritizing risk

The second step of the ERM framework involves assessing risks against defined criteria (rating the consequence of an event against its likelihood of occurring), selecting the top corporate risks, and identifying risks that require additional actions, controls, or monitoring. Prioritizing corporate risks is important because it helps companies focus their resources on the most critical threats affecting their business objectives and strategies. By prioritizing risks, companies can allocate resources more effectively and efficiently to manage those risks.

When assessing risk, consider the consequences of not meeting the organization's objectives: residual risk (are there gaps that need to be filled?), time horizon (could this occur in the short- or mid-term?), and urgency (how quickly might the crisis occur, if it does?).

My participation in ERM projects has shown me that visualization of risks helps people focus on what's important. Once the risks have been assessed, select the high-priority ones based on significance and the ability to take action by plotting them on the assessment matrix (Figure 7). It is crucial to step back from the matrix (Figure 7) and associated plotting and ask yourself whether they make sense. Are they relevant to the organization's goals and objectives? How do the risks impact the organization's strategy?

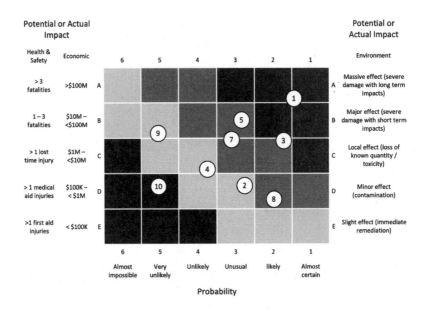

Figure 7: Enterprise risk assessment matrix

CASE STUDY
A recipe for sweet success at chocolate company Mars, Inc.

Mars Incorporated is one of the largest privately held companies in the United States, with annual sales exceeding $47 billion in 2023.[122] Mars owns and markets a wide range of very popular brands, including M&M's, Snickers, Dove, Mars, Wrigley's, Orbit, Masterfoods, Extra, Ben's Original, Pedigree, Whiskas, Royal Canin, CocoaVia, TWIX, and more.

Like many global companies, Mars faces diverse risks, notably in the variability of cocoa production due to climate change. As the leading worldwide chocolate producer, over 70 percent of Mars's cocoa comes from the West African cocoa belt, where erratic rainfall patterns and rising temperatures threaten future growth. The company also contends with regulatory and policy risks, including changes in tax policies, trade controls, and legislation related to employment, competition, and health and safety. Mars's intricate global supply chain is also vulnerable to disruptions from natural disasters, geopolitical tensions, and other factors impacting production and distribution.

To help deal with such difficult external risks, Mars developed an ERM process. The company piloted and deployed the initiative through workshops with geographic, product, and functional teams, engaging deep and wide within the organization.[123]

Driven by a desire to frame risk as an opportunity and to work within the company's decentralized structure, Mars created a process that asked participants to identify potential risks and vote on which had the highest probability. The teams listed risk mitigation steps, then ranked and colour-coded them according to probability of success. This process led to the creation of an ERM dashboard that listed risks in prioritized order, with the profile of each risk faced in the quarter, the risk profile trend, and a comment column for a year-end view.

According to Larry Warner, a Mars risk officer at the time, the key success factor for ERM at Mars was that the initiative focused on achieving operational and strategic objectives rather than compliance. The program also evolved, often based on requests from business units, and incorporated continuous improvement. Furthermore, the ERM team did not overpromise but set realistic objectives and periodically surveyed business units, management teams, and board advisors.

3. Managing and controlling risk

The third step, managing and controlling risk, involves deciding on an individual or team to develop an action plan and identify key indicators. The first step is assigning an owner to each risk. The "owner" is responsible for validating the significance of risk, documenting information, and creating action plans to address it, as well as identifying individuals to take accountability for activities within the action plan, monitoring the execution and status of the action plan, and obtaining additional support as required.

Once ownership has been established, risk-specific action plans can be developed using the following steps:

a. Identify and select strategies for managing the risk (see below).
b. State action plans in specific terms (actions, accountabilities, milestone targets).
c. Identify key risk indicators that will demonstrate change in the level of risk.

d. Obtain buy-in from key stakeholders (e.g., executive team).
e. Be proactive, start now, and course correct as required rather than over-planning.

Risk management strategies I've discovered over the years are as follows:

- *Mitigate*: Reducing the probability of the risk
- *Transfer*: Having a third party take responsibility
- *Accept*: Accepting that the risk will occur
- *Eliminate*: Focusing on avoiding the cause of risk
- *Increase*: Eliminating uncertainty by making the risk happen rather than remaining uncertain
- *Reduce*: Making the negative outcome less likely to occur

Once the appropriate action plans have been completed, it's vital to identify key risk indicators (KRIs) that predict unfavourable events that can impact organizations. KRIs monitor changes in the levels of risk exposure and serve as early warning signs that enable organizations to report and either mitigate or prevent risks.

CASE STUDY
Risk management recovery at Toyota supports market share dominance

Things can quickly unravel in complex global businesses. In 2009, Toyota's world-class production methods and reputation for manufacturing quality cars pushed it past GM to take the lead as the world's number one vehicle seller. But its time at the top would not last long. Jammed gas pedals that caused a sudden and unstoppable acceleration were first discovered in its Lexus brand vehicles. After several fatalities, Toyota was ordered to recall over four million cars and replace the faulty pedals. Subsequent recalls spread to other Toyota brands and pushed the total much higher. The recalls were costly, but despite independent analysis that suggested that driver error may have been equally the cause of the accelerator crisis, the worst of the damage was done to Toyota's reputation for quality, which had been central to its success.

An unplanned disaster of a different sort hit Toyota in 2011: the magnitude nine earthquake and tsunami in eastern Japan. The Tohoku region is an auto-making centre that suffered significant damage and loss of life, and Toyota had to shut down four assembly plants that made vehicles for Japan. On top of that, many of the small suppliers in the region used by Toyota to source parts and components had to close their doors. This greatly strained Toyota's supply chain, which had to be reconfigured.

It was clear by then that risk management and control would need a new emphasis at Toyota. To give risk management visibility, Toyota appointed a C-level executive, the global chief risk officer (CRO), to lead the management and control of risks from the inside out. At the company headquarters, each department appointed a risk manager to coordinate and cooperate with the global CRO. As part of the corporate governance function, meetings are held where all risk managers worldwide assemble to identify new risks and review and report on current risk items.[124]

According to Statista, after years of risky failures, by 2022 Toyota once again occupied the number one spot in market share globally at 11.5 percent.[125]

4. Monitoring and reviewing changes

Once risks are identified, you need to monitor them closely. The key activities I've used with success for this phase are outlined below and focus on the continual monitoring, improvement, and communication of an organization's risks and risk management approach:

- *Managing and improving*: Prepare mitigation and management plans, implement, monitor, and report on the status. Remember that too many important things are forgotten about in the face of urgent issues.
- *Monitoring and reviewing*: Continually check to determine the status of the existing risk significance, put in place objective measures based on data, and watch out for emerging risks that need quick action.
- *Communicating and reporting*: Create a reporting and escalation process for the board (or alternative leadership team). Ensure the

perception that stakeholders have of risk is addressed and look for opportunities to streamline and coordinate reporting.

- *Creating the culture*: To prevent "fizzling out" over time, openness must be continually cultivated. For example, create open communication channels and a culture that allows people to discuss risks without fear of personal consequence. It's also essential to maintain a disciplined approach to executing the process of monitoring and reviewing changes to risks so that it becomes routine to employees.

CASE STUDY
Risk culture challenges at General Motors

In 2012, G. Mustafa Mohatarem, then chief economist at General Motors, said, "There is a tendency to underestimate the risk . . . It is relatively easy to say, 'Well, it's a low-probability risk; let's go on.' It may be a low-probability event, but those low-probability events have a way of materializing, and we've got to understand what happens if we do it." Unfortunately, despite this caution from within, this enormous multinational got caught in a strategic failure—resulting in a recall of 3.1 million vehicles and a cost of $300 million—that materialized from a seemingly "low-probability" event.

The communication and evaluation of internal risks—in this case, faulty ignition switches—did not occur for 10 years. The US Justice Department subsequently launched a criminal investigation to determine if GM knowingly withheld information about defective cars from consumers. The question asked was whether GM was taking its inside-out risk management process seriously. Was everybody in or not? Or was it more of a check-the-box type of activity?

According to Global Risk Insights, GM's risk management culture was not as developed as it should have been. Exposing individuals at various levels of management to the goals and objectives of the ERM program is not the same as promoting and embedding risk awareness. The company was not as adept at spotting, assessing, and mitigating risks as imagined, and no one in the firm seemed to own the risk, so no plans were developed to manage it. It appeared that GM underestimated the probability of the risks associated with the defective engineering and failed to recalculate risks in a Bayesian fashion.

GM experienced an accumulation of bad decisions controlling these factors because the problems were entirely internal to company operations. The weaknesses in their risk assessment and performance review processes contributed to a significant failure. Further, these weaknesses thrived despite a "model" company-wide ERM process under the direct and active supervision of the company's top management and board.[126]

◆ ◆ ◆

CONSIDERATIONS

Risk must be ingrained in the strategy development process and the strategic plan to ensure success. ERM is an inside-out process that helps organizations identify, assess, and manage risks that could impact their ability to achieve their strategic objectives. Here are some key considerations when performing ERM:

- *Perform regular risk assessments*: The world does not stand still, so it's important to conduct a comprehensive risk assessment regularly, identifying all the dangers that could impact an organization's ability to achieve its strategic objectives. This should include internal and external risks, such as operational, financial, legal, regulatory, reputational, technological, environmental, and strategic risks.
- *Integrate strategy and risk management*: Risk management can help prioritize strategic initiatives (Chapter 12) through this quantification. An organization's risk management should align with and support a company's strategic plan (Chapter 1) and business model. It is important to us as strategists to help our stakeholders understand the risks they're exposed to strategically and how that aligns with strategic planning. Bottom line is that risks not properly managed can prevent strategic outcomes from being achieved. The updated COSO definition emphasizes the connections between risk, strategy, and value, illustrating how risk informs strategic decisions.
- *Build a straightforward process and governance structure*: Ensure a clear and well-defined risk process and governance structure is in place to support ERM. If it's not simple and easy to understand

leaders and employees won't use it. This includes identifying key stakeholders and defining their roles and responsibilities, establishing risk processes, policies, and procedures, and ensuring regular communication on risk management activities. It's also important to understand who makes the key decisions, with a clear chain of command. Based on data gathered from 123 organizations, research has shown that the presence of a chief risk officer, board independence, CEO and CFO support for ERM, and the engagement of a Big Four auditor are all critical for success.[127]

- *Understand your risk appetite and tolerance*: Define the organization's risk appetite and tolerance levels and ensure they align with its strategic objectives. This includes establishing clear risk limits and ensuring decisions are made within these parameters. For example, a low-risk company likely should not invest in cryptocurrency and blockchain.

- *Focus risk mitigation and response*: Develop a plan outlining how the organization will respond to different types of risks, including the appropriate allocation of resources. This should include a range of options, such as risk avoidance, risk mitigation, risk transfer, and risk acceptance, based on a clear understanding of each risk's likelihood and impact. It's essential to remember that not all risks can or should be mitigated against.

- *Prioritize monitoring and reporting*: Implement a robust monitoring and reporting process that enables the organization to track and report its risk management activities. This should include regular reporting to key stakeholders, such as senior management and the board of directors, and ongoing monitoring and review of risk management processes to ensure relevance. Risk management must be part of the inside-out process.

- *Drive continuous improvement*: ERM is an ongoing process. Organizations should continuously review and improve their risk management framework to ensure it remains effective and aligned with their strategic objectives. This includes regularly updating risk assessments, revising risk response plans, confirming risk tolerance levels, and incorporating stakeholder feedback. It's also important to consider how ERM effectiveness will be measured.

CHAPTER 8

BUSINESS PERFORMANCE, PERFORMANCE MANAGEMENT, AND SCORECARD MANAGEMENT

"However beautiful the strategy,
you should occasionally look at the results."
—WINSTON CHURCHILL, FORMER BRITISH PRIME MINISTER

WHEN IT COMES TO INFRASTRUCTURE, YOU ARE WHAT YOU MEASURE

One of the globe's most significant infrastructure firms is in the business of delivering design, planning, engineering, consulting, and construction management solutions. It focuses on solving complex problems for its clients worldwide. With over 50,000 employees and billions in revenues, focus areas include asset management, construction, environmental services, operations and maintenance, technical services, and more.

A joint venture division of the organization in North America needed a corporate strategy but also key performance metrics to help management understand if the strategy was progressing. Prompted by, as the CEO said, "substantial change," including a change in leadership, the organization initiated a project to help redefine the performance management process. He added that management was engaged and realized the importance of adequately defining KPIs aligned with the strategy to help "steer our organization toward success." Given the company's planned growth, it was essential to get this right.

Strategic focus is always the starting point. Initially, it was vital for my team to work with management to understand the strategic objectives of the business unit within the broader group of companies. Time was spent articulating the outcomes critical to success and where they wanted to focus their attention. Through a series of workshops, the organization started to align around the importance of safe operational excellence, commercial innovation, labour market flexibility, alliances, an integrated approach to maintenance and project services, and seamless transitions between client projects.

KPI development was accomplished through leading practice analysis, interviews, and workshops to create a selection of value drivers and key performance indicators aligned with the strategic objectives. Value drivers were defined as the measurable factors that influence strategy execution and shareholder value; these "levers" impacted the achievement of the strategy, describing the things the company had to get right for the strategy to work. Furthermore, they were both financial and non-financial as well as mutually exclusive. As a KPI initiative, it was exhaustive.

Engagement builds buy-in, and the strategy workshop was also critical to bring the team together to synergize and share findings from the current state KPI assessment. It also helped explore the implications of those findings. The sessions assisted in identifying the primary value drivers for each of the strategic objectives, agreeing on the validity of each of them as they pertained to the goals (we removed some that were deemed less necessary), and selecting the drivers that should be kept and used for KPI development.

A balanced scorecard was eventually achieved through several late nights and a two-day strategic offsite at a secluded mountain resort. We struck the appropriate focus across the four key KPI dimensions: financial, customer, internal business process, and innovation and learning.

In a *Forbes* article titled "You Are What You Measure," Jacob Drucker claims you can't improve what you don't measure. This quote has elicited plenty of admiration as well as ire. When measurements become an end in and of themselves, they consign themselves to irrelevance. Indeed, many critical factors, including confidence, integrity, and collaboration, can't be easily measured. Nonetheless, more than enough can, and should, be routinely tracked and monitored.

Drucker claims that KPIs are crucial for successfully growing a business. Identifying the right metrics, breaking numbers down into smaller drivers, and being willing to shift focus to new KPIs are all essential elements in successfully scaling a company. Without detailed performance metrics, zeroing in on the most influential business strategies becomes little more than a guessing game.[128]

The infrastructure company has continued to cement its position in the construction and maintenance-related services market. It regularly measures and reports progress using a balanced company-wide scorecard and cascades measures into individual employee performance scorecards to help drive consistent behaviour down to the front line toward the shared strategic goals of the organization.

Managing performance is a multifaceted endeavour when using the holistic outside-in, inside-out approach. As indicated in Figure 1 in the Introduction, this approach spans strategy development (business performance), preparing for execution (performance management), and execution (scorecard management). So, for simplicity, this chapter covers broad aspects of how you measure and manage performance across the entire strategic planning process and highlights how to develop the all-important balanced scorecard with examples of success stories from Fitbit, Inc. and Buffer.

◆ ◆ ◆

WHAT IS BUSINESS PERFORMANCE, PERFORMANCE MANAGEMENT, AND SCORECARD MANAGEMENT?

Managing performance starts with measurement—across the enterprise and throughout the integrated process of strategic planning and execution. Performance drivers are the measurable factors that influence shareholder value. I always say they create the link between the strategy and the key performance metrics. They're the glue. Effective performance management helps measure an organization's performance relative to its strategy and goals and aids in determining where course correcting might be needed if targets are not being met.

So, what is performance measurement? I see it as collecting, analyzing, and reporting information regarding the performance of an individual, group, organization, system, or any component inside the organization. It can be input-based, output-based, outcome-based, process-based, quality-based, or financial-based and aims to clearly understand how well an organization or individual performs and identifies areas for improvement.

Performance measurement can help improve accountability, decision-making, motivation, and resource allocation. It also sets out to define quantitative and qualitative performance metrics and enable the dissemination and ·

monitoring of goals within an organization. This is usually measured and managed through key performance indicators (Kpis), which provide consistent, objective performance monitoring against goals. Key performance indicators allow organizations to define their performance and value as well as track their success and help determine a company's strategic, financial, and operational achievements, especially compared to other businesses within the same sector.

Performance management and KPIs are both methods of performance measurement. Performance management refers to setting inside-out goals and regularly checking progress toward achieving those goals. It is a continuous process feedback loop whereby the outcomes are continually measured and compared with the target objectives. KPIs are quantifiable measurements showing how well an organization, team, or individual performs against a pre-determined goal or objective. KPIs can be applied to any performance area and should align with the organization's critical success factors, vision, and strategy.

Through many projects in this space, I've learned that KPIs should be tied to your core business. Electronics giant Intel Corporation heavily leverages KPIs to measure the efficiency and effectiveness of its manufacturing processes, research and development operations, and financial performance to measure progress toward achieving its strategic goals and objectives. The company uses a variety of KPIs across different areas of the organization to ensure that it is meeting its targets and identifying opportunities for improvement. For example, they use customer performance indicators (CPIs) to help focus on customer-centric outcomes, such as traffic inside stores, customer retention, average amount spent per customer, availability of products in demand, and customer satisfaction rankings.[129]

HOW TO APPROACH BUSINESS PERFORMANCE, PERFORMANCE MANAGEMENT, AND SCORECARD MANAGEMENT

KPI development approach

Any successful KPI development approach starts with agreeing on some principles. In the fall of 2019, social media giant Snapchat wanted to help create more consistency and trustworthiness in metrics used in the tech industry. Working with a consortium of industry peers, it established a set of best practice guidelines for building quality into metrics, especially crucial business and product metrics used publicly. Social technology operating measures principles—or STOMP—was the set of principles developed by this group to facilitate the standardized reporting of key operating measures applicable to organizations in the technology industry that develop mobile and other social applications and platforms. There is a degree of overhead associated with applying the principles, and it is expected that only some metrics should follow STOMP. Snapchat takes a risk-based approach, applying the STOMP principles to its most critical business metrics.[130]

There are several essential steps involved in the formal KPI development process that I've used with success. These include:

- *Identify strategic objectives*: High-level activities are required to realize the strategy. Align them to a firm's vision and mission, support differentiators, and address the SWOT. Have you defined specific goals with clear outcomes and a deadline? For example, achieve long-term commercial agreements with customers, locking into sustainable revenue.
- *Identify performance drivers*: Performance drivers, also referred to as value drivers, derive from the strategic objectives within the organization's strategic articulation map. They are factors impacting the achievement of the organization's strategy (quantitative or qualitative). For example, related to achieving long-term commercial agreements, performance drivers could be the ability to foster and develop the right client prospects that are willing to engage in long-term relationships, or the ability to deliver against contract expectations, resulting in repeat business.
- *Shortlist KPIs*: Evaluate KPIs against the KPI success factors to help prioritize which metrics to focus on. For example, rate the degree to which each KPI is aligned with the strategic objectives (high, medium, and low). It's important to prioritize KPIs based on the needs of the business and shortlist them to narrow the scope. Remember that less is more as you transition to a performance management system and culture.
- *Develop KPI scorecard and reporting criteria*: Determine who is responsible for each KPI. Establish a formal communications structure and cadence for reporting and discussing each KPI with

the leadership teams responsible. Decide how frequently reports will be issued and reviewed.

- *Document KPI definitions and calculations*: Explicitly define what each KPI is intended to measure. Determine which calculations are required for each KPI. Document the terms of measurement associated with each calculation.
- *Set KPI targets*: Benchmark industry-leading practices. Determine a target value for each KPI calculation.

KPI practicality assessment criteria

There is some science behind designing good KPIs. I typically use a fact-based approach to assess KPIs for practicality, scoring each shortlisted KPI based on predefined criteria. This can be done by engaging working groups in discussion to select final KPIs using a scoring mechanism for various measures:

- *Leading/lagging score*: It's essential to strike a good balance of leading and lagging KPIs.
- *Ease of measurement and data capture*: KPIs must be easy to measure and data readily available to help calculate the KPIs. What's easy gets done within an organization.
- *Quality of data feed*: Data quality can vary for many reasons, but data feeding into enterprise-level KPIs must be accurate to enable sound decision-making.
- *Frequency of data feed*: Data is most useful when relevant and up-to-date. However, it is not always possible to collect data in real time, and it is essential to factor this into the scoring.
- *Ease of communication and understanding*: The metrics selected must be straightforward and easy to explain so that people can understand the results the organization is trying to achieve and how the metrics are aligned with the strategic goals.
- *Transparency and consistency of calculation*: It is essential to understand how metrics are being calculated and which factors contribute to the performance of the metric to create buy-in throughout an organization.
- *The ability of employees to impact*: It is crucial to understand how

metrics are being calculated and which factors contribute to the metric's performance so that employees know how they can influence that performance.

- *The ability to drive positive behaviours*: Metrics can be used to drive behaviours, but to prevent unintended consequences ensure that the selected metrics incentivize the correct behaviour.

CASE STUDY
Buffer's Happiness KPI enables customer satisfaction

Take care of your customers, and they will take care of your business. One innovative example of a company using KPIs to measure performance against strategic goals is Buffer, a social media management platform.

Buffer uses a unique KPI, called Happiness, which measures customer satisfaction with the product and service. Buffer's Happiness KPI is based on a weekly survey sent to customers, asking them to rate their satisfaction with the platform on a scale of 1 to 10. Buffer then calculates the average score, and the result indicates customer satisfaction. The Happiness KPI is innovative because it measures a crucial aspect of the business that is often overlooked in traditional KPIs. Customer satisfaction is a critical factor for any business's success and by measuring it, Buffer can make data-driven decisions that improve the customer experience and drive business growth.

Buffer's Happiness KPI is also flexible; the company adjusts it based on customer feedback and changes in the business environment. For example, Buffer recognized that failed key actions significantly influence customer happiness. By addressing the causes of failed posts (such as authentication issues on the Buffer platform), they aimed to directly impact customer happiness. By analyzing these specific pain points and adapting KPIs to address user concerns, this adaptable focus allowed them to improve the overall user experience.

Furthermore, the KPI is updated regularly and shared with the entire team, creating an inside-out culture of transparency and accountability. Buffer uses the Happiness KPI to demonstrate the importance of developing KPIs relevant to the business and aligned with its strategic goals. The KPI has helped the company grow its customer base and increase revenue while maintaining high customer satisfaction.[131, 132]

CASE STUDY
Performance management challenges at Wells Fargo and Amazon

Specific to behaviour, one cautionary tale about tracking KPIs is the story of Wells Fargo, the massive financial services company embroiled in a scandal in 2016. The company's sales targets were so aggressive that some employees resorted to unethical practices to meet them. Employees had opened millions of unauthorized bank accounts, including fake accounts, and signed up customers for products without their knowledge.

The root cause of this scandal was the company's focus on short-term results. To boost sales, Wells Fargo had created a culture in which employees felt pressured to do whatever it took to meet their targets, leading to widespread misconduct. This serves as a reminder that it's essential to set clear expectations for ethical behaviour and to ensure that hitting specific KPI targets is not prioritized over doing the right thing.[133]

A further example of behaviour-driven metrics gone wrong is Amazon, which has faced criticism for its treatment of its warehouse workers. In 2020, the company was accused of using a metric called "time off task" (TOT) to track the productivity of its workers. The TOT metric measures the time an employee spends not working, and employees who consistently have high TOT scores are at risk of termination.

While businesses need to track the productivity of their employees, the issue with the TOT metric at Amazon was that it didn't consider the many factors that can impact an employee's ability to work, such as breaks for rest, bathroom breaks, or addressing personal issues. As a result, many workers felt pressured to work at an unsustainable pace to avoid being flagged as unproductive. This led to accusations of poor working conditions and the mistreatment of employees.

The Wells Fargo and Amazon examples highlight the importance of using KPIs from the inside out to measure and drive the *right* behaviours and being careful and thoughtful in the design process.

Balanced scorecard framework

Organizations are complex multidimensional systems, so the measurement approach should factor this in. For example, FMC Corporation is one of the most diversified companies in the US, producing more than 300 product lines in 21 divisions. A change in strategy and a vast diversity of initiatives, each with their own slogans, created confusion and mixed signals. Leaders realized that if you are going to ask a division or the corporation as a whole to change its strategy, you had better change the measurement system. FMC's leaders implemented a balanced scorecard with colossal success.[134]

A balanced scorecard is a management system that provides feedback on both internal business processes and external outcomes to continuously improve strategic performance and results. The balanced scorecard involves measuring four main aspects of a business: financial, customer, business processes, and innovation and learning. If KPIs track and incentivize performance on specific measures from the ground up, the balanced scorecard is the big-picture, top-down tool that ensures an appropriate mix of KPIs across the enterprise.

One benefit I've found of using a balanced scorecard is how it helps organizations align their business activities with their strategy and vision. It also provides a framework for measuring and monitoring performance and supports organizations in identifying areas for improvement and in prioritizing their efforts. The creators of the balanced scorecard argue that it provides a more comprehensive view of organizational performance and helps managers align their strategic objectives with their operational activities.[135] Further to alignment, it also allows organizations to communicate their strategy and vision to employees and other stakeholders, using KPIs to set their targets and track progress, thus focusing on the key drivers of success.

CASE STUDY
Driving behaviour at Fitbit, Inc. with performance management balance

Employee behaviours are crucial to company culture, and performance management systems drive behaviours. One example of a company that has successfully integrated scorecard management into its company culture is Fitbit, Inc., a technology company specializing in wearable fitness devices.

Fitbit used a balanced scorecard approach to align strategic objectives, monitor performance, and drive continuous organizational improvement from the inside out. The company's scorecard system focused on various strategic objectives, including product innovation, customer satisfaction, operational efficiency, and financial performance. Fitbit conducted regular performance reviews to track progress against the established KPIs. These reviews involved managers and employees discussing company performance against the strategic objectives, identifying areas for improvement, and collaboratively setting action plans to address gaps or challenges. Fitbit emphasized the use of data to inform decision-making. The company collected and analyzed relevant data to measure performance, identify trends, and uncover insights. This data-driven approach ensured that decision-making was based on accurate information and supported continuous improvement efforts. Fitbit recognized and rewarded employees who achieve outstanding results and consistently contributed to the company's scorecard goals. This recognition took the form of incentives, performance bonuses, or public acknowledgement and was intended to motivate employees and reinforce the importance of scorecard management in the company culture.

By effectively integrating scorecard management, Fitbit aligned its organization with strategic objectives, tracked performance, and fostered a culture of accountability and continuous improvement.[136, 137] Since 2010, Fitbit has sold over 136 million devices worldwide and counted around 120 million registered users in 2022.[138]

Figure 8 illustrates how creating a balanced scorecard establishes a formal inside-out reporting structure for the four classic areas of focus—financial, customer, business process, and innovation and learning—along with target audiences for each area. It ensures that management's reporting focuses on the most critical strategic issues and helps companies monitor the execution of their vision and strategy. Other slightly differing versions of this scorecard model exist. For example, researchers published a paper in *Strategy & Leadership* describing resource, capability, leadership, and process as the balanced approach, particularly when trying to drive innovation.[139]

◆ ◆ ◆

CONSIDERATIONS

Examining existing performance measurements and developing new ones should be part of strategy development and execution. Using KPIs without

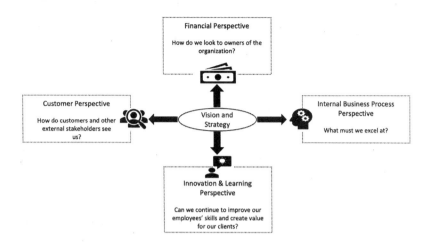

Figure 8: Balanced scorecard

concrete measures makes it hard to tell whether your strategy is successful. Developing effective inside-out KPIs for a business requires careful consideration of several critical elements, including:

- *Align to business goals*: You are what you measure, so KPIs should align with the organization's strategic objectives and goals. It's essential to identify which metrics matter most for the company's success.
- *Ensure relevance*: KPIs must be relevant to the business, measurable, and actionable. Choose metrics that provide valuable insights into the company's performance, so that leaders and employees pay attention to those metrics and align behaviours toward them.
- *Build timeliness into the KPI system*: KPIs should be regularly updated, in real time, to reflect current performance levels, giving leaders a pulse on the company and enough time to course correct when required, to keep things on track.
- *Support consistency*: KPIs should be consistent across different departments and levels of the organization and provide a reliable performance measurement across other business areas. When

measuring business unit performance this consistency supports fair comparisons.

- *Provide clarity*: KPIs should be specific, simple, and straightforward. Avoid using technical jargon or complex language that may confuse stakeholders. Ultimately, KPIs are about driving behaviours to achieve strategic outcomes, so clarity supports understanding, making buy-in by employees far easier.
- *Benchmark against others*: Benchmarking compares your KPIs to industry standards or competitors. It helps identify areas where the company is underperforming and provides insight into how to improve. It is important to not focus too much on the competition and forget to improve yourself.
- *Support flexibility*: KPIs should be adaptable to changing business conditions, reflect the company's evolving priorities, and be adaptable to new opportunities or challenges. As the business context and therefore strategy changes so do the KPIs need to change.
- *Build balanced metrics*: KPIs should measure different aspects of the business performance, that is, they should not be too focused on the financials. Using the balanced scorecard previously explained in this chapter as an additional measurement tool can help to ensure an appropriate mix of KPIs.
- *Ensure KPIs are actionable*: Decision-makers should quickly be able to see if they are succeeding and feel like they can directly influence the KPI.
- *Ensure KPIs are measurable*: That said, gathering data should not be a complex, difficult process.

CHAPTER 9
PORTFOLIO ANALYSIS

*"Business is often about killing your favourite children
to allow others to succeed."*

—RICHARD KOCH, VENTURE CAPITAL INVESTOR & AUTHOR

CHANGE IS CONSTANT WHETHER YOU LIKE IT OR NOT

Marathon Petroleum Corporation (MPC) is a leading, integrated down-stream energy company headquartered in Findlay, Ohio. The company owns and operates the United States' most extensive refining system; gathering, processing and fractionation assets; as well as crude oil and light product transportation and logistics infrastructure. MPC's marketing system comprises locations across the United States, including Marathon brand retail outlets.

In the summer of 2020, the company announced the changing of its portfolio by selling its Speedway gas stations to 7-Eleven's parent for $21 billion. The sale of Speedway, one of the country's largest convenience store chains with nearly 4,000 outlets, was the most significant corporate deal in the oil sector since the coronavirus slashed demand for fuel early that year.

At the time, MPC had been struggling financially and had shuttered operations at two refineries. It had been seeking to spin off Speedway for months. The deal brought approximately $16.5 billion in after-tax cash proceeds to pay down debts and support dividend payments. The deal included a 15-year agreement in which Marathon would provide 7.7 billion gallons of petroleum annually to the Speedway chain.

Diving deeper, it became apparent that Marathon agreed to spin off its Speedway chain partly under pressure from activist investors, including the Elliott Investment Management hedge fund.[140]

An activist investor is an individual, or institutional, investor who seeks to acquire a controlling interest in a target company by gaining seats on the company's board of directors. Activist investors want to change the target company significantly and unlock perceived hidden value. In an article in the *Financial Times*, Jonathan Guthrie wrote that Elliott Management had yet to dispense french fries with its slide decks, but in investor activism, the New York hedge fund group had become everything McDonald's is to burger restaurants—completely dominant.

As founder, president, and co-CEO of Elliott Management, Paul Singer is among the world's most feared activist investors. When he and his team get involved, they mean business, and shares generally rise when Elliott declares an exposure. They recently showed their reach and capacity by launching simultaneous campaigns in Germany, Japan, and the US, investing in Vantage Towers, Dai Nippon Printing, and Salesforce. During 2022, Elliott launched 13 campaigns, roughly double the tally of larger rivals, according to financial advisory firm Lazard.[141]

Elliott is always on the prowl for underperforming stock. For example, when San Francisco–based software giant Salesforce, Inc., initiated layoffs as its stock value fell, Elliott took a multi-billion-dollar activist stake. The move by Elliott adds to activist pressure on Salesforce to boost profits and shareholder returns after a half-decade of fast hiring and significant acquisitions, including the purchase of Slack in 2021 for $27.7 billion. Following the move, Salesforce said it was reducing its real estate footprint and cutting 10 percent of a workforce that had almost tripled in the previous four years. Salesforce currently has a market capitalization of $151 billion, down from a peak of more than $300 billion in 2021.[142]

The Marathon Petroleum and Salesforce examples demonstrate the importance of proactive portfolio management. If you don't do it yourself, someone else might force you. Success is all about aggressively evaluating from the inside out how your different products, business lines, and services perform and maximizing your portfolio to drive shareholder return. This chapter explores these success factors, including the disciplined process of reviewing portfolio holdings to identify where management should focus its investments and strategies to reduce risk.

♦ ♦ ♦

WHAT IS PORTFOLIO ANALYSIS?

Companies make bold moves when they change direction with a significant commitment of resources. These manoeuvres typically involve a different set of products or services, a new customer base, or new ways of operating. For example, Nokia Corp.'s shift in the early 1990s from forestry, TVs, and tires to mobile phones was a dramatic move. Such strategic shifts are risky; companies that attempt them often fail to meet their stated objectives. Yet they are essential for value creation in the long run. Although organizations may have long periods of incremental growth, the constantly changing business environment periodically forces corporate leaders to reposition their business portfolios in fundamental ways.[143]

So, what is portfolio analysis? It is the disciplined process of reviewing portfolio holdings for appropriateness and to reduce risks. By evaluating a company's products and services, portfolio analysis can be used to develop and compare alternate strategies that a company might pursue.[144] Such a review aims to determine where a company should focus its investments and business activities, and allocate capital (Chapter 14). Business analysts within a company and external market analysts may offer opinions as part of the business portfolio analysis, pointing to specific products and services that would yield better returns with more investments. Business portfolio analysis can lead businesses to better performance through categorizing products, evaluating investment opportunities, and identifying potential cuts.

Organizations execute their strategy on three primary levels: portfolio, programs, and projects. These three levels have distinctly different objectives but should work coherently. While project management is focused on delivering a tangible outcome, portfolio management is focused on the decision-making process around programs and projects. It should be executed based on its alignment with the goals and objectives of the organization. Program management is the intermediate layer that is focused on the delivery of business benefits.

Business portfolio optimization is important because it helps businesses make informed, inside-out decisions about allocating resources—such as capital, time, and personnel—among different business units, products, or markets. It involves analyzing and evaluating a company's portfolio of products, services, and business units to determine which ones are performing well and which ones are not.

Successful strategies are driven by top-line and bottom-line growth. As I said in a recent article for *Chief Executive* magazine, by optimizing the portfolio, businesses can maximize their return on investment, reduce risks, and ensure that resources are used effectively and efficiently.[145] This can increase profitability, better allocate resources, and improve competitiveness. Moreover, a well-optimized business portfolio can help a company adapt to changing market conditions, customer needs, and emerging technologies. It can also help companies identify potential gaps in their product or service offerings and provide a framework for making strategic decisions about entering new markets or developing new products.

In summary, business portfolio optimization enables businesses to make data-driven, inside-out decisions that lead to improved resource allocation, profitability, and long-term competitiveness.

CASE STUDY
Aligning portfolio management to strategy at apparel and gear company Patagonia

It's critically important to align the portfolio approach to core business and strategic goals. One example of a company with a well-structured inside-out business portfolio approach is the outdoor apparel and gear company Patagonia. As an avid mountaineer and outdoors adventurist, I found this example interesting. Patagonia was founded by a rock-climbing enthusiast named Yvon Chouinard as a small company in Ventura, California, making high-quality climbing gear. But, over the years, it expanded its product line to encompass a range of recreational outdoor apparel and gear, including food products.

Despite this expansion, Patagonia effectively managed its business portfolio approach, staying true to the core goals of sustainability and environmentalism, which are critical to the company's brand identity. In fact, the founder once said, "A company doesn't last 100 years by chasing endless growth."[146] Keeping the company private gave Chouinard far greater control over his maverick management approach.

Patagonia's portfolio management strategy also involves investing in innovation and R&D to create new products and technologies that align with its goals. For example, the company has developed new materials such as recycled nylon and pioneered the use of Fair-Trade Certified products to reduce its environmental impact and promote sustainable practices throughout its supply chain. This is not to say that Patagonia is perfect; it has been criticized for allowing microfibres to seep into the water system and ignoring questionable labour practices in less developed countries that produce some of its apparel, but there are attempts to improve.

Another aspect of Patagonia's business portfolio management strategy is its commitment to transparency and accountability. The company regularly communicates with customers and stakeholders about its sustainability initiatives, including its environmental impact and progress toward its sustainability goals.

Overall, Patagonia's success in managing its business portfolio can be attributed to its strong commitment to its core values and mission and its strategic investments in innovation and sustainability. By staying true to its brand identity and investing in products and technologies that align with its values, Patagonia has maintained its competitive edge and continued to grow its business while staying true to its mission.[147]

True to form, in 2022, Chouinard, along with his wife and their two adult children, transferred their ownership of Patagonia, valued at around $3 billion, to a trust and a non-profit organization called Holdfast Collective to ensure that future profits are used to fight climate change.

HOW TO APPROACH PORTFOLIO ANALYSIS

Portfolio optimization approach through three steps

The portfolio optimization approach drives closer alignment between the company's strategic objectives and its assets. I've found the EY approach, illustrated in Figure 9 below, to involve three vital steps. Firstly, a strategic review (knowing your core business). Secondly, a portfolio review (helping make better-informed decisions). And, finally, implementation (taking action).

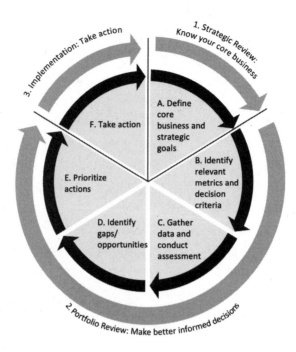

Figure 9: Portfolio management approach

1. Strategic review

A. Define core business and strategic goals

I believe in starting with what you're trying to achieve. The strategic review lets a company objectively assess its operations against a defined set of strategic priorities. The first step requires a deep understanding of the group's position, or core business, within the sector and a clear view of future growth opportunities and threats to align with the goals. The focus will be on ranking and rating the performance of the existing portfolio and identifying any shortcomings, weaknesses, and significant gaps. According to *Investopedia*, one company that understands its business is General Electric. It has successfully managed its portfolio by consistently focusing on its core and divesting non-core businesses.[148]

To complete this step, I've found the following aspects should be considered:

- Identify key industry trends and disruptors.

- Understand the latest competitive position and benchmark against peer groups.
- Assess performance against KPIs at multiple levels (company, region, project).
- Identify gaps in the portfolio that need to be filled to meet medium- and long-term KPI targets.
- Understand existing and future financial capacity and constraints.
- Assess existing capital structure and allocation.

Once the above is assessed, it's essential to define a clear set of strategic goals for the portfolio in line with KPIs and long-term strategy. For example, CAPEX profile, ROIC, competency alignment, geographic scale, commodity mix, and technical mix. Further to these strategic goals, it is argued that relative competitive position and actual and potential growth are additional parameters that must be considered in determining the strategy an individual business should follow when viewed within the context of the company's overall business portfolio.[149]

2. Portfolio review

B. Identify relevant metrics and decision criteria, and C. Gather data and conduct assessment

This step is about creating a scorecard to rank and assess assets. You then need to develop criteria based on strategic goals and relevant industry performance and gather robust and timely data to conduct a review. Once this is done, you can begin to analyze the strategic cohesiveness of the current portfolio.

One example of a company that has done portfolio management well by defining clear and vital decision criteria is Procter & Gamble. Its leaders have successfully focused on core brands and divested of non-core brands—an essential element of their assessment approach. This has allowed them to focus on their most profitable brands and increase overall profitability.[150]

It's also vital to consider the combined use of a large variety of analytic methods to understand the whole market mix, the strategic position held by every business unit within a market, the performance potential of the portfolio, and the financial aspects related to the allocation of resources for the business units within the portfolio. Note that the business portfolio's usual methods of analysis should not be relied on as the only tools for analysis and decision-making—different methods offer different advantages and disadvantages. Standard business portfolio analysis does not always provide accurate answers, but the main virtue is simplicity.[151]

The BCG Matrix is a famous and straightforward portfolio analysis method that I've used extensively over the years.[152] It classifies an organization's products and services into a two-by-two matrix. Each quadrant is identified as low or high performance, depending on the relative market share and growth rate. The four quadrants are defined as follows:

- *Question Marks*: There is a low market share in a high-growth industry. These categories require considerable cash to maintain or gain market share. Question marks are generally goods and services new to the portfolio with potential for high growth and share in the future.
- *Dogs*: These are categories where the business has a weak market share in low-growth markets. They neither generate cash nor require vast amounts of money. Due to low market share, these categories face cost disadvantages. Generally, cost-cutting strategies are needed to keep these business areas afloat, as these categories drain valuable resources.
- *Stars*: Categories with a significant market share in a fast-growing industry. They may generate cash, but stars require considerable investments to maintain their lead because of the fast-growing market. If successful, a star will become a cash cow when the industry matures.
- *Cash cows*: These are categories where the organization has a significant market share in a mature, slow-growing industry. These require little investment and generate cash that can be used for investment in other areas. They support the rest of the organization.

I've found that the BCG Matrix helps businesses decide where to allocate resources by identifying which products or business units are most valuable and which are not. For example, a company might invest in its question marks to turn them into stars or divest its dogs to free up resources for more profitable ventures.

D. Identify gaps and opportunities

Gaps create opportunities in the portfolio. Following the review, the team can examine these opportunities and ask some important strategic questions, such as what the group's critical growth areas and threats are (for example, regions, commodity prices, products, and political constraints). The team can assess the group's operational positioning relative to its competitors and its ability to lead and react. You also ask questions about which assets do not support your strategic objectives and should be divested. What are the gaps in the portfolio of business operations? Can the gaps be filled?

In 2016, Unilever identified a gap in its portfolio: a lack of products catering to the needs of consumers concerned about the environment. To address this gap, Unilever launched a new hair and skin care line called Love Beauty and Planet. The launch was successful and this became one of the company's most popular product lines.[153]

E. Prioritize actions

Without action, portfolio analysis is a theoretical activity which achieves nothing. At the action stage, my participation in portfolio-focused projects highlights that the team needs to do the following:

- Assess potential actions.
- Evaluate the likelihood of success.
- Secure support from critical stakeholders.
- Agree on actions, timing, and measurements of success.
- Validate agreed-upon actions against strategic goals and decision criteria.

In terms of potential actions, there are three possible options that I typically see:

- *Strengthen or grow existing assets*: Invest in upside opportunities through performance improvements or additional development. Consolidate interests and/or acquire small-scale bolt-on assets to leverage existing operations. Improve financial and operational performance (optimize working capital, reduce costs, right-size capital expenditures, and track performance).

- *Evaluate selected divestment candidates*: Base decisions on the likelihood to succeed, complexity to divest, impact on the portfolio, and impact on management. Then, review and agree on the divestment approach and preferred structure(s) and, accordingly, accelerate or decelerate making decisions on critical assets to keep, and less-critical assets to divest.
- *Grow through acquisition*: Consider transformational growth and core portfolio strengthening opportunities through material investments, including corporate takeovers, asset acquisitions, and partnerships. Define available acquisition capital and preferred funding method. Identify an optimal strategy to execute transactions.

3. Implementation

F. Take action

At this stage, forming an execution team and creating a detailed action plan is essential to optimize the portfolio. To do this, it's vital to identify internal leadership, sponsors, and key stakeholders for each action. You must also form steering committees and execution teams and engage external advisors. The action plans should include critical dependencies, resource requirements, timelines, and success measurements.

The team then executes the plans by regularly validating against original assumptions, critical drivers, and decision criteria. This ensures that sponsors and key stakeholders remain engaged throughout the exercise. During the execution process, it's essential to measure whether the actions deliver the expected results (and any unexpected results) as well as how the portfolio scores.

◆ ◆ ◆

CONSIDERATIONS

Understanding your portfolio is a critical part of the inside-out analysis regarding how the business performs. Companies can make informed decisions to allocate resources, maximize profitability, and drive sustainable growth by conducting a comprehensive business portfolio analysis. While performing the analysis, it's essential to do the following:

- *Align portfolio to strategy*: It is important to clearly understand the overall strategic goal and how all products or services within the portfolio fit into that strategy. You must treat portfolio management as a strategic imperative.
- *Assess market trends*: Neglecting market trends results in investment gaps, poor risk management, and missed opportunities, so the outside-in perspective is a critical part of regular portfolio reviews although portfolio analysis is primarily an inside-out process overall.
- *Get data gathering and analysis right*: Ensure your data and analytics challenge your portfolio and explore different scenarios. Consider the current market position of each product or service in terms of market share, competition, growth potential, customer satisfaction, cost to support, resource requirements, risk, and profitability. Ensure portfolio data is consistent across projects, functions, and business units, so that you are comparing apples with apples. Build effective reporting.
- *Evaluate from different perspectives*: Understanding different perspectives is a key leadership skill. Evaluate portfolio decisions in both absolute and relative terms and on a stand-alone and aggregated level. Measure them against specific criteria (hurdles) as well as each other (ranking).
- *Support routine leadership behaviours in decisions to divest, invest, or retain*: Each leadership team, project team, and business unit (individually or at a group level) should feel comfortable deciding whether to invest in, divest, or keep an asset. The "retain" decision should be a conscious one, not a convenient one. Doing nothing is often a higher-risk strategy that can lead to business decay.

- *Ensure speedy and flexible decision-making*: When required, one should have alternative strategic options or a fast process for developing and approving them. Don't wait, but act in an agile way.
- *Be prepared to make tough decisions*: Take the necessary actions while considering the broader portfolio. For instance, be ready to shut down or significantly amend a project or business unit that does not meet portfolio objectives, even if you've substantially invested in it, and it's been part of the business for a long time.
- *Be proactive on governance management*: Build effective governance to avoid poor-performing assets or projects and ensure business cases are critically analyzed and the benefits are real. Be deliberative about including business-as-usual activities in the portfolio analysis and not just special one-off projects and business units. It can be easy to get stuck in the trap of not critically reviewing those business units and projects that are long-standing within the company. Everything should be on the table—old and new.
- *Focus on management and capabilities*: Build the right level of experience and ability within the portfolio management function. Make sure project management and financial skills are seen as a critical success factor. Also, ensure the organization can absorb change.
- *Maintain alignment*: Be sure that capital allocation is aligned with the strategic value of portfolio components.

CHAPTER 10

MERGER, ACQUISITION, AND DIVESTMENT STRATEGY

"I'm not looking to make huge acquisitions. I'm looking for small companies that are compatible with what we do."
—MARK CUBAN, OWNER OF DALLAS MAVERICKS AND
CO-FOUNDER OF BROADCAST.COM

M&A LESSONS FROM A SOCIAL MEDIA GIANT

Facebook (now Meta Platforms, Inc.) is a powerful social media company with a large and loyal user base, a sophisticated data collection and analysis system, a diversified portfolio of products and services, and a dominant position in the digital advertising market. These factors give it a vast reach and influence over people's opinions, behaviours, and preferences as well as a competitive edge over other platforms. With its approximately 2.8 billion monthly active users, it is the largest social media platform in the world.[154]

In 2014, Facebook acquired WhatsApp's popular messaging app for $19 billion, which was one of the most significant tech acquisitions of that year. It was more than 20 times larger than Facebook's acquisition of Instagram two years earlier. WhatsApp had an immense and loyal user base of over 400 million monthly active users at the time of purchase and a high daily engagement rate of 70 percent.

This acquisition showcased a unique M&A strategy and had several key objectives. First and foremost, Facebook aimed to leverage WhatsApp's technology and expertise to expand its presence in the mobile messaging market, which is rapidly growing and attracting a large user base. WhatsApp had already gained significant popularity, especially in international markets, and Facebook wanted some of that action.

In addition, WhatsApp's user base was primarily younger users who were increasingly moving away from traditional social media platforms like Facebook. By acquiring WhatsApp, Facebook aimed to tap into this demographic and ensure its relevance among younger users. WhatsApp also had a strong presence in emerging markets, particularly in countries like India, Brazil, and Mexico, so the acquisition allowed Facebook to expand its reach in these markets and gain a competitive advantage. It also integrated WhatsApp's features—such as end-to-end encryption and cross-platform functionality—into its messaging services.

While WhatsApp was initially free to use, Facebook envisioned future monetization opportunities for the platform, such as introducing business accounts, advertising, and other revenue streams.

Since the acquisition, WhatsApp has grown from 400 million monthly active users to an impressive 2 billion as of 2023. Facebook has also reported that WhatsApp contributes to its overall revenue growth by increasing user engagement and retention across its family of apps. WhatsApp was a strategic fit for Facebook's vision of enhancing global connectivity and expanding into emerging markets with limited or expensive internet access. (WhatsApp uses minimal data and works on various mobile platforms, making it popular in regions like India, Brazil, and Africa.) By acquiring WhatsApp, Facebook also eliminated a potential competitor and threat to its Messenger app, which had fewer users and features than WhatsApp.[155, 156, 157, 158]

The acquisition's scale and strategic implications were significant. This case exemplifies how inside-out M&A strategies can drive market growth, tap into new user bases, and leverage synergies between technologies and platforms. The flip side of M&A is divestment, whereby a company aims to dispose of a piece of the enterprise in order to achieve its strategic objectives.

Chapter 10 examines different M&A and divestment strategies and provides a guide to executing them, highlighting the importance of always remembering to align these moves with an overall corporate strategy. The chapter also looks at alternatives to M&As, such as joint ventures, licensing agreements, and strategic partnerships.

◆ ◆ ◆

WHAT IS MERGER, ACQUISITION, AND DIVESTMENT STRATEGY?

Mergers and acquisitions (M&A) are transactions in which the ownership of companies, other business organizations, or their operating units are transferred to, or consolidated with, other entities. A divestment is a business unit's partial or complete disposal through sale, exchange, closure, or bankruptcy. Divestment most commonly results from a decision to cease operating a business unit because it is not part of a core competency.

Mergers, acquisitions, and divestments allow enterprises to grow or downsize and to change the nature of their business or competitive position. Many leading organizations derive substantial value from their acquisitions and divestments and recognize that a disciplined, agile, and repeatable approach to transaction strategy, planning, and integration prevents costly problems and elevates deal value.

The life cycle of M&A and divestments starts with strategy, from the inside out, and in the case of M&A is followed by target identification. Acquiring organizations begin this process by understanding internal capabilities, including gaps and opportunities, and then move on to target-company screening (Chapter 4), in particular, identifying and assessing the potential synergies of bringing two organizations together. In the case of divestments, a similar process is used in separating businesses within an organization to create value. In either case, a high-level assessment of future potential risks and current real issues is usually performed.

If a potential target of interest is identified for acquisition—or a business, service, or product line is selected for divestment—a pre-deal evaluation and due diligence will occur. Due diligence is about understanding the differences between the organizations or business units and the impact that integration or divestment could have. Valuation modelling, tax structuring, and research into financials, operations, and HR are performed. Workstream leads and support needs are identified during and after the transaction. Commercial due diligence during this phase is essential to turn up any financial skeletons in the closet.

Once a deal is publicly announced, pre-close planning can begin, which is explained in more detail in Chapter 17. At a high level, this is where the integration or divestment approach is established (that is, how to integrate or separate different assets and/or companies), and the organizations prepare for day one and stabilization. If required, transition service agreements are implemented, a detailed integration or separation plan is defined for day 1 and 100 days after, and functional dependencies are addressed. Risks are carefully managed, and the team develops a high-level plan for long-term integration and optimization. For example, making sure employees and suppliers get paid is a must.

My participation in various deals has illustrated that from the close of the deal and day one, the focus shifts to stabilization and short-term integration when the combined organizations operate together, or separated businesses operate apart. Integration and separation plans get executed at this point, synergies are captured, and the team monitors, measures, and reports on progress. In the case of M&A, financial statements at the quarter-end get consolidated, interim management is established, and the focus is on retaining key talent and cultural integration, which takes longer to achieve.

The final step of optimization and long-term integration or divestment usually occurs 100 days after day one. At this time, in the case of M&A the synergies from the integration are realized and execution of the long-term integration plan begins. The end-state target operating model, including process, technology, people, and data, is usually established at this point. These same principles also apply to divestments and separation situations, whereby 100 days after day one of operating separately, stabilization, value creation, and optimization should have been achieved.

CASE STUDY
Switching to high-volume acquisitions at Cisco Systems

One example of a company that quickly expanded and integrated a high volume of acquisitions as part of its core inside-out strategy is the California-based multinational technology company, Cisco Systems. Since its inception in 1984, Cisco has acquired a mammoth 200 companies, representing 50 percent of its business activity. It rapidly integrated these acquisitions by maintaining a dedicated team focused on post-merger integration.

By evaluating its own internal capabilities, when assessing acquisitions, Cisco looks for businesses that complement its existing product lines, fill gaps in its technology portfolio, and provide access to new markets and consumers. The company segments acquisitions into three categories: market acceleration, expansion, and new market entry. The target companies might bring different assets to Cisco, including great talent and technology, mature products, or new go-to-market models. The strategy is mainly focused on acquisitions with the potential to reach billion-dollar markets.

After an acquisition is completed, Cisco focuses on integrating the newly acquired company's operations into its existing business. This involves consolidating overlapping functions, streamlining operations, and integrating systems and processes. Of course, it is critical to ensure that the acquisition delivers the intended synergies and benefits.

Cisco has a reputation for succeeding in a process that challenges all companies making acquisitions, and because of this, IT market leaders and others frequently seek Cisco's advice on acquisition integration. That's because Cisco consistently and strategically seeks acquisitions with a strong business case, a shared business and technological vision, and a compatibility of core values and culture to foster an environment for success.[159]

HOW TO APPROACH MERGER, ACQUISITION, AND DIVESTMENT STRATEGY

Overview of different M&A and divestment strategies

As Larry Ellison, co-founder of Oracle, famously said, "Everyone thought the acquisition strategy was extremely risky because no one had ever done it successfully. In other words, it was innovative." Having consulted on many transactions, I've learned in the case of M&A that strategies vary based on the relative size of the acquired entity and the degree of difference between the two companies.

It's vital to understand from the inside out what type of M&A and divestment deals might make sense for the organization, can be integrated or separated with success, and help further the business's strategic objectives. It starts by understanding your internal capabilities, service, and product performance; evaluating gaps; and exploring opportunities to further performance through an M&A or divestment deal of some kind.

Consolidation occurs when the acquired company's size relative to the acquirer is high, and the difference in business products and services is low. The focus is on increasing market presence, so full integration is needed to drive operational alignment and lower costs. Research shows that when you

143

acquire another company that provides similar products and services, the cost savings tend to be much more significant than acquiring a company in an unrelated industry.[160]

Transformation is when the size of the acquired company is large compared to the acquirer, and the two companies have different business models, products, and services. Combining the organizations creates a new transformative organization with a new stand-alone business model, and new revenue-generating sources and cost-saving opportunities.

A tuck-in is when the size of the acquired company is small compared to the acquirer, and the difference in business model, products, and services is negligible. This type of acquisition might occur when another organization divests of a particular asset, business service, or product line. The focus for the acquiring company then becomes transferring core strengths to the target business; full integration occurs by embedding the skills and capabilities of the acquiring company into the acquired business to support improvements.

Strategic growth occurs when the size of the acquired company is tiny. Still, the acquired company has different services and products, which provides the acquirer with expanded offerings or helps it reach a broader geographic base of consumers. This is where hybrid integration is needed.

Finally, divestment in business refers to the process of selling off a portion of a company's assets, investments, or divisions. The goal is to maximize the overall value of the parent company. Companies often use divestment to streamline operations, regain focus on their core business, or achieve strategic goals. This can involve selling subsidiaries, business departments, real estate holdings, equipment, or other financial assets.

Now let's look at each of the four main types of M&A deals, as well as divestment deals (illustrated in Figure 10), in more detail.

Consolidation

A consolidation M&A deal is when a company acquires another company to expand its product or service offerings or enter new markets. The acquiring company wants to diversify its portfolio and expand its revenue streams.

For consolidations, I've learned that a winning strategy typically involves fully integrating business models as quickly as possible. It's essential to promptly arrive at a combined organizational structure to eliminate redundancies and

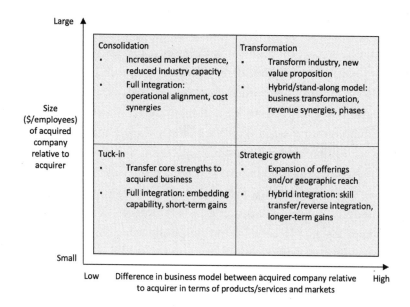

Figure 10: M&A strategies quadrant

avoid productivity losses. It involves adopting and fully integrating the acquirer's, or acquired company's, business model or inventing a new one. (However, the latter can be disruptive and impact the speed of integration.) It's essential to consider qualitative measures, such as employee and customer satisfaction, as well as quantitative measures, such as revenue per employee, cost of goods sold per employee, downtime, and employee turnover. Furthermore, it's worth thinking about using standardized systems to enforce processes and capture efficiencies, focusing on "quick wins" in the back office and shared services structures. It's also essential to clearly and consistently communicate the strategic goals of the combined company to mitigate employee disengagement and undesired turnover.

In my mind, perhaps one of the most famous consolidation M&A deals in history was between Exxon and Mobil. This merger occurred in 1999, creating a black gold superpower in the energy industry. At the time, oil prices were consistently low, and energy companies were taking a hit. This prompted Exxon and Mobil to merge in a deal that *Yahoo Finance* called "one of the most successful in M&A history." The US government approved the deal after assurances that the two merging companies would sell more than 2,400 gas stations nationwide. According to CNN Money, "Exxon defended the deal, the largest in a string of consolidation moves in the industry, citing price pressure on crude oil, the need for greater efficiency, and new competitive threats overseas."[161]

The food industry is already highly consolidated, so when Heinz and Kraft Foods announced in 2015 the most significant consumer goods deal in history, questions were asked. This was considered more a merger of equals than an acquisition per se. When the $100 billion deal was announced, it made everyone in the food industry—P&G, Mars, Nestlé, Danone, and others—sit up and take notice. However, despite creating one of the world's undisputed food industry giants, the deal wasn't successful. It was followed by starved sales, shareholder lawsuits, and even shadows hanging over the firm's accounting practices.[162] The lesson is that not all consolidations make sense, they are sometimes not well executed, and it's always important to keep a sharp eye on the value of bringing two companies together before embarking on something of this size and scale.

Transformation

A company typically pursues transformational deals to disrupt an entire industry. The acquiring company is usually a smaller, innovative firm seeking to challenge larger, established competitors. An industry-disruptor M&A aims to gain a competitive advantage by acquiring new technology, intellectual property, or a talented workforce to help the acquirer gain a foothold.

An example of a transformational deal is when, in 2020, Costco acquired Innovel Solutions for $1 billion. Innovel Solutions is a logistics and supply chain management company that helps retailers deliver products to customers more efficiently. The acquisition allowed Costco to improve its delivery capabilities and compete more effectively against Amazon.[163]

I've come to appreciate that transformational deals involving legacy businesses require a phased integration to maintain consistent performance. To do this, the acquired company should operate independently of the acquiring company, especially in terms of product development and service delivery to customers during the transition period. It's essential to take time to understand the acquired business and gradually implement a combined operating model or way of working. However, not everything should be completely stand-alone from the start. For example, there might be some immediate cross-selling opportunities, and these should be captured. It is also necessary to develop interim financial and operating reporting structures.

I've found that success is about designing the new go-to-market model of the combined company to capture revenue synergies. Because of this, strategic planning should focus on creating a differentiated value proposition that is unique to the new entity. The team should blend the quantitative and analytic integration tasks with the inspirational and creative functions of creating a new vision. Finally, transformational deals must retain the acquired business's leadership team to enable knowledge transfer.

Tuck-in

Tuck-in deals involve larger companies acquiring smaller companies in the same industry. I've worked on a few tuck-ins, and this type of M&A aims to increase market share and reduce competition. The acquiring company is usually an established player in the industry looking to absorb smaller players and consolidate its position in the market.

Tuck-in deals are often found in emerging industries where intellectual capital is essential to stay competitive. For example, in 2019, Microsoft acquired Mover, a cloud migration start-up that helps businesses move their workloads to the cloud. The acquisition was part of Microsoft's strategy to expand its Azure cloud platform. Mover was integrated into Microsoft's Azure platform and became part of the Azure migration centre.[164]

Focusing on critical employee retention is vital to this strategy. It's essential to identify and incentivize star performers and other employees whose experience is required for successful integration. One technique is to collaborate with HR and the functional executive to design bonus awards to achieve specific integration milestones and metrics. You also need to develop individual retention plans for key employees that go beyond financial incentives. Most acquired employees leave due to uncertainty about their role in the new organization as opposed to pure economics. To benefit from "quick hit" cost savings and achieve cultural integration, start planning as early as possible to have the back office fully integrated on day one.

Strategic growth

Strategic growth deals seek to transfer skills from the acquired company to develop a new or non-core business. For example, think Google's 2014 acquisition of Nest Labs, a company specializing in smart home devices such as thermostats, smoke detectors, and security cameras. This acquisition gave Google new skills and capabilities in the emerging smart home technology market that it did not previously have.[165] To accomplish this kind of acquisition successfully, it's crucial to leverage relationships with the target company's key employees, customers, and suppliers to retain knowledge and ensure continuity. Furthermore, I've come to appreciate through trial and error that the team must exploit longer-term gains by expanding offerings and geographic reach. This includes two-way skill transfer between the acquiring and acquired company and integration of back-office finance, supply chain, human resource, and technology functions.

The team must also develop interim financial and operating reporting structures while planning and designing the longer-term structure. Pay particular attention to aligning the cultures between the organizations by identifying synergy opportunities, with significant participation by the relevant business unit and the acquired entity. Failure to do so could engender resentment and create unattainable, or detrimental, synergy targets.

What's notable about the lists of the largest M&A deals over the past 50 years is how few countries were involved outside the United States, Canada, and a few European nations until the beginning of this century. That has started to change rapidly, with giants from emerging markets now competing on the world stage. The biggest such deal to date was the acquisition of TNK-BP by Russian oil giant Rosneft in 2013 for a fee of $55 billion, creating yet another Russian national champion in the oil and gas industry.[166]

Divestment

Although not covered in Figure 10, which focuses on different M&A deals, divestments are equally important to consider as part of the strategy development process from the inside out. Divestment refers to the process of selling off a subsidiary, business unit, asset, or investment. It is a strategic decision that companies make to streamline operations, focus on core activities, raise capital, or respond to regulatory or market pressures. Just like M&A deals, divestment is a complex process requiring careful planning and execution to maximize value and achieve strategic goals. Companies often engage financial advisors, legal experts, and consultants to assist with various aspects of the divestment process.

A good example of a notable divestment deal was in 2011, when GE divested its majority stake in NBC Universal to Comcast. This allowed GE to reduce its exposure to the media industry and concentrate on its core industrial businesses. The deal was successful for both companies, with Comcast gaining control of NBC Universal's media assets and GE streamlining its portfolio.[167] In a more recent example, in 2020, VF Corporation, the clothing and footwear company, successfully completed the divestment of its Jeanswear business into a separate public company, Kontoor Brands. This allowed VF Corporation to double down on its core active and outdoor lifestyle brands and Kontoor Brands to operate separately with a focus on denim.

Aligning corporate strategy with deal strategy

My exposure to various deals has shown me that aligning the merger, acquisition, and divestment focus (deal strategy) with the overall corporate strategy is vital to success. There needs to be strategic coherence between the two.

Critical considerations related to this alignment include the following:

- *Support the overarching strategy*: M&A and divestment deals should support the overarching strategy to ensure that all business activities are moving in the same direction. Misalignment can lead to acquisitions or divestments that do not fit with the company's strategic priorities, potentially wasting resources and creating disjointed acquired product and service lines that don't align strategically with what the company is trying to achieve. Salesforce, Inc., is an example of a company that has made acquisitions a central part of its overall growth strategy with tight alignment between the two. Its acquisition of Slack for $27.7 billion in July 2021 was made after the company realized that the workplace had changed forever due to the COVID-19 pandemic.[168]
- *Focus on shareholder value*: It's also important to consider that when doing deals the organization must create value for

shareholders. This value creation focus is maximized when the acquisition target complements and enhances the acquirer's core competencies and strategic objectives. For instance, if a corporate strategy focuses on technological innovation, acquiring a company with cutting-edge technology can drive this goal forward. Morgan Stanley's acquisition of E*TRADE in 2020 could be considered a synergistic acquisition or an acquisition aimed at acquiring technology, as there is considerable overlap. From the synergies perspective, the $13 billion deal provided new capabilities and allowed Morgan Stanley to tap into $56 billion worth of low-cost deposits, data about E*TRADE's millions of customers, and a powerful new tool to add to Morgan Stanley's existing portfolio.[169]

- *Integrate the risk profile*: Corporate strategies also often include risk profiles and mitigation plans that are crucial during deal activities. Acquiring companies that fit within the strategic risk parameters of the corporation helps in managing uncertainties and potential downsides associated with the deal. As an example, if strategically the risk profile of the acquiring company is low, then acquiring a very risky business likely does not make sense. However, the divestment of a high-risk business product or service line probably does.

- *Create competitive advantage*: Maintaining and enhancing a competitive advantage is a key aspect of corporate strategy. M&A and divestment deals should strengthen the company's market position, complementing its competitive strengths. For example, if a company's strategy is to dominate a specific market segment, acquiring competitors or complementary businesses in that segment can fortify its market position. Tight alignment is vital and misaligned acquisitions can dilute competitive strengths and confuse market positioning.

- *Define the nature of the deal*: The nature of the deal is also important to define and align on as part of the overall company strategy. For example, Spanish bank Banco Santander adopted what they call a roll-up deal strategy as part of its corporate strategy, emphasizing a geographic-centric investment. Banco

Santander didn't let Spain's relatively tiny population of fewer than 40 million people limit its growth prospects. It looked to the Latin American and later European markets, where cultural and economic links gave it an advantage. An example of an acquisition (or series of investments) to enter a new geographic area is well exhibited by Banco Santander's investments in Argentina. Beginning in 1963, it entered the Argentinian market by buying a series of small banks: Banco El Hogar Argentino, Banco Mercantil de Rosario y de Santa Fe, and Banco Comercial e Industrial de Córdoba over four years. In 1996, it acquired Banco Tornquist, beefing itself up to become Argentina's most significant private banking entity, a market with more banking consumers than Spain, according to Statista.[170]

◆ ◆ ◆

CONSIDERATIONS

Growth can be achieved through organic or inorganic means. Either way, the deal strategy must be integrated into the overall strategy so the corporate development team understands their options from an inside-out perspective. Some of the most critical merger, acquisition, and divestment strategy considerations include the following:

- *Think about strategic fit*: An acquisition target should be evaluated based on its strategic fit with the acquiring company's overall goals and objectives. Similarly, when evaluating potential divestments of businesses within a company, considering strategic fit of potential parts of the business under consideration for divestment is also vital.
- *Focus on future value*: Traditional due diligence approaches often place extreme weight on the past performance of assets targeted for M&A or divestment. Instead, deal teams must shift their mindset toward a forward-looking view of value and ensure the integration or divestment strategy and process deliver long-term value. This is particularly important in an era of rapidly changing

economic conditions, vast shifts in technology and society, and rapidly developing decarbonization and tax regimes worldwide that continuously create new risks as well as opportunities.

- *Use market analysis to understand targets*: The target company's market position, assets, customer base, and competitive landscape should be thoroughly analyzed to ensure that the acquisition will provide growth and expansion opportunities for the future. See Chapter 4 for more details on performing comprehensive competitor analysis.

- *Do detailed due diligence*: The acquiring or divesting company should conduct thorough due diligence, sometimes using independent third parties, including financial analysis, to identify potential risks or liabilities associated with the target company for acquisition, or opportunities to create value through the divestment of a specific business within the company.

- *Investigate regulatory and legal requirements:* The acquisition or divestment may have regulatory or legal implications that must be carefully considered, such as compliance with antitrust regulations or licensing requirements. Involving the legal team early is smart.

- *Consider various financing options*: The financing options available to the acquiring company should be evaluated, including using debt or equity financing, to determine the most cost-effective approach that uses the company's balance sheet in the right way.

- *Build a communications strategy*: A communication strategy is needed to ensure that all stakeholders, including employees, customers, and investors, are informed of the acquisition or divestment and its potential impacts once you're ready to go public. Business continuity is critical and communications can help.

- *Consider cultural integration as vital to success*: The cultural differences between the acquiring and target companies should be evaluated and addressed to ensure the successful integration of the two organizations. Remember that usually one culture needs to prevail. It's also important to consider the culture of the divested business relative to the company acquiring it.

- *Challenge hidden bias*: The propensity to make acquisitions or divestments can be influenced by experience, which needs to be kept in check. Researchers from the National Dong Hwa University in Taiwan found that business acquisition experience positively influences the acquirer's inclination to pursue a subsequent acquisition.[171] But just because a company experiences one positive acquisition success does not mean the same organization should jump into another without doing as much due diligence.

- *Explore customer impacts*: Lastly, the acquiring or divesting company's leaders must understand how the merger or divestment impacts customers and other stakeholders and what communication strategies will be used to manage these impacts.

KEY CONVERGENCE 2

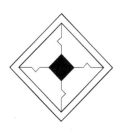

STRATEGIC CHOICES

CHAPTER 11
STRATEGIC CHOICES

"The essence of strategy is choosing what not to do."
—MICHAEL PORTER, HARVARD BUSINESS SCHOOL PROFESSOR

TRANSFORMATIONAL CHOICES THROUGH THE SHARING ECONOMY

Airbnb is one of the fastest-growing tech companies. Shortly after its initial public offering (IPO) in December 2020, it reached a US$100 billion-plus valuation, and the company has quite possibly changed forever how we travel. But did you know that Airbnb started as low-tech as you can get?

It all began in 2007 when co-founders Brian Chesky and Joe Gebbia decided to rent three air mattresses on their apartment floor in San Francisco. They charged $80 per guest and thought it seemed like an excellent idea for a start-up so, in 2008, with a third partner, Nathan Blecharczyk, they launched a website called Airbed and Breakfast and invited others to list their mattresses for hire. They got a few bookings here and there, but things didn't go well for the most part. They had plenty of listings on the site and plenty of site traffic, so potential customers were out there, but they weren't making enough bookings.

To make ends meet, they dreamed up a stunt: creating custom cereal boxes featuring then-presidential candidates Barack Obama and John McCain ("Obama Os" and "Cap'n McCains"). They ended up selling 1,000 boxes at $40 apiece and raised enough financing to keep Airbnb afloat a bit longer. But, more importantly, their gimmick attracted media attention. Paul Graham, of the start-up accelerator Y Combinator, invested in Airbnb in part because he thought that if these young guys could do it with cereal boxes, they could do it with Airbnb.

Meanwhile, the partners realized their biggest market was New York City, so they relocated there and identified the most likely problem. The low-quality listings needed to be enticing. So, they grabbed their cameras, visited every one of their New York listings, and persuaded the owners to let them take many photographs of their places. After touching them up, they replaced their website's old, mostly poor-quality photos with the new ones. Within a month, sales doubled. Then tripled. The rest is history.

What I love the most about this story is that it flies in the face of one of the most commonly stated principles of building a tech start-up: "Everything must be scalable." What Brian and Joe did was anything but scalable (least of all the cereal boxes). But it got them enough traction to prove that their concept could work.

Later, they scaled their initial solution by making the strategic but risky choice to hire young photographers in significant locations and pay them to take professional photos of owners' listings (at no charge to the owners). They also added a bunch of guidelines and articles on the site to educate owners on how they can make more money by taking better photos.

Airbnb's story shows that business strategies don't have to be grand, long-term affairs. The right strategy, focused on a specific challenge that is preventing the business from taking off and executed relentlessly, can be all it takes. Once the challenge is solved, the company progresses on its roadmap and integrates the solution into the revamped business strategy.[172]

Airbnb's success can be attributed to its disruptive business model, user experience, brand recognition, personalization, price, and community. The company generated $5.9 billion in revenue in 2021, a 73 percent year-on-year increase. It had 150 million users and 300 million bookings, representing a 55 percent increase from 2020. Its founders started with three mattresses and grew into a business with over seven million listings run by four million hosts.[173]

This chapter is vital and stand-alone, sitting at the crux of the strategic planning process between strategy development (described in Parts 1 and 2), and execution (described in Parts 3 and 4). Once the upfront strategy development work is completed and the external and internal information, facts, and know-how are gathered, choices need to be made on where to play and how to win. It is critical to make these strategic choices about what your business will be—and won't be—*before* you undertake the challenge of strategy execution. This chapter combines the inputs from the outside in (Chapters 2–5) and inside out (Chapters 6–10) analyses and will evaluate how several approaches— executing a SWOT analysis, a Buy, Build, Partner matrix, McKinsey's 7S model, or simply using a company's existing strategic plan—can help leaders make the best strategic choices, just like Airbnb.

◆ ◆ ◆

WHAT ARE STRATEGIC CHOICES?

Once the outside-in and inside-out analyses have been completed, the information and insights gathered must be synthesized into a clearly defined strategy, including the company's vision, mission, values, and strategic objectives. When making these strategic choices, remember that strategy is just as much about choosing what *not* to do as it is about selecting objectives; it is essential to choose a distinct goal and not try to be "all things to all people." Workshops are great places to have these discussions.

A strategic business choice determines the direction and scope of a company's activities to achieve its long-term goals. It involves identifying opportunities and threats in the external environment, as well as strengths and weaknesses within the organization, and then developing a plan to capitalize on opportunities and overcome challenges.

Making a strategic choice is the second key convergence in the integrated strategic planning process, bringing together several aspects in an important point of fusion. It typically involves outside-in analysis of market trends, competitive forces, and customer needs, as well as assessment of internal capabilities from the inside out, and then selecting a course of action that aligns with the company's vision, mission, and values. This could involve expanding into new markets, developing new products or services, repositioning the company's brand, or pursuing a merger or acquisition. Ultimately, a strategic business choice is about determining the most effective way to allocate resources and create value for customers while also achieving sustainable growth and profitability over the long term.

After 25 years of working as a strategist, perhaps one of the most important things I've come to understand is the importance of keeping a strategy simple so employees can understand and remember it. For example, McDonald's strategy is simple: to provide fast food at a low price and still make $20 billion annually. This strategy is reflected in everything the company does, from its menu to its operations. McDonald's has successfully executed this strategy (albeit with different revenue targets each year) and become one of the most popular fast food chains in the world.[174]

A strategy articulation map (illustrated in Figure 11) is a visual tool I've used extensively to clarify and communicate a company's strategic choices. It helps to align the organization around a common understanding of the company's vision, mission, values, and goals, and provides a clear framework for decision-making and action planning.

The map typically includes the following key elements:

- *Strategic objectives*: The goals or outcomes the company wants to achieve should align with the overall mission and vision.
- *Value proposition*: This refers to the unique value the company offers its customers and should be based on a deep understanding of customer needs and preferences.
- *Target market*: The specific group of customers the company targets with its products or services. It should be based on a thorough analysis of market trends and customer behaviour.
- *Competitive advantage*: This refers to the factors that give a company an edge over its competitors, such as cost leadership, differentiation, or innovation.
- *Strategic initiatives*: The specific actions or projects the company will undertake to achieve its strategic objectives. They should be aligned with the overall strategy and be designed to deliver customer value.

Overall, a strategy articulation map helps to bring clarity and focus to the strategic planning process and provides a roadmap for the organization to follow as it makes choices and takes action to achieve its goals.

Values

The core principles that embody an organization's essence, acting as a moral compass for the behaviour of the organization and its employees.

KPIs

Quantifiable metrics used to evaluate progress of the focus areas and strategic objectives.

Strategic Objectives

More specific strategic goals that support each of the focus areas.

Mission

A concise explanation of an organization's reason for existence.

Vision

A forward-looking view of the ideal state that the organization wants to achieve, summarized into an aspirational statement.

Focus Area

High-level buckets of work have been identified as high-priority areas that the company will align its strategic objectives around.

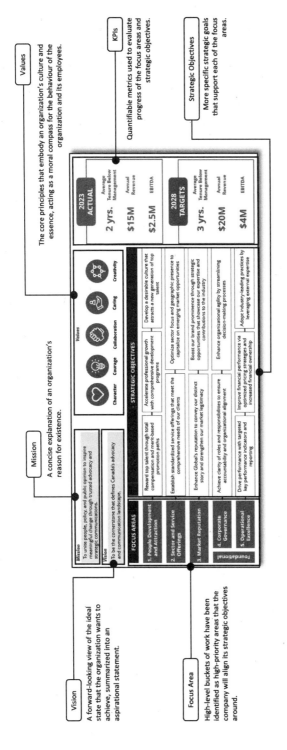

Figure 11: Strategy articulation map

CASE STUDY
Making strategic choices at Recess, makers of CBD-infused sparkling water

Making the right strategic choice can have a powerful impact on a business. Recess, a New York-based company producing CBD-infused beverages, was founded in 2018 and quickly gained popularity as a wellness-focused beverage brand. However, by mid-2019, the company faced increased competition from other CBD-infused beverage brands and needed to make critical strategic choices to stay competitive and grow.

So, Recess began by focusing exclusively on its CBD-infused sparkling water product, discontinuing its other product lines. The company believed focusing on its core product could better differentiate it and build a stronger brand. Recess revamped its branding and packaging to better appeal to its target market—health-conscious millennials who value wellness and self-care. The new branding featured bright, pastel colours and minimalist designs.

The company's leaders also shifted their distribution strategy, moving away from traditional retail channels and focusing on direct-to-consumer (DTC) sales through their e-commerce platform. They believed that DTC sales would allow them to control the experience better and build stronger customer relationships. Recess invested in marketing campaigns targeted at its core audience, using social media and influencer partnerships to build brand awareness and generate buzz. The company also launched a pop-up shop in New York City, a physical manifestation of the brand and a way to engage with customers in person.

By making these strategic choices, from the outside in and inside out, Recess bubbled to the top in the crowded CBD-infused beverage market, built a strong brand, and continued to grow its business.[175,176]

HOW TO APPROACH STRATEGIC CHOICES

Leveraging the SWOT analysis framework to uncover choices

This tool can help a company better understand its internal and external environment by analyzing its strengths, weaknesses, opportunities, and threats. A SWOT analysis effectively summarizes all the insights from outside-in and inside-out analyses, making it easy to identify areas to pursue and avoid and generally inform critical strategic choices.

Here are some ways that I've used a SWOT analysis to inform strategic choices:

- *Strengths*: A strength in this context is what a company is known for. A company can capitalize on these areas of core strength to create a competitive advantage. For example, a company with solid customer relationships in the market could leverage a strength by offering personalized services or developing loyalty programs to keep customers engaged and buying its services.
- *Weaknesses*: By identifying its shortcomings, a company can work to improve these areas, close gaps, and mitigate any risks they may pose. For example, a company with poor financial management could implement tighter financial controls or hire an expert financial controller to improve its performance in this area. Another example might be launching a new service or product to address a market gap or reshaping the organizational structure to reduce costs and increase profitability.
- *Opportunities*: By identifying opportunities in the external environment, a company can develop strategies to capitalize on this information. For example, if there is a growing demand for sustainable products, a company could develop new eco-friendly products to meet this demand by leveraging recycled materials, transforming supply chains, capturing emissions, and improving overall environmental, social, and governance (ESG) performance.
- *Threats*: By identifying hazards in the external environment, a company can develop strategies to mitigate these risks. For example, a company operating in a highly regulated industry could invest in compliance programs to minimize the risk of legal or regulatory issues. Having a focused relationship management approach with regulatory stakeholders could also help.

When making strategic choices, you need to look under the hood. Knowing what a company is good at and where to improve is essential to developing a successful strategy. A SWOT analysis also helps a company evaluate external factors impacting its business, such as market trends, competition, and regulatory changes. Understanding these factors can help a company make informed decisions about how to respond to changes in the market.

CASE STUDY
Hitting the right note at online streaming powerhouse Spotify

Understanding the competitive threats and opportunities is essential to a successful strategy. Spotify successfully combined both outside-in and inside-out thinking to do this and to create a unique competitive advantage. Before Spotify came along, online music streaming needed to be improved. Sure, you had platforms like Napster and the Pirate Bay, but they were illegal, and you never knew when they would get shut down. And even if you did use them, you were still limited in what you could listen to, creating a massive opportunity for a new entrant.

Spotify nailed its core strength by putting its customers at the forefront of its business strategy. They saw that people were fed up with the limitations of other music streaming platforms and decided to create a service that put the customer's needs and wants first (developing their strategy from the outside in).

Spotify also invested in inside-out technology and engineers to ensure the experience was seamless and easy for listeners. As a result, consumers flocked to Spotify like bees to honey because it gave them the freedom and control over the music choices they craved.

Another inside-out component of Spotify's success and core strength was (and still is) its "freemium" business model. They offered a free version of the service but also had premium options for those who wanted more features and services. This allowed them to attract a huge user base and generate revenue from free users through advertising and from paying users through a subscription model. This model helped Spotify grow its user base and revenue stream quickly, more than exceeding its business goals.

Let's also remember Spotify's data-driven approach. They invested heavily in data analysis and machine learning, which allowed the company to create algorithms predicting which songs and artists users would like and recommend them accordingly (going one step further into user personalization). They didn't miss a beat, as the outside-in, inside-out analysis and investment helped to drive engagement and loyalty, making Spotify the go-to platform for discovering new music and creating playlists.[177]

Overall, a SWOT analysis is critical to strategic choices in a firm's business strategy because it helps a company understand its position in the market and develop a plan to achieve its goals while minimizing risks and leveraging opportunities.

Linking the strategic plan components with strategic choices

Building on details explained in Chapter 1, a well put together strategic plan outlines the strategic choices that a company has made and provides a roadmap for how those choices will be implemented. In advising many clients over the years, I've found that the strategic plan combines the analysis and execution aspects of strategic planning into a single, concise document. It makes the essential strategic choices very clear.

Here are some ways that a strategic plan combines outside-in, inside-out analysis with key strategic decisions to chart a clear course forward to execution:

- *Mission and vision statement*: The strategic plan should include a clear and concise mission statement outlining the company's chosen purpose, vision, and values. This statement should be aligned with the company's strategic choices and serve as a guiding principle for decision-making.
- *Market analysis*: The strategic plan should include a thorough examination of the company's target market, including customer demographics, market trends, and competitive landscape. This external analysis should inform the strategic choices that the company has made from a market perspective and provide insight into how those choices will be implemented.
- *Marketing strategy*: The strategic plan should outline the company's marketing strategy, including how it plans to reach its target market, promote its products or services, and build brand awareness. This strategy should align with the company's strategic decisions and provide a clear roadmap for implementing those choices.
- *Operational plan*: The strategic plan should include an operational strategy that outlines how the company will achieve its strategic objectives. This plan should draw on the inside-out

analysis to include details on how the company will allocate resources, manage its operations, and measure its progress toward achieving its goals.

- *Financial plan*: The strategic plan should include a financial plan that outlines the company's revenue projections, expenses, and expected profitability. This plan should be based on the company's strategic choices and provide a clear blueprint for how those choices will be translated into financial results.

Overall, a strategic plan serves as a critical tool for combining all four aspects (or quadrants) of the strategic planning process (as described in Chapter 1 and shown in Figure 1). It outlines and communicates strategic choices based on thorough outside-in and inside-out analysis, as well as providing a clear roadmap for turning strategy development into execution to achieve the company's goals.

Strategic growth options leveraging the BCG tool

Strategic growth options refer to a company's choices for achieving growth and increasing its market share. The BCG (Boston Consulting Group) Growth Options tool,[178] which I've used extensively with much success, helps companies evaluate their growth opportunities and determine the best approach for achieving their objectives. Like the SWOT analysis and development of the strategic plan, this matrix brings together outside-in and inside-out factors for the most complete picture possible. The framework consists of two main components: "where to play" and "how to win."

Where to play

This component involves identifying the most alluring market segments and product categories for the company to focus on for growth. To identify these segments, the company must evaluate the market size, growth potential, profitability, competition, and existing capabilities and resources. Based on this analysis, the company can elect to focus on one or more of the following growth options:

- *Market penetration*: Increasing the company's market share in its existing markets by selling more of its current products or services. This can be achieved by increasing advertising, offering promotions or discounts, or improving customer service.

- *Market development*: Expanding into new markets with the company's existing products or services. This could include targeting new customer segments, entering new geographic regions, or developing new distribution channels.
- *Product development*: Introducing new products or services to the company's existing markets. This might be achieved by improving current products or developing new ones through innovation (further described in Chapter 18) to meet changing customer needs or preferences.
- *Diversification*: Entering new markets with new products or services. The company might expand into related markets or completely new industries.

How to win

This component involves developing a winning strategy to capture the identified growth opportunities. The company must evaluate its competitive position, unique strengths, and resources to determine the best approach for winning in the chosen markets. Based on this analysis, the company can focus on one or more strategies:

- *Differentiation*: The company distinguishes its products or services from those of its competitors through unique features or benefits.
- *Cost leadership*: Competing based on price by offering products or services at lower prices than competitors.
- *Focus*: Focusing on a narrow market segment or product category and becoming a specialist.
- *Integration*: Vertically integrating the company's operations by acquiring or partnering with suppliers or distributors.

Each of these strategic growth choices carries different risks and rewards. The decision will depend on several factors, such as the company's existing strengths and weaknesses, the level of competition in its markets, and the availability of resources. Overall, I've come to appreciate that making strategic growth choices is a critical aspect of a company's long-term success and requires careful analysis and planning, both from the outside in and the inside out, to ensure that the chosen strategy is aligned with the company's vision, mission, and values and can deliver sustainable growth and profitability over time.

The Build, Buy, Partner Matrix

The Build, Buy, Partner (BBP) Matrix is another tool that helps companies evaluate the strategic choices available when considering expanding the business or entering new markets.[179] The BBP Matrix consists of three main strategies:

- *Build*: Developing capabilities in-house through internal development, R&D, and talent acquisition. It is best suited for companies that have existing capabilities or resources that can be leveraged to develop new products or services.
- *Buy*: Acquiring a company or product line to access new capabilities, technology, or markets quickly. It best suits companies that need more resources or capabilities to develop new products or services in-house.
- *Partner*: Collaborating with another company to share resources, knowledge, or technology. It's best suited for companies that want to enter a new market or expand their business while avoiding committing significant resources or taking on the risk of acquiring a company.

It is important to note that it doesn't always make sense to buy. One example of a strategic buy choice gone wrong is an acquisition by Hewlett-Packard (HP). HP is a technology company specializing in hardware and software development. In its prime, HP oversaw the development of computers, printers, and software, but in 2011, the company acquired Autonomy, a British software company specializing in enterprise search and knowledge management, to help HP expand its software business. However, it turned out that Autonomy had been overvalued and had misrepresented its financial performance, leading to an $8.8 billion write-down for HP.[180] This example points to the vital importance of doing your due diligence, as explained in

Chapter 10, to fully understand the financial and operational details of the acquired company before closing the deal.

CASE STUDY
Learning from failed strategic choices at P&G to eventually achieve success

An excellent example of earlier strategic choices gone wrong goes back to the late 1990s when consumer products company Procter & Gamble (P&G) struggled to sustain success in the skincare market—a sector with powerful customer loyalty that can be very profitable. At the time, people referred to P&G's established brand Oil of Olay as the "oil of old lady." It was cheap, sold primarily at drugstores, and was perceived as boring and associated with grandmothers. As more skincare products entered the market, its sales plummeted.

P&G executives discussed their options. They considered the build strategy of launching a new line, but that would take time and money; they could use a buy strategy to acquire an existing, more "fun," product line, which, again, would be very costly; or they could try to rebrand Oil of Olay. Using the cascade strategy, they decided to rebrand.

The five steps of the strategic choice cascade they followed included defining the winning aspiration, assessing the current state, developing a strategic choice, creating a plan to win, and executing and adjusting as necessary.[181] The strategic rebranding pivot targeted a new demographic with premium products, raising the price from $3.99 to $18.99. The result, post-2000, was that Olay enjoyed a resurgence, eventually spinning off an array of new products and evolving into a $2.5 billion powerhouse.

The Build, Buy, Partner Matrix evaluates each of these different strategies based on their fit with various outside-in and inside-out factors: the company's existing capabilities, market opportunities, and resource constraints. It's a valuable tool for companies to evaluate the strategic choices available when considering expanding their business or entering new markets. I've learned that companies can profitably use the BBP Matrix to identify new growth opportunities and determine how to best invest for the future.

The McKinsey 7S Model

Through my experience executing over 200 strategy-related projects, I've found that the alignment of supporting systems with strategy is critical. The 7S Model is a strategic planning tool developed by McKinsey that helps businesses align their strategy with their internal resources, capabilities, and organizational structure.[182] Although the seven components all focus primarily on inside-out factors, this model provides a great way of articulating all the integrated strategic choices that flow from a detailed outside-in, inside-out analysis and serves as a bridge to execution.

The 7S Model consists of seven interrelated elements:

- *Strategy*: The plan that outlines how a company will achieve its goals and objectives.
- *Structure*: The formal and informal organizational structure, including reporting relationships, hierarchies, and communication channels.
- *Systems*: The processes, procedures, and policies that enable a company to operate effectively and efficiently.
- *Shared values*: The core values, beliefs, and culture that guide a company's behaviour and decision-making.
- *Style*: The leadership style and management practices influencing an organization's operations.
- *Staff*: The skills, knowledge, and experience of an organization's employees.
- *Skills*: The competencies and capabilities essential for an organization to succeed.

The 7S Model helps businesses to identify areas of misalignment among these seven elements, which can hinder the achievement of strategic goals. By analyzing and aligning these elements, companies can improve their performance, increase efficiency, and enhance their competitive advantage.

The model also helps businesses assess the impact of changes in one element on the others and make strategic choices that consider the interdependencies between the different aspects of the organization. For example, if a company changes its strategy, it may need to restructure its organization, develop new skills and competencies, and create new systems and processes to support the new direction.

◆ ◆ ◆

CONSIDERATIONS

Leaders must be prepared to make tough and unpopular choices to move the needle forward. Strategic decisions combine all the outside-in and inside-out analyses to make a move toward execution.

When making strategic choices in business, several key points need to be considered:

- *Start with purpose*: Making strategic choices starts with articulating an organization's purpose and why it exists. As Michael Nemmers, professor of strategy at Kellogg School of Management, and Paul Leinwand, global managing director at PWC, explain in an article on purpose, it's what matters most and provides clarity to leaders, managers, and employees on how to focus amid the cacophony of daily, competing demands.[183]
- *Remain fact-based*: While experience and intuition play a role, it is essential to ensure sufficient analysis and data to support all the strategic choices. Additionally, the analysis must be quantitative and fact-based so that the organization is confident in its strategic direction.
- *Ensure buy-in*: The strategic choices must be effectively communicated and explained to ensure organizational alignment and buy-in. My experience has helped me appreciate that strategies need to be communicated numerous, sometimes an uncomfortable, number of times before they are understood by front-line employees.
- *Keep it simple enough to be understood and remembered*: The strategy must be articulated in a way that is clear, concise, and easy to understand. A long-winded, overly complex strategy is much more likely to be forgotten or not implemented at every level of the organization. The strategy articulation map is an

effective way to summarize the strategy, for easier understanding, implementation, and measurement.

- *Combine internal and external analysis*: A thorough analysis of internal and external market factors, including the company's strengths, weaknesses, opportunities, and threats, including competition, should be conducted to identify potential growth areas and risks.

- *Consider resource allocation*: Strategic choices should effectively consider, and allocate, the company's available financial, human, and technological resources. Choice is about prioritizing the valuable business resources and not trying to do it all and then do it poorly.

- *Put considerable effort into the implementation plan*: A detailed implementation plan, including timelines, milestones, and performance metrics (see Chapter 8), should be developed to ensure the effective execution of the strategic choices. You can have a thoughtful and well articulated strategy, but if it's not implemented it's worthless.

- *Perform regular reviews and adaptation*: Strategic choices should be regularly reviewed and adapted to ensure they remain aligned with the company's mission and values and continue supporting its long-term vision. Strategic flexibility is key.

PART 3

PREPARE FOR EXECUTION

CHAPTER 12

INITIATIVE PRIORITIZATION AND ROADMAP DEVELOPMENT

"Initiative prioritization is the key to driving results in a fast-paced business environment. It ensures that resources are aligned with strategic goals and focused on the most important activities."
—BRIAN HALLIGAN, CEO OF HUBSPOT

AVOIDING INITIATIVE OVERLOAD THROUGH PRIORITIZATION

As Michael Porter famously said in a seminal 1996 *Harvard Business Review* article, "The essence of strategy is choosing what not to do." That sounds straightforward enough, but it's surprisingly hard for business leaders to kill existing initiatives, even when they don't align with new strategies and the company's future direction. Instead, leaders keep adding on initiatives, which can lead to severe overload at levels below the executive team.

In another well-known *HBR* article, published in 2018 by strategy gurus Michael Watkins and Rose Hollister, the authors describe how most organizations struggle with initiative management. Unaware of the cumulative impact or unwilling to part with pet projects, senior leaders increasingly pile on, expecting managers and their teams to absorb it all.

Yahoo, Inc., is an example of a company that lacked focus. In the early 2000s, Yahoo expanded into a wide range of industries, including search, email, and e-commerce. However, the company's diversification strategy led to a lack of focus and resulted in poor financial performance. Unable to correct the problem, the company was acquired by Verizon Communications in 2016.[184]

In the course of my consulting, I, too, have seen the consequences of failing to cut underperforming projects and establish clear priorities for those that remain. Failing to do so can lead to severe overload, and productivity, engagement, performance, and retention suffer as a result. By understanding the root causes of initiative overload, leaders can better diagnose the risks to their organizations and make smarter decisions.

So, what are the root causes of initiative overload and how can leaders avoid them?

- *Overlooking initiative impact*: It's essential to understand the demands on employees and managers of all the initiatives that leaders want to move forward. That means understanding the organizational capacity to execute initiatives and the potential impact on employees.
- *Cross-functional effect of initiatives*: Remember that by prioritizing initiatives collectively, as a leadership team for the entire organization, we should consider how an initiative needed in one function impacts another in terms of broader resources required to execute it across multiple functions.
- *Political logrolling*: Avoid backroom deals on projects that should be killed; have the conversation in the room and prioritize and agree as a whole.
- *Unfunded initiatives*: Ensure that projects are adequately funded and that no pet projects exist that force managers and employees to take on extra work in addition to their existing duties to deal with poorly sanctioned initiatives.
- *Band-Aid initiatives*: Avoid limited fixes to significant problems when the root causes should be addressed. Review initiatives to ensure the company has the right skills to complete the work successfully.
- *Cutting people without cutting work*: Beware of reducing your workforce without simultaneously reducing the workload.
- *Initiative inertia*: Evaluate existing initiatives rather than simply allowing them to carry over from one year to the next.

Of course, the best way to avoid initiative overload is not to allow it to happen in the first place. Easier said than done. That means preparing to build in rigorous prioritization reviews to impose discipline on when and how the organization launches initiatives and keeping close tabs on those whose time they consume. For companies already experiencing initiative overload, focusing on the benefits of cutting back can make the path forward somewhat easier. As Steve Jobs once said, organizations are at a great advantage when they learn to say no to the "hundred other good ideas that there are." They can then use their creative and productive energy more wisely, foster outstanding employee commitment and loyalty, and accomplish more in the areas that matter.[185]

This chapter helps management diagnose the root causes of initiative overload, make smarter decisions about which projects to keep or kill, and follow through by allocating talent and other resources to the right places.

◆ ◆ ◆

WHAT ARE INITIATIVE PRIORITIZATION AND ROADMAP DEVELOPMENT?

If the strategy is the *why* and *what* roadmapping, initiatives are part of the *how*. Effective initiative identification and prioritization take a holistic view of ongoing projects and prioritize them based on the value they add to the organization. Selecting the highest priority initiatives and mapping them out creates a clear path forward for the organization and its employees. That way, everyone is kept focused on what is most important and how it will get done. As the vice president of design and artificial intelligence at Microsoft, John Maeda, once said, "People who can focus, get things done. People who can prioritize, get the right things done."

My work as a consultant has helped me understand that initiatives are the projects, programs, or priorities—and there are usually quite a few of them—that can overburden an organization and cause it to lose track of what adds value. To prioritize initiatives, companies pick essential criteria (for example, cost to implement, level of complexity, and financial benefits) and rank the pool of initiatives against them. Only those deemed urgent are moved forward to the roadmap; others are dropped.

At its simplest, a roadmap takes the most critical initiatives and sequences them over a defined period. For added clarity, it can include roles, responsibilities, and associated deliverables. Roadmapping has emerged as a best practice, particularly for large, global organizations, providing the framework for aligning on a complex set of business-wide initiatives that must be executed successfully. An organization can fully exploit its entire spectrum of capabilities and drive growth by employing roadmapping from an enterprise perspective. Critical functions in the business "own" their strategies, which are fully integrated as needed to meet business priorities.[186]

In my experience, strategic initiative prioritization and roadmaps are essential. They help organizations focus on the most critical initiatives and save resources by eliminating low-priority projects.

I know that prioritization and roadmapping also enable organizations to allocate their resources efficiently and effectively. By focusing on high-priority initiatives, organizations can ensure that they invest their time, money, and personnel in the areas that will deliver the greatest return on investment, in support of the strategic plan (Chapter 1).

I've also come to appreciate that engaging in a disciplined prioritization process and roadmapping support is a way for organizations to demonstrate their commitment to achieving their goals by communicating their strategic goals and objectives to internal and external stakeholders. It helps organizations remain agile and responsive to changing market conditions, customer needs, and other external factors. Also, organizations can adapt quickly to changing circumstances by regularly reviewing and prioritizing initiatives and adjusting their strategies.

To summarize, strategic initiative prioritization and roadmapping are essential processes that help organizations focus efforts, allocate resources, manage risk, communicate priorities, and remain agile and responsive to changing conditions.

HOW TO APPROACH INITIATIVE PRIORITIZATION AND ROADMAP DEVELOPMENT

Prioritization matrix approach

Initiatives likely originate from either outside-in or inside-out analysis and define some kind of opportunity, or an improvement in the business to advance performance. Strategic initiatives can be prioritized using various frameworks and methods, depending on an organization's needs, goals, and resources. A common practice in all frameworks and methods is to start by bringing everything together, that is, mapping in one place all initiatives for the entire organization.

Businesses also need some mechanism to rank initiatives. A grid (illustrated in Figure 12) prioritizes initiatives based on their effort (time, resource requirements, complexity, or a combination of these) and benefit (financial or otherwise). This is an effective tool that I've often used in workshops, and it can help force a firm's leaders to prioritize when everything has ended up being "high priority."

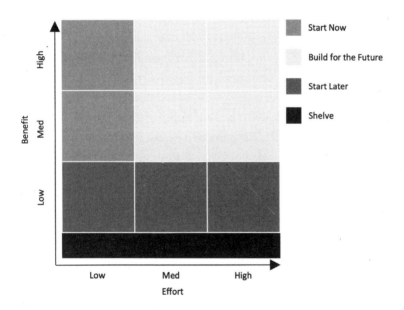

Figure 12: Prioritization matrix

Other common approaches to prioritizing strategic initiatives include the following:

- *Value-based prioritization*: This approach identifies the initiatives and prioritizes those that deliver the most value to the organization, such as revenue and sales growth, profitability, cost savings, customer satisfaction, ESG performance, or employee engagement. Value-based prioritization can involve analyzing financial metrics, customer feedback, market research, or employee surveys to determine the potential impact of each initiative.

- *Risk-based prioritization*: Focuses on identifying the initiatives that address the most significant risks to an organization, such as competition, regulatory changes, technology disruptions, environmental damage, or reputational damage. To get to the required outcomes, risk-based prioritization can involve conducting a risk assessment, scenario planning, or stakeholder analysis to determine each risk's likelihood and potential impact on the organization.

- *Resource-based prioritization*: This is about understanding the organizational constraints and identifies the initiatives that align with the organization's available resources, such as budget, personnel, assets, or technology. It typically involves analyzing the organization's capacity, skills, or technology infrastructure to determine the feasibility and scalability of each initiative.

- *Time-based prioritization*: In this case, the focus is on identifying the initiatives that align with the organization's strategic timeline, such as short-term, medium-term, or long-term goals, or as I like to say, the now, next, and beyond. Time-based prioritization can involve analyzing the organization's strategic plan, market trends, or customer behaviour to determine the urgency and importance of each initiative to optimize the business.

- *Stakeholder-based prioritization*: This approach focuses on identifying the initiatives that align with the needs, preferences, or expectations of the organization's stakeholders, such as customers, employees, investors, or partners. It can involve conducting surveys, focus groups, or interviews to determine each stakeholders' level of interest and support.

Ultimately, the best approach to prioritizing strategic initiatives depends on an organization's specific circumstances, goals, and resources. Combining multiple techniques or tailoring them to fit the organization's needs is often helpful.

Organizations have finite resources. McKinsey claims that some transformation efforts flounder because too many initiatives spread an organization's resources too thinly. Accordingly, what an organization chooses not to do is every bit as important as what it does. The starting point in any vital prioritization process is a robust study to clearly understand the size and nature of a firm's opportunities, their timing, and any impediments that might affect delivery. Usually, prioritization applies the twin lenses of value (financial and non-financial benefits to the organization) and ease (how many resources an initiative would consume and the complexity of its execution). While this approach can be practical, the "ease" criteria are often subjective and reinforce bias. As a result, teams may underestimate risk on projects they deem attractive and undervalue opportunities that superficially seem less promising.

Prioritization should not be a one-time event but rather should serve as a core tool to assign resources flexibly, as dictated by available facts. Effective implementation pilots are, therefore, a significant investment. Organizations that successfully execute these typically have well-grooved approaches that manage pilots tightly and ensure that key lessons are drawn from the experience. Rather than using the pilot as a box-ticking ritual, successful organizations use it both as an opportunity to refine an initiative and as a critical go/no-go gate.[187]

At best, prioritizing, in my experience, enhances strategic dialogue and the alignment of an initiative at the top level of management that is then communicated down through the rest of the organization. Once an executive team understands and accepts this, priorities become embedded in the organization and its corporate culture.[188]

Sequencing initiatives and roadmap development to drive pace

Another workshop exercise I have a lot of experience in is plotting an organization's initiatives in the period they will get done. This is typically completed only after initiative prioritization. Only those initiatives identified as high-priority items will be plotted when creating the roadmap. Subcategories can be used to theme initiatives on the roadmap into different groups, different goals of the company, and different value streams. For example, some initiatives could be grouped into the technology category with a focus on improving how new digital solutions enable the business. Another group might be focused on people, talent, and capability. This type of grouping exercise helps with understanding, integration, and accountability for execution of the initiatives down the road. Furthermore, this is a starting point for sequencing and can subsequently be used to develop a detailed project work plan.

Strategic alignment of the *what* and the *how* is essential. Microsoft used a strategic initiative roadmap to transform its business model from software licensing to cloud-based subscription. The roadmap helped the company determine and prioritize key initiatives to help it achieve its goals. It also helped Microsoft communicate its vision and strategy to its employees and stakeholders.[189]

Here are some best practices for roadmapping strategic initiatives that have worked for me:

- *Define the scope*: Start by defining the scope of the roadmap, including the initiatives, programs, or projects that will be incorporated and the timeframe for implementation. The scope should be aligned with the organization's strategic objectives and stakeholders' needs.
- *Develop milestones*: Break down each initiative into specific milestones, or deliverables, that will be achieved over time. These milestones should be specific, measurable, achievable, relevant, and time-bound (SMART).[190] But, as I also explain in a recent article with *Take It Personel-ly*, milestones or goals should also be visible, positive, prioritized, hierarchical, aligned, flexible, up-to-date, monitored, and celebrated.[191]
- *Allocate resources*: Identify the resources, such as budget, personnel, or technology, required to achieve each milestone. Allocate the resources based on the priorities of the initiatives.
- *Identify dependencies*: Identify the dependencies among the initiatives, including technical, financial, or operational dependencies. Determine how they will impact the roadmap and how they will be managed.
- *Manage risks*: Identify each initiative's potential risks and challenges and develop contingency plans to address them. Monitor the risks and adjust the roadmap as needed to mitigate the impact of the risks.

- *Communicate the roadmap*: Clearly communicate the roadmap to stakeholders, such as executives, employees, customers, or partners. Explain how the roadmap aligns with the organization's strategic goals, the benefits it will deliver, and the roles and responsibilities of each stakeholder.
- *Monitor progress*: Monitor the progress of the roadmap against the milestones and adjust it as needed to ensure that the initiatives remain aligned with the organization's strategic goals and priorities. This step is described in more detail in Chapter 20.

A strategy roadmap of sequenced initiatives helps bridge the gap between vision and actions, and between strategy development and implementation. It gives you a visual guide for executing a strategy and outlines key targets in an appropriate timeframe. In 2009, Coca-Cola created a strategic roadmap to help it achieve its goal of doubling revenue by 2020. The roadmap included initiatives such as expanding its product line, increasing its marketing efforts, and improving its supply chain.[192] While Coca-Cola did not achieve this target in 2020, in 2023 revenue was up to $45.75 billion, representing a 6.39 percent growth compared to the previous year, an impressive achievement in a very competitive and dynamic market where resilience is key.[193]

CASE STUDY
Product roadmapping at marketing company Mailchimp

An excellent example of monitoring roadmap progress and course correcting along the way was demonstrated by Mailchimp, the all-in-one marketing platform for small businesses.

Mailchimp experienced significant growth, expanding from email marketing to a full-fledged marketing platform with various features and capabilities. To effectively plan and prioritize its strategic initiatives, Mailchimp uses a framework called the Mailchimp Product Roadmap, a multi-year plan that outlines the company's strategic initiatives, product releases, and technology advancements. It is divided into multiple phases, each corresponding to a specific period, typically spanning several years. Each phase includes a set of objectives and key results (OKRs) that align with the company's overall strategy and mission: to allow its customers to open, click, and buy.

Mailchimp's Product Roadmap is also heavily focused on customer feedback and market research. The company conducts extensive research to understand its customers' needs and incorporates that feedback into its roadmap planning process. This allows Mailchimp to prioritize the most relevant and valuable initiatives for its customers. In addition, Mailchimp regularly reviews and updates its execution roadmap based on market changes and evolving customer needs. This allows the company to remain prepared, agile, and responsive to changes in the business environment.[194]

With robust tools to create compelling campaigns, automate delivery, track metrics, and integrate campaign data, Mailchimp in 2024 remains one of the best email marketing software organizations in the world according to *PC Magazine*.[195]

Overall, roadmapping strategic initiatives is a collaborative process that requires input from various stakeholders and continuous monitoring and adjustment. By following these best practices, organizations can ensure that their roadmap aligns with their strategic goals, stakeholders' needs, and available resources and puts them on the path to successful execution of their strategy.

Business case development

You cannot always prioritize based on high-level descriptions of various initiatives; diving a little deeper can help. A business case is a document that outlines the rationale for undertaking a particular initiative, including the expected benefits, costs, risks, and timeline. I've used business cases in the process of prioritizing initiatives to gain a deeper understanding of the resources required to implement an idea. For each opportunity that is more significant than the dollar value threshold (determined by the organization in the prioritization process), owners complete business-case templates to increase their understanding of what it will take to deliver. I've also found that business cases are critical in defining high-priority strategic initiatives because they help organizations assess their feasibility, impact, and value.

According to a June 2016 article by the Project Management Institute, incorporating a business-case template into the initiation process for significant initiatives can help project teams gather the information they need to make the right decisions. For example, at American finance company MSCI, the business-case template relies on data collected to address several issues, including explaining why the project is necessary; recommending business solutions; defining organizational benefits; determining how much money, resources, and time are required; identifying risks; and measuring the financial impact. This detailed information feeds into the initiative prioritization process.[196]

♦ ♦ ♦

CONSIDERATIONS

The prioritized initiatives on a roadmap represent a crucial aspect of strategy execution. Both must form part of the preparation for execution. When prioritizing and sequencing strategic initiatives, there are several key considerations that organizations should take into account to ensure the most effective use of resources:

- *Use a defined set of criteria to prioritize*: The same criteria should be used for all projects and initiatives, potentially including financial criteria. This helps ensure apples to apples comparison. For example, net present value/internal rate of return (NPV/IRR), resource capacity, change capacity, complexity, and value-add.
- *Take an enterprise view*: Ensuring that all the enterprise initiatives are included in the prioritization gives an accurate and complete picture of what is currently on the table and what is urgent. Hidden projects and initiatives can suck value capacity, and with limited resources and capacity, organizations must pick only the projects that add the most value. Companies often layer initiative upon initiative, which leads to many things being done poorly instead of a few important things being done well.
- *Align initiatives to strategy*: Companies using a strategy articulation map (SAM) should prioritize items that align with the strategy's pillars. The initiatives should match or enable the organization's strategic goals, vision, and mission to ensure that resources are focused on the most critical activities. Initiatives essentially describe how elements of the strategy get done.

- *Learn when to say no*: Most companies struggle with the art of saying no, but it's a necessary discipline to seriously consider which projects will add the most value and either delay, or abandon, all other initiatives. Constantly layering new initiatives without eliminating any leads to overload and strategic failure.
- *Have a plan for "break-in work"*: Different projects will come up after prioritization and roadmapping are done, and the organization should have a plan for dealing with these, remembering that if something is being added to the roadmap, something else must be taken off (or new resources must be added to account for the extra effort required). Roadmaps rarely work out as expected.
- *Consider impact and urgency*: It is critically important to prioritize initiatives based on their potential impact and urgency. The initiatives that have the most significant potential impact on the organization's goals and objectives, or require urgent attention to address a pressing issue, should be prioritized.
- *Keep feasibility in mind*: The organization should assess whether it has the resources and capabilities to execute the initiatives successfully. The ones that are the most feasible to accomplish, given the organization's current resources and capabilities, should be prioritized.
- *Evaluate available resources*: When prioritizing initiatives, the organization's budget, personnel, and technology should be considered to understand what's possible; the initiatives that require fewer resources, or can be executed with existing resources, should be at the top of the list. A typical trap that many organizations fall into is asking the same high-performing resources to be involved in many different initiatives, limiting progress and causing burnout.
- *Build dependencies*: Dependencies between initiatives should be considered when sequencing strategic initiatives; if the start of one initiative is dependent on the completion of another, ensure they are sequenced in that order.
- *Ensure balance*: Balance the priorities and sequencing of strategic initiatives across different areas of the organization. Prioritizing

initiatives across multiple areas, such as customer experience, technology, or operations, will help ensure the organization is well-rounded, adequately paced, and focused on delivering value across the board. If initiatives exist in support of one strategic pillar and not another, then rebalancing should be considered.

- *Align to metrics*: Consider the potential impact of each initiative on the organization's KPIs, such as revenue, profitability, market share, or customer satisfaction.

CHAPTER 13
CAPABILITY AND TALENT DEVELOPMENT

"Talent management is not just an HR function. It's a strategic imperative that must be integrated into every aspect of the business."
—JOSH BERSIN, INDUSTRY ANALYST AND
FOUNDER OF BERSIN & ASSOCIATES

BUILDING DREAMS WITH WORLD-CLASS TALENT MANAGEMENT STRATEGIES

In the arid desert of the Middle East, Dubai, the largest city in the United Arab Emirates, is known as the "City of Dreams." It rose from a small pearl-fishing village and trading post to a vibrant urban centre emphasizing luxury tourism. Unlike many of its regional peers, which developed unstable regimes and oil-dependent economies, the Emirate of Dubai has embraced diversification to become a politically stable economic powerhouse. The desert oasis thrives on trade, tourism, transportation, mass communications, construction, finance, and a host of other growing sectors, all in a business climate of optimism and expansion.

One ambitious project is known as Bluewaters Island, located off the coast of Jumeirah Beach Residence. One of several manufactured islands created by dredging sand from the floor of the Persian and Arabian Gulf, it features many attractions, including Ain Dubai, the world's largest observation wheel (at 250 metres); the Green Planet, an indoor rainforest attraction; and many luxury retail outlets, hotels, restaurants, and residential buildings. The project was developed by Meraas, a Dubai-based conglomerate known for its innovative properties.

The big question is: How did Dubai achieve such a diversified economy and a high degree of political stability, making it one of the most attractive destinations in the world, not just for visitors but also for expatriate residents? How did it break out of the oil curse to create one of the fastest-growing economies in the world?

In 2016, the city-state launched its Dubai Future Foundation with the ambitious goal of anticipating, preparing for, and responding to socioeconomic difficulties by shaping the economic and industrial landscape of the future. The winning formula involved a compelling, low-cost, and differentiated value proposition following a Blue Ocean Strategy, a concept first introduced by Chan Kim and Renee Mauborgne in their bestselling books *Blue Ocean Strategy* (2004) and *Blue Ocean Shift* (2017). The authors described Blue Ocean Strategy as a "systematic process to move your organization from cutthroat markets with bloody competition—what we think of as 'red oceans' full of sharks—to wide open 'blue oceans,' or new markets devoid of competition."

Dubai's Blue Ocean Strategy required the alignment of three strategy propositions—value, profit, and people (talent). From a people perspective, the Dubai job market is highly competitive, with many professionals from around the world seeking opportunities in the city. This means that companies operating in Dubai need to be highly skilled at attracting and retaining top talent. The Blue Ocean approach to developing a unique and innovative project in Bluewaters was seen as a way to attract and retain talent by offering exciting and challenging work.

Additionally, companies in Dubai are often focused on developing a diverse workforce. This is partly because of government initiatives aimed at promoting diversity but also because of the benefits of having a workforce comprising different perspectives and backgrounds. Finally, the Dubai job market is highly competitive in terms of compensation and benefits. Companies operating in Dubai typically offer generous salaries, tax-free income, and other benefits such as healthcare, housing, and transportation allowances. The Blue Ocean approach was seen as a way to justify these high compensation packages by offering challenging and rewarding work unavailable elsewhere.

In summary, the highly competitive nature of the job market, the focus on bringing talented workers from many countries, and the generous compensation packages offered in the city all played a role in how talent was managed for this strategic project.[197]

This chapter provides a step-by-step guide to creating the most effective capability and talent plan or fine-tuning an existing one. The chapter also includes case studies of firms that are doing it right, such as BlackRock, Inc., the world's largest asset manager, and Fevertree Drinks plc, the British maker of premium mixes for alcoholic beverages.

◆ ◆ ◆

WHAT IS CAPABILITY AND TALENT DEVELOPMENT?

My work in business has taught me that a strategy can be successful only if the people responsible for executing it have the required capabilities. Capability and talent development seeks to identify gaps in an organization's human resources and create a plan to address them. For example, when Disney+ launched in 2019, offering a vast library of Disney content including original series and movies, they needed new streaming service capabilities. They built the new capability, and in 2023 Disney+ generated an impressive $8.4 billion in revenue, a 13 percent increase compared to the previous year.[198] At Disney, the team was only as good as its members. For a company to have a team that works like a finely oiled machine, it must align its business goals with its available talent. This alignment goes deeper than just putting people into positions where they are best suited. An aligned strategy looks at the business's mission and vision and actively recruits and develops people who can direct the company to attain both.[199]

A focused talent strategy is something most businesses ignore. "While most organizations have a business strategy and a financial plan to support it," says Mike Zani, CEO of the Predictive Index, "our State of Talent Optimization report finds only 36 percent have a talent strategy—and a mere 12 percent align their talent and business strategies. However, those with talent strategies designed to hire, manage, and engage their people in a way that aligns with business objectives significantly outperform other companies. The essence of leadership is aligning employees with the business strategy to achieve maximum success."

The business case is clear, as outlined by Zani's "The State of Talent Optimization" report: companies that align talent with their business strategy outperform others by 16 percent, retain 30 percent more top performers, and see 34 percent higher employee performance.

For the report, 600 executives across 20 industries were surveyed. The results confirm that companies with aligned talent and business strategies are more likely to outperform other companies, retain top talent, see higher employee performance, and achieve strategic success rates of nearly 90 percent.[200]

Capability and talent development are crucial for successfully implementing an organization's business strategy. Here are some reasons I've come to understand and appreciate this through my work:

- *Alignment*: Strategy outlines the long-term goals and objectives of an organization. By developing the capabilities and talents of employees, organizations ensure that they have the right people with the right skills to execute the strategy effectively. It helps align the workforce's competencies with the strategic direction.

- *Competitive advantage*: Developing capabilities and nurturing the right talent can provide a significant competitive advantage. Firms that invest in developing their employees' skills and knowledge create a more innovative, adaptable workforce capable of driving positive change.

- *Agility and adaptability*: In today's rapidly changing business landscape, organizations must be agile and adaptable to survive and thrive. Capability and talent development contribute to building a more flexible and resilient workforce. Employees who are continuously learning and evolving are better equipped to navigate uncertainties, embrace new technologies, and adapt to shifting market conditions.

- *Succession planning*: Developing capabilities and talent ensures a pipeline of skilled individuals who can take on key leadership positions. This approach minimizes disruptions, maintains continuity, and supports the organization's long-term sustainability.

- *Employee engagement and retention*: Capability and talent development programs demonstrate a business's commitment to employee growth and professional advancement. Employees with opportunities to enhance their skills and pursue career development are more engaged, motivated, and loyal. This focus on development can contribute to higher employee retention rates and attract top talent to an organization.

- *Innovation and creativity*: Developing capabilities and fostering a culture of continuous learning and development can fuel innovation and creativity within an organization. Employees who are encouraged and supported to enhance their skills are more likely to generate fresh ideas, challenge the status quo, and contribute to the organization's innovative endeavours.

The difference between capability and competency

Although capability and competency can sometimes be interchangeable, they have different meanings and implications in the context of talent management.

Talent competency refers to specific skills, knowledge, abilities, and behaviours essential for success within a particular job or role. Competencies are often used in talent management and human resources to assess and evaluate an individual's performance, potential, and development needs.

Talent capability refers to the abilities, skills, and competencies that a person possesses, or an organization requires, to perform specific tasks, achieve strategic objectives, or gain a competitive advantage in the marketplace. It encompasses a range of personal and professional attributes, including technical expertise, leadership skills, problem-solving abilities, communication and interpersonal skills, adaptability, creativity, and a willingness to learn and grow. Talent capability is often evaluated through assessments, performance reviews, and other measurement tools to identify strengths and areas for improvement and to guide training and development initiatives. Ultimately, talent capability aims to enable individuals and organizations to perform at their best and achieve their goals.

In summary, capabilities are broader and more encompassing than competencies, which are focused on specific skills and abilities. Capabilities reflect the overall capacity of an individual or organization, while competencies are the specific skills and abilities required for successful performance in a particular role or task. It's imperative to align competencies, capabilities, and resources.[201]

HOW TO APPROACH CAPABILITY AND TALENT DEVELOPMENT

Competency model development approach

Creating a competency model is integral to enhancing talent and aligning with strategy. A competency model is a body of knowledge, skills, abilities, and other characteristics (KSAOs) required to succeed in a particular job or role. Developing a competency model involves a few steps, which are explained below:

- *Identify the job or role*: Identify the job or role for which the model will be created, whether it's a specific job title or a broader category of roles. It's important to note that you can have a job with a title—for example, vice president of sales—but you might fill a variety of roles encompassed by that title, such as sales strategy, relationship management, sales operations, revenue generation and forecasting, negotiation and deal closure.
- *Conduct a job analysis*: This involves gathering information about the job or role from sources such as job descriptions, interviews with subject matter experts, and observation of job activities, aiming to identify the specific KSAOs required for successful performance in the job or role.
- *Define the competencies*: KSAOs are then grouped into competencies, which are clusters of related KSAOs that are necessary for effective performance in the job or role. For example, project management is a competency that clusters a number of related KSAOs, including understanding project management methodologies; knowledge of risk management; skills in planning, scheduling, communication, risk management, and problem-solving; and abilities in leadership, adaptability, and decision-making.
- *Validate the competencies*: Get feedback from subject matter experts, job incumbents, human resources, and other stakeholders. This can be done through tools like surveys, engagement meetings, and focus groups.
- *Develop proficiency levels*: Proficiency levels describe the level of mastery required for each competency and are often described

as essential, intermediate, or advanced. Either way, some kind of
scale should be developed to help with measurement.

- *Communicate the model*: Communicate the competency model to
relevant stakeholders, such as HR professionals, hiring managers,
managers, and employees through training sessions, workshops,
or other communication channels.

Perhaps one of the more novel approaches to competency development I've
encountered is Google's g2g training method. This volunteer teaching network of
over 6,000 Google employees dedicates much of their time to helping their peers
learn new competencies. Volunteers, known internally as g2g'ers can participate
in various ways, such as teaching courses, providing one-on-one mentoring, and
designing learning materials. People come to this forum from every department
of Google in search of impactful and practical learning experiences.[202]

Competency assessment

Next comes the review. A competency assessment evaluates an individual's
knowledge, skills, and abilities against predefined competencies. The evaluation
can be used to identify an individual's strengths and weaknesses, as well as to
guide performance improvement and development planning.

Here are the typical steps I've used in conducting a competency assessment:

1. *Choose an assessment method*: There are several methods for
assessing competencies, including self-assessments, supervisor
assessments, peer assessments, and 360-degree assessments. The
method chosen will depend on the purpose of the evaluation and
the resources available.

2. *Collect data*: Data can be collected through surveys, interviews,
observation, or performance reviews. The data should
be collected from as many sources as possible to ensure a
comprehensive assessment.

3. *Analyze the data*: Once the data has been collected, it should
be analyzed to identify strengths and weaknesses in each
competency area. This can be done through statistical analysis,
content analysis, or a combination of both.

4. *Provide feedback*: The assessment results should be provided to the individual. Feedback should be specific, constructive, and focused on improvement.

5. *Create a development plan*: Based on the assessment results, the plan should help individuals improve their competencies. It should be specific, actionable, and measurable.

6. *Monitor progress*: The individual's progress should be monitored over time to ensure they progress toward their development goals. The assessment may be repeated periodically to measure progress and identify areas for further improvement.

The assessment aims to identify strengths and weaknesses in an individual's competencies and guide their development and growth in a way that aligns with the broader organizational strategy and objectives.

CASE STUDY
Competency assessment at professional services firm Accenture

Accenture uses a competency-based assessment approach to evaluate its employees' skills and knowledge. The company has identified a set of core competencies essential for success in various organizational roles. These competencies are used to evaluate employees' performance and identify areas where they need to improve and be better prepared to support the company's strategy execution. Accenture's competency-based assessment approach helps ensure its employees have the skills and knowledge for the individuals and the organization to succeed.

The company's competency framework is based on four key areas: business acumen, client value creation, technical and functional expertise, and professionalism. Each of these areas is further divided into sub-competencies that are specific to different roles within the organization. For example, the business acumen area includes sub-competencies such as financial acumen, market insight, and strategic thinking.

Accenture's competency-based assessment approach is used to evaluate employees at all levels of the organization, from entry-level positions to senior leadership roles. It helps ensure that employees have the skills and knowledge needed to succeed in their roles and helps identify areas where additional training or development may be required, keeping talent and strategy aligned.[203,204] Accenture has evolved into a massive company over the decades, with over 742,000 employees, serving clients in more than 120 countries.[205] With that many people working for the organization, managing employee competency is central to the strategy.

I've learned that many successful organizations use the competency-based approach today and for a good reason. It works. However, you must align your competency model with your business strategy or objectives for this approach to work for your organization. To do this, it's important to take the time to determine which significant behavioural themes or competencies—for example, innovation, customer engagement, and action orientation—need to be demonstrated across your organization for your business strategy to work.[206]

Integrated talent and competency management

The process of competency management, however, is not as simple as just defining and assessing competencies and ensuring alignment with the business strategy. There is simply more to it. Once competency gaps have been identified, there are several things to consider while developing a go-forward strategy to address them.

My project work has revealed that all of the different facets of talent management shown in Figure 13 are interrelated, and they must be aligned with the strategy and each other to manage and close the gaps of the talent and competencies of the organization successfully. Integrating talent and competency management into strategy development and execution can bring several benefits to organizations.

Competency management helps identify specific skills and abilities that employees need to succeed. In contrast, talent management is broader, and focuses on attracting, developing, and retaining employees with the right skills and abilities. Integrating both can help organizations align their talent strategies with business goals and objectives. Competency management also helps identify performance gaps and provides targeted training and development opportunities to build new capabilities to support strategic

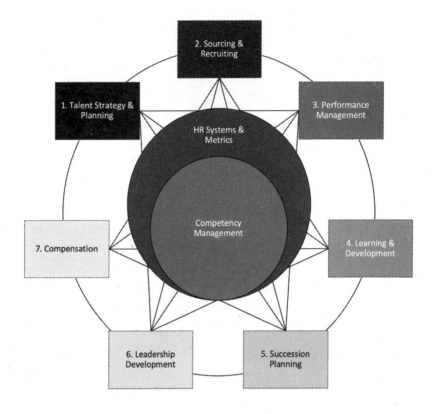

Figure 13: Talent management approach

success. Talent management helps identify high-potential employees and provides career development opportunities to retain them. Integrating both can allow organizations to create a more comprehensive approach to improving performance.

Integrating talent and competency management can also help streamline HR processes by eliminating redundancies and reducing data entry. For example, competencies can inform job descriptions, performance evaluations, and training and development plans, which can be managed in a single system. Competency management can help identify the skills and abilities critical for leadership roles and support succession planning. Talent management can help identify high-potential employees who can be developed for leadership roles. Integrating both can allow organizations to create a more robust succession planning process.

BlackRock, Inc., the world's largest asset manager, is focused on delivering high performance and has four guiding principles that its 11,000-plus professionals abide by: to be fiduciaries to the company's clients, passionate about performance, innovative, and part of the inclusive, collaborative team known as One BlackRock. The company has a talent management strategy aligned with these principles that, for example, ensures its policies toward employees respond to changing conditions on the ground and to cultural differences across the globe. The company also prioritizes leadership behaviours and focuses on a rigorous and extensive talent development, review, and succession planning process. Furthermore, BlackRock continually refreshes its systems, processes, and strategic initiatives.[207]

CASE STUDY
Holistic talent management at Fever-Tree

I've always enjoyed a tasty gin and tonic, which leads us to another excellent example of a business with an integrated talent management strategy. Fever-Tree produces premium mixers for alcoholic drinks. Its corporate strategy centres around product innovation, brand development, and global expansion. The company's talent management practices are designed to support these objectives and ensure its workforce aligns with its strategy.

Getting the right people in the door is step one of being prepared. Fever-Tree has a robust recruitment process that focuses on attracting and hiring individuals who are passionate about the company's brand and products. The company seeks innovative, customer-focused people with a proven record of delivering results. Once employees are hired, Fever-Tree invests in their potential through various training and development initiatives. For example, the company has an internal academy that provides ongoing training and support to employees at all levels of the organization.

Fever-Tree also has a performance management system that ensures individual goals and objectives match the company's strategy. This helps ensure that employees execute toward common goals and objectives and that their performance is directly tied to the company's success. In addition, Fever-Tree has a strong culture of collaboration and teamwork. It encourages employees to share their ideas and work together to develop new products and strategies supporting Fever-Tree's growth and expansion plans.

Finally, recognizing that hiring a range of people from different social and ethnic backgrounds and of different genders and sexual orientations is critical to its success, Fever-Tree strongly emphasizes diversity and inclusion, and it has implemented initiatives to ensure that all employees feel valued and included. Overall, Fever-Tree's talent management practices are aligned with its corporate strategy, helping to ensure that the company has the right people in the right roles and working toward common goals.[208, 209]

◆ ◆ ◆

CONSIDERATIONS

People are central to bringing a strategy to life. Talent development is challenging but very important for successfully preparing for strategy execution. Here are some critical considerations as organizations look to effectively implement capability and talent development:

- *Identify strategic goals and objectives*: It's essential for talent management and capability development to understand the organization's mission, vision, and values and translate them into specific goals and objectives from a talent and capability perspective. Furthermore, understanding the critical competencies required to execute the strategy is also essential.
- *Understand the current state*: The organization must assess its talent and capabilities to create the required baseline. This involves identifying the skills, knowledge, and abilities needed to achieve the strategic goals and objectives and comparing them to the existing talent and capabilities. It also consists of an employee assessment.
- *Explore external forces*: It's important to be aware of the forces transforming competencies in the workforce and understand and prepare for them in advance, such as economic shocks, technological disruptions, and environmental and regulatory pressures.

- *Perform leadership validation*: Get leadership and employee validations of the core competencies required to execute the strategy successfully. Tone from the top is vital.

- *Integrate leadership development*: Implement proper leadership development strategies for high-performing individuals. It helps retain these individuals and propels the organization forward.

- *Consider the presentation lens*: Present the competency assessment through a development lens rather than a performance review lens to encourage employees to self-assess more accurately and enable the right high-performance behaviours.

- *Integrate succession planning*: Develop succession plans for areas with two or fewer specialists. This is vital to future-proof the business.

- *Embrace knowledge management*: Promote knowledge sharing across enterprise teams; proper learning and development structures and culture must be ensured so employees can develop their capabilities, and learn from and help others to be successful.

- *Perform regular assessments*: Conduct periodic reviews to determine progress in critical knowledge and skill areas. It's essential to have a culture of continuous improvement and to truly focus on ongoing progress management.

- *Integrate sourcing and recruitment*: Ensure sourcing and recruiting can fill immediate capability gaps. It's about finding and getting the right talent in the door.

- *Identify gaps and prioritize areas for development*: Based on the analysis of current talent and capabilities, the organization needs to identify the gaps between the current and the desired state and prioritize areas for development. This involves identifying the critical skills and capabilities required to achieve the strategic goals and objectives and focusing on developing or acquiring them.

CHAPTER 14

CAPITAL ALLOCATION AND ONGOING CAPITAL MANAGEMENT

"Capital allocation is one of the most important jobs of any CEO.
How you allocate your capital will ultimately determine
your company's success or failure."

—WARREN BUFFETT, CEO OF BERKSHIRE HATHAWAY

SEARCHING FOR ACCELERATED GROWTH AT CAPITALG

According to *Fortunly*, artificial intelligence will be worth a massive $422.4 billion by 2028, with emerging titans like ByteDance, one of the world's highest-valued unicorns at around $140 billion, set to take over.[210] These are staggering numbers. Growth in this sector is partly driven by emerging niches, including search engine algorithms, self-driving vehicles, medical services, and robotics, which all belong under the AI umbrella.

One powerful and interesting tech-focused venture capital company fulfilling this growth is CapitalG which, like Google, is owned by parent company Alphabet, Inc. CapitalG is Alphabet's venture capital arm, operating independently of Alphabet's investment decisions. (Alphabet is the single limited partner of the fund, providing "patient, long-term capital.")[211] Focused on cyber security, data, automation, and AI, CapitalG was founded in 2013 to empower entrepreneurs with Alphabet's and Google's unparalleled expertise in growth. Early on, CapitalG appointed its star investor, Laela Sturdy, as managing partner, making her one of the few female leaders in the sector. She had been at Google since 2007, and since joining CapitalG has led some of the firm's most notable investments in companies such as Stripe, UiPath, Inc., and Duolingo,

Inc. The organization has always been willing to share the lessons learned from helping to scale Google, Airbnb, CrowdStrike, Databricks, and Zscaler with the next wave of tech entrepreneurs.

CapitalG maintains a small, concentrated portfolio, so every company receives substantial capital and hands-on support, which helps leaders accelerate the growth of their businesses. It focuses on growth-stage companies, leveraging a dedicated in-house team and Google's world-class expertise to guide entrepreneurs through the shift from start-up to scale-up. The results are staggering: $4 billion invested in 55 companies, meaningful investment of resources to help companies grow (typical cheque sizes of $50 to $100-plus million), 16 initial public offerings and 9 merger and acquisition exits, and 3,000 Googlers have advised 4,500 portfolio employees.

CapitalG seeks to accelerate and amplify each company's success. For example, CapitalG helped Duolingo develop its successful monetization model and scale its marketing channels; Credit Karma refresh its HR operations; and Gusto revamp its payment system. The CapitalG advisors even incubated CrowdStrike's inside sales team, frequently hosting events in their offices to facilitate C-level buyer introductions. The company also helps consumer companies expand their marketing channels and enterprise companies build sales pipelines with qualified leads, generating an average of $10 million in incremental pipeline revenue per company within the first year alone.

CapitalG directs its support for maximum impact. Immediately after each new investment, dedicated growth account teams establish tailor-made connections and programming designed to accelerate each company's growth. Typical engagements include business model development, qualified customer introductions, executive or technical recruiting support, security reviews, marketing channel revamps, and leadership and engineering training. Some engagements involve a few sessions with Google experts, others span many months.[212]

CapitalG takes a long-term view of capital allocation and investments, looking for companies with the potential for sustained growth over many years. This means that the fund is willing to allocate capital to companies that may not be profitable in the short term but have a clear path to profitability in the future. CapitalG is also patient with its investments, taking the time to understand the market and the company's competitive position before committing capital.

Once an investment is made, the fund provides ongoing support to help fledgling companies achieve their growth objectives—capital management. CapitalG often forms strategic partnerships with the companies in which it invests. These partnerships provide additional resources and support to help the companies achieve their growth objectives. There is also a team of professionals with deep operational expertise in product development, sales, and marketing. This expertise is leveraged to help portfolio companies optimize their operations and achieve sustainable growth. Finally, CapitalG carefully constructs their portfolio to ensure diversification across industries and stages of development. This helps to mitigate risk and maximize returns over the long term.

Like CapitalG, individual companies in all sectors must consistently make the right capital allocation decisions, investing in areas that align with, and further, the company's objectives and ensure they generate the expected returns. This chapter uses examples like Bank of Australia, Texas Instruments, and others to help readers recognize where to allocate capital by looking at three criteria—strategic fit, risk, and financial return—within the overarching framework of what a company wants to achieve.

◆ ◆ ◆

WHAT IS CAPITAL ALLOCATION?

Once strategic choices are made, explained in Chapter 11, companies want to spend cash or capital on those areas that align with, and further, their objectives. A rigorous, consistent, enterprise-wide approach to allocating capital can help companies make unbiased investment decisions, stave off disruption, and return more cash to shareholders. Ongoing capital management also helps meet expense obligations while maintaining sufficient cash flow.

My best definition of capital allocation is distributing an organization's financial resources. When allocating capital, it's essential to consider the expected returns and maintain a balance between short-, medium-, and long-term demand, investment performance, and opportunities for reprioritization and reallocation. Capital is allocated to portfolios and, ultimately, projects. But the question is: *How* do you decide which projects?

I've found that many executive teams consider available investment options—such as providing shareholder dividends, purchasing stock shares, investing in growth initiatives, or increasing research and development budgets—and analyze the effects each has on the organization to ensure profitability. There are plenty of value-creation opportunities, and it's essential to know your options before making important financial decisions. However, that on its own is not enough.

My experience is that these projects should also be evaluated and prioritized based on three criteria:

- *Strategic fit*: How well does the project align with the business unit/division/corporate strategy?
- *Risk*: How risky is the project, taking into account execution as well as organizational and external threats?
- *Financial return*: What is the probable return? Is it enough to justify capital allocation?

CASE STUDY
Capital allocation challenges at Commonwealth Bank of Australia

One example highlighting the consequences of poor capital allocation decision-making is the Commonwealth Bank of Australia's acquisition of Colonial Limited. On March 10, 2000, under the leadership of CEO David Murray, CBA announced it had reached an agreement to acquire Colonial Limited, a life insurance, funds management, and banking group created through the amalgamation of 18 different businesses over the five years prior. In consideration, CBA issued 351 million new Commonwealth Bank shares and paid $800 million in cash to the rebranded Colonial First State Limited's income security holders. The equity issuance represented 39 percent of CBA's preacquisition issued capital.

The rationale for the acquisition was that the merger provided a robust platform for future international revenue growth. It would also increase revenue potential from opportunities to offer customers a greater number of products via a broader, more diverse distribution network. Furthermore, the deal had all the hallmarks of many "top-of-the-cycle" transactions, with equity markets at all-time highs and asset managers trading at record multiples.

The deal ultimately did not close, and destroyed $53 billion in CBA's shareholder value compared to the investment records of the other major Australian banks, roughly equal to $30 per CBA share.[213] There were various deal preparation challenges, including conflicted remuneration and loss of focus on essential customer needs during the transaction, and the Australian Securities and Investments Commission brought legal proceedings against CBA and Colonial. Although this M&A deal may have seemed like a good strategic fit, CBA failed to assess the potential risks adequately, losing transparency and the trust of key stakeholders in the process, which in the financial world is everything.

What is ongoing capital management?

Capital management refers to an organization's set of processes, policies, and procedures to manage and optimize its capital resources, including capital allocation. The term *capital* can refer to financial resources, such as cash, investments, and debt, as well as non-financial resources, such as intellectual property, human capital, and physical assets.

In my experience, capital management typically involves the following activities:

- *Capital planning*: Assessing an organization's current and future capital needs and developing strategies to meet those needs.
- *Capital allocation*: Determining how much capital to allocate to different parts of an organization and prioritizing investment opportunities.
- *Capital monitoring*: Tracking and evaluating the performance of an organization's capital investments and making adjustments as necessary.
- *Capital reporting*: Communicating information about an organization's capital resources and performance to stakeholders, such as investors, regulators, and internal management.

In the big picture, effective capital management can help organizations optimize their use of capital resources, minimize risk, and achieve their strategic objectives. It also guides the development, approval, execution, and monitoring of specific projects.

- *Developing projects*: Creating a financial business case for a project throughout its life cycle.
- *Approving projects*: Reviewing, evaluating, and supporting a portfolio of projects, taking into account the merits of individual projects and the impact of each on the portfolio.
- *Executing and monitoring*: Evaluating project performance during implementation and comparing it to expectations. This includes revisiting the initial business case and incorporating the impact of change requests.

HOW TO APPROACH CAPITAL ALLOCATION AND ONGOING CAPITAL MANAGEMENT

Capital allocation and ongoing capital management design principles

Senior executives across industries know that wisely managing capital investments means better cash flow, faster growth, and a competitive advantage. Many organizations, however, have hundreds or even thousands of capital projects on the go at once; it's easy for them to miss substantial growth and profitability opportunities, and they generally need help managing spending on their vast portfolio. As I've said earlier in this book, overarching principles define your goal. Executives can improve capital management performance by mastering several principles and adopting a capital portfolio management system powered by a comprehensive digital application.

McKinsey highlights the importance of prioritizing the capital portfolio, tapping into the organization's wisdom, and setting clear investment objectives. Matt Banholzer, Ashish Chandarana, and David Straden, authors of a 2017 McKinsey report, also stress the importance of scrubbing the business case for each project multiple times, using ROI throughout the investment life cycle, and streamlining approvals. Finally, they focus on forecasting more frequently to enable tactical shifts, implementing a unified cross-platform approach, and adopting a culture of continuous improvement.[214]

CASE STUDY
Capital management at Texas Instruments drives sustainable competitive advantage

You might be wondering what laser-guided bombs and calculators have in common. The answer is the American technology company Texas Instruments (TI), which has produced both. It is also an excellent example of a company with pinpoint capital management at its best.

Everyone should look through TI's investor relations materials, particularly those dedicated to capital allocation. This company is well prepared and even has presentations and videos on YouTube to reinforce the significance of this strategic process: "At Texas Instruments, we as managers think that allocation of capital is one of the most important jobs that we have." That statement is as straightforward as you'll ever see, and you rarely see it.

The business model is built around four things the company calls its sustainable competitive advantage: manufacturing and technology, broad product portfolio, reach of its market channels, and diverse and long-lived positions. It has the discipline to allocate the capital to the best opportunities, but not based on gut feel or where someone thinks it should go. There is a strict hierarchy for these opportunities, and it's clear where and how the company measures outcomes. It has targets and publishes the results, which is fantastic.

Over a 10-year period, Texas Instruments allocated $72 billion of capital. If executives had said in 2008, "Guys, we need to sit down and allocate $72 billion of capital over the next decade," it probably would have been a pretty sobering thought at the time. But this challenge is real and essential, and every company has some version of this to think about.[215]

The semiconductor industry is dynamic, heavily influenced by technological advancements, market demand, and global economic conditions. Despite these market headwinds, Texas Instruments has built a $145.32 billion giant through smart allocation of capital, with a total return of 373 percent over the last 10 years. Impressive on any scale.[216] The company is also potentially poised for further growth, as it seeks to take advantage of the $53 billion CHIPS Act introduced into the US with hopes of ending Chinese dominance in chip manufacturing.[217]

Learning from the past through historical capital allocation analysis

Why do people seem to fail to remember the lessons of history? Maybe it's because they think it's boring or because people adjust predictions based on new information. Or it could be that there is so much available information to learn from that it all becomes overwhelming. But, as philosopher George Santayana famously said, "Those who cannot remember the past are condemned to repeat it."[218]

In business terms, looking back on the past can give clues to where future value may lie. Historical capital allocation analysis is a process that helps understand how a company has allocated its capital over time. For example, Morgan Stanley's research arm, Counterpoint Global, delves into historical capital allocation in a big way. They've analyzed how companies in the Russell 3000 Index have allocated capital since 1985.[219] I've come to appreciate this practice; the problem is that only some companies spend the time doing this.

The steps involved in historical capital allocation are as follows:

1. *Collect data*: Collect historical data on the company's capital expenditures. This should include information on the amount and timing of capital expenditures and details on the projects and investments that were funded over as long a period as possible.

2. *Merge datasets*: Merge the data into a single dataset. This can involve combining data from multiple sources, such as financial, social, technological, environmental, operational, and project-related reports as well as accounting systems.

3. *Identify outliers*: Identify any outliers in the data. Outliers are data points that fall outside the normal range and can skew the analysis. You want the data to be clean. Outliers can be caused by errors in data collection or by unusual events, such as a significant but atypical acquisition or a natural disaster that does not happen very often.

4. *Analyze historical actual vs. budget capex variance*: Compare the actual amount spent on capital expenditures to what was initially budgeted so you can identify areas where the company may have overspent or underspent on capital expenditures. Look to understand the root causes for the change.

5. *Rank investments by profitability*: Rank investments by profitability by calculating the return on investment (ROI) for each project or investment. Projects with a higher ROI are typically more profitable and should be prioritized.

6. *Perform detailed analysis on the few largest projects with readily available data*: Review the project's financial and operational performance and any challenges or risks encountered. By analyzing the most significant projects in detail, it's possible to gain understanding and insights that can be applied to other projects and investments in the future. Try to uncover the lessons learned.

Capital allocation governance

My engagement experience has uncovered the vital importance of deciding who is doing what. Capital allocation governance involves a structured approach to managing capital allocation within an organization.

The steps involved in capital allocation governance are as follows:

1. *Document current state*: Gather information on how an organization's capital is currently allocated, who is responsible for making investment decisions, and how those decisions are made.

2. *Conduct stakeholder interviews*: Talk to key stakeholders to understand their perspectives on the current state of capital allocation and identify any pain points or areas for improvement.

3. *Review process and policy documentation*: After conducting stakeholder interviews, the process and policy documentation should be reviewed to ensure that it aligns with the current state of capital allocation.

4. *Hold working sessions to understand the current state*: Schedule working sessions that bring together key stakeholders to review the documentation, discuss pain points, and identify opportunities for improvement.

5. *Develop a playbook of FP&A activities*: A playbook of financial planning and analysis (FP&A) will ensure all stakeholders understand their responsibilities and expectations. This playbook

should outline the key steps involved in capital allocation, including the roles and responsibilities of each stakeholder.

6. *Align stakeholders on future-state responsibilities and process expectations*: Once the playbook is developed, it should be shared with all stakeholders so they are on board with future-state responsibilities and process expectations.

7. *Analyze outputs from historical analysis*: Identify process inefficiencies and weaknesses by reviewing past investment data and comparing actual and expected outcomes.

By following these steps an organization can establish a structured approach to capital allocation governance that aligns stakeholders and improves the efficiency and effectiveness of the capital allocation process.

◆ ◆ ◆

CONSIDERATIONS

Capital allocation and ongoing capital management are essential steps leading to a successful execution of strategy. There are several key considerations, including the following:

- *Align allocation to strategic goals*: Put your money where your mouth is. An organization's priorities should guide capital allocation decisions. It is essential to align capital investments with the overall direction of the organization and its long-term objectives.
- *Consider risk appetite and management*: Capital allocation decisions should also consider each investment opportunity's risk level. Organizations need to consider each investment's potential risks and rewards and weigh them against the organization's overall risk tolerance. High-risk investments probably don't work in a conservative business culture.
- *Use financial performance as a critical input*: Capital management requires careful monitoring of an organization's financial performance, including revenue, sales, profits, cash flow, and debt

levels. Organizations must have sufficient capital resources to fund both their operations and investments.

- *Consider non-financial data*: Do non-financial benefits justify the additional capital allocation? It's important to consider broader areas like social, technological, operational, environmental, and more when considering capital investment decisions.

- *Evaluate each opportunity's potential return on investment (ROI)*: Organizations need to consider the expected returns of all investments and compare them to the cost of capital.

- *Consider the capital structure*: Capital allocation decisions should also consider an organization's capital structure, including its mix of debt and equity. Organizations need to determine the optimal combination of these to minimize their cost of capital and maximize shareholder value.

- *Remember that cash is king*: Effective capital management requires monitoring an organization's cash position. What is our current cash balance, and what are our anticipated cash flows over the short and long term?

- *Ensure regulatory compliance*: Capital allocation and management decisions must also comply with relevant regulations and laws, including accounting standards, tax laws, environmental requirements, and securities regulations.

- *Evaluate consistently:* Use consistent methodologies to evaluate portfolios to ensure apples to apples comparison when making important decisions.

- *Build objective criteria*: Develop objective assessment criteria before gathering information. Avoid using noncomparable information and develop multiple models/spreadsheets to determine where to allocate capital.

- *Manage data quality*: Garbage in means garbage out from a data perspective. Data quality is based on factors such as accuracy, consistency, reliability, and validity. Be sure the data meets these measurements when using models/spreadsheets.

- *Be careful of bias*: It's not uncommon that individuals may become overly optimistic about a particular course of action, rely too much on specific pieces of information while overlooking others, or interpret the objective through too narrow a lens. Try to anticipate and avoid biases when allocating capital.

- *Drive ongoing monitoring and control*: After allocating capital, be sure you have set up a continuous monitoring and control system.

CHAPTER 15
OPERATING MODEL DEVELOPMENT

"Truly comprehensive corporate governance can support companies in achieving a balance between business and reputation, always taking sustainability and long-term value creation into account."
—SUSANA SIERRA, CEO OF BH COMPLIANCE

AN OLYMPIC APPROACH TO DESIGNING GOVERNANCE

The Winter Olympic and Paralympic Games are the premier competitions for sports played on ice or snow; among the most popular are ice hockey, skiing, and figure skating. They are held every four years and feature participants from across the world.

A city-wide Bid Corporation (BidCo) was developed to steer the bid process for the Olympic and Paralympic Winter Games. As part of its mandate, BidCo proposed how a Host Corporation (HostCo) would be created, governed, and organized if the bid for the Games was successful. But the BidCo board of directors soon faced challenges related to decision-making and execution. The voting structure made it difficult for critical decisions to be made promptly, and unclear roles and responsibilities between the board and an external coordinating committee had the potential to cause confusion. Additionally, the board was overrepresented by some levels of government and underrepresented by members of the business community, which meant the board was lacking some of the critical skills it needed to govern effectively.

The BidCo board required recommendations on how to fix its existing issues and advice on structuring the HostCo board to avoid the same problems and learn from similar organizations. BidCo and I engaged a small project team to determine high-level recommendations for board governance for the city Host Corporation. The aim was to assess the current board governance model and understand how other similar organizations within the significant sporting events area, and similarly funded non-sporting organizations, structure and manage their board governance.

The team and I developed a report that provided deep analysis and insights into board governance models. Leading board governance practices as well as external research directly informed the recommendations related to board size, structure, composition, representation, supporting/coordinating bodies or functions, policy, and process. Furthermore, the team benchmarked the current state against similar entities worldwide (sporting and non-sporting), including the Vancouver 2010 Olympic and Paralympic Winter Games and Toronto 2015 Pan Am and Parapan Am Games. The report also included a series of recommendations and options for the BidCo CEO and board to review, which guided how to fix existing board governance issues within BidCo and inform the HostCo board governance model.

Despite the good governance model adopted by BidCo in support of a successful strategy execution, past Olympic failures loomed large. Issues like hosting costs, the potential effect on the city's security and budget, and environmental and other social priorities were at the top of the public's mind (although all of these were addressed in the bid). As a result, the agenda never resonated in the city. Following a public vote, the city decided not to bid on the Winter Olympics. The results were decisive: 43.6 percent supported the bid while 56.4 percent were against it. Some say the public was given too much information and was too influential in the decision, while others argue that the bid process was rushed and locked out the public.

This chapter explores the development of a robust operating model, including the governance element illustrated in this Olympic management example. Furthermore, this chapter describes how to study an organizational continuum of four strategic operating models to identify the right one to focus on, drawing on examples such as Sears, Tower Records, Ford, Nestlé SA, Barclays Bank, and Tesla.

♦ ♦ ♦

WHAT IS OPERATING MODEL DEVELOPMENT?

Chapter 6, part of the inside-out analysis, described the approach to assessing the current state operating model using a maturity model–based approach. This chapter takes it to the next level, elaborating on that analysis to design a future-state operating model. Creating the optimal operating model to enable the strategy is vital in preparing for execution.

Through my involvement with 80-plus organizations, I've learned that an operating model bridges the *why* of strategy with the *how* of day-to-day operations, translating the organization's higher-level strategy into a more defined model that employees can follow daily. An operating model is designed to improve decision-making, lines of communication, investment oversight, and reporting. Ultimately, as an outcome of the operating model, an organization can define what excellence means and how it underpins its future-state focus areas: transparency, engagement, and measurables.

An operating model consists of various elements that interact with each other and combine to paint the picture of how work gets done within an organization. As part of a robust strategic planning process, enterprises often wisely choose to revisit their organizational model and redefine it for an aspirational state. A target operating model (TOM) aligns an organization's operating capacities and strategic objectives to execute future projects.

An operating model is essential to successfully execute a strategy. In fact, a global survey of more than 4,000 senior managers by the Economist Intelligence Unit (EIU) found that the majority (54 percent) favoured new business models over new products and services as a source of future competitive advantage. EIU analysts concluded that, "The overall message is clear: how companies do business will often be as, or more, important than what they do." In a similar global study conducted by IBM, in which over 750 corporate and public sector leaders were interviewed on innovation, researchers found that "competitive pressures have pushed business model innovation much higher than expected on CEOs' priority lists."[220]

Operating model alignment to strategy

I've worked on several operating model projects and have come to understand the critical importance of aligning this component with an organization's strategy. Business strategy and operating model are two interdependent aspects of any organization.

A business strategy defines a company's goals, objectives, and approach to achieving its mission and vision, with a focus on *why* it does this. An operating model focuses on *what* a company does, translating strategic intent into operational capabilities. It serves as the foundation for execution and provides a clear guide for the leadership, line managers, and operational teams. Furthermore, an operating model defines how a company will organize its resources, processes, and people to execute the strategy effectively. The business strategy and operating model must stay integrated and aligned because they work symbiotically to achieve the organization's goals. I've learned that a misalignment between the two can lead to inefficiencies, floundering due to misallocation of resources, and missed opportunities.

CASE STUDY
Operating model struggles at Sears led to bankruptcy

Here is a cautionary tale about how, when strategy changes, so should the operating model. Founded in 1893, Sears became synonymous with the middle-class American dream of the 20th century. It smartly leveraged customer data, creative marketing, and a large store count to become a formidable juggernaut that would dominate the US retail landscape during the postwar boom of the 1940s and 1950s. The company helped develop many brands that consumers still know and love. Brands like Whirlpool appliances, Craftsman tools, Schwinn bicycles, and Allstate insurance owe much of their success to Sears.

At its peak, Sears sales alone accounted for 1 percent of the entire US economy, and two-thirds of Americans shopped there in any given quarter. Sears was America's largest retailer because it predicted the trends shaping the latter half of the 20th century. For example, it correctly anticipated the importance of mail-order retail, suburbs, and the American mall.

However, by the first decade of the 2000s, Sears needed to pivot its operating model away from the mall-based store model as malls began to decline due to competition from online retailers and big-box stores. Although the company experimented with smaller format stores, the brand didn't invest heavily enough in the new formats even though smaller stores were twice as profitable. Even more disastrous for Sears, an online retail operating model was outside its strategy. Sears Holdings filed for Chapter 11 bankruptcy on October 15, 2018, ahead of a $134 million debt payment due that day. It was a sad end to an American icon that failed to rethink the operating model.[221]

Operating model design elements

A few critical elements in an operating model were initially described in Chapter 6: the strategic foundational elements establish the overarching direction for the organization, and the business architecture elements outline how work will get done day-to-day.

Strategic foundational elements include the following:

- *Strategy and design principles*: This is the organization's mission, vision, and goals, as well as the strategies and tactics used to achieve them. The design principles define how the organization should operate and provide rigour, consistency, and structure to guide the design process.
- *Service delivery*: Defines critical service areas, high-level and functional activities, and core competencies and describes the required changes to move to a future state.
- *Governance and risk management*: The policies and procedures that ensure the organization's activities align with its objectives and values, including the oversight and decision-making structures that guide the organization. This provides a framework that balances stakeholder interests and mitigates risk.
- *Stakeholder relations and engagement*: Documents key stakeholder groups outside the company that must be managed. Typically, critical needs, relative influence, and interaction mechanisms need to be defined.

Business architecture includes the following:

- *Organization design, people, and culture*: Defines organization structure, responsibility, and accountability within the structure, required skills to bring the structure to life, and culture and values as a foundation. This element also defines the organization's leadership style, including how people will be managed (e.g., command and control, team-based, etc.).

- *Process*: The set of activities the organization uses to create value, including the design, implementation, and management of these processes.

- *Information technology*: The systems and tools—including hardware, software, and data management—used to support an organization's processes and achieve its goals.

- *Performance management*: A comprehensive set of key performance measures for an organization's business processes that align them with its strategic objectives and create the capability of measuring process performance against its past, industry peers, and strategic objectives.

CASE STUDY
Facing the music at Tower Records

Tower Records is another unfortunate example of getting an operating model's service delivery component wrong. This retail music franchise was founded by Russell Solomon in 1960. After enjoying 40 years of continuous growth, the company filed for bankruptcy in 2006 and 2008.

Tower Records' aggressive expansion strategy was based on CD sales remaining high indefinitely. Despite the likes of Sir Elton John, Bruce Springsteen, and other high-profile artists being loyal customers, market share was first eroded by big-box competitors and then by the digital music revolution.

Tower Records was especially blind to, and ill-prepared for, the impending digital revolution. Consumers stopped buying music from physical stores, instead preferring to purchase albums from iTunes, which was cheaper and more convenient. According to subject matter experts, one of the main reasons behind Tower Records' failure was poor leadership, but the operating model was also a fundamental flaw.[222]

HOW TO APPROACH OPERATING MODEL DEVELOPMENT

Operating model design and implementation approach

Through my consulting work, I've determined that a workshop-focused method tasked with identifying the strategy within the organization and defining the target operating model elements in detail is a practical approach. You get the key players together to agree on a target future state. This approach increases organizational buy-in since those developing the TOM will be part of the group using it.

Designing and implementing a new operating model can be a complex process requiring careful planning and execution. Here's a step-by-step guide on how to initiate, assess, design, and implement a new operating model:

1. *Initiate and scope*: The first step is identifying the need for a new operating model. This can be driven by internal factors, such as changing business goals, or external factors, such as changes in the competitive landscape and overall market conditions. Once the burning platform is identified, the next step is to create a team or a project group responsible for overseeing the development and implementation of the new operating model and to appoint a leader to drive the effort overall. Deliverables in this phase include project charter, team roles and responsibilities, stakeholder analysis, and business case.

2. *Assess current state*: As described in Chapter 6 (Operating Model Analysis), this step focuses on assessing the current operating model to identify core strengths to retain, gaps, and opportunities for improvement. It comprehensively analyzes the organization's business processes, systems, and structure to evaluate how things are working. The assessment should also include an external environment analysis, including market trends and competitor analysis. Deliverables in this phase include a current state assessment report, gap analysis, opportunity analysis, and risk assessment. My experience has shown the importance of understanding observations, insights, and recommendations when developing the current state assessment report.

3. *Design future state*: Design the new operating model based on the current state assessment and gap analysis findings. This involves defining the target operating model, which is the future state of the organization's operating model. The target operating model should be aligned with the organization's business strategy and goals, and importantly identify some key principles of success. Deliverables in this phase include target operating model design, operating model roadmap, business process maps, organizational design, and culture, performance management, governance, and technology architecture. It's also important to consider partnerships with third parties when developing future-state operating models in terms of what activities to insource vs. outsource.

4. *Implement and monitor*: Implement the new operating model, transitioning from the current state to the target operating model. The implementation plan should include detailed activities, timelines, work effort, and responsibilities and have a communication and change management strategy to ensure the new operating model is successfully adopted. It's also important to monitor and manage implementation risks. Deliverables in this phase include an implementation plan, change management plan, communication plan, training plan, process and technology migration plan, and post-implementation review report.

CASE STUDY
Assessment and redesign of the operating model at Chipotle with a four-step approach

Fast-food chain Chipotle Mexican Grill is an example of getting the assessment and redesign of the operating model bang on. In 2015, the company dealt with many scandals, such as an *E. coli* outbreak and similar food safety issues. A negative reputation harmed the company's sales, which fell by one-fifth the following year.

However, the Coronavirus pandemic allowed Chipotle to regain its reputation and strengthen its revenue. Namely, it significantly changed its food preparation processes. Practices recommended by the Centers for Disease Control and Prevention, such as washing hands between tasks and applying hand sanitizer, became mandatory for its employees. During the COVID-19 lockdown, Chipotle also focused efforts on a new service delivery method: orders for pickup. It created digital kitchens that organized online orders for pickup at restaurants that did not already have a system to do so. The number of digital orders skyrocketed. The company hired 8,000 new employees in May 2019 and 10,000 more in July.[223] That helped Chipotle gain a competitive edge and hit new all-time highs in the turbulent COVID-19 era when many restaurants struggled to survive. Chipotle tweaked its customer experience strategy to meet market demand by effectively redesigning the operating model.[224]

Following the four-step approach outlined, Chipotle understood the scope (food preparation and service delivery). It went deep on issue identification and root cause as part of the current state assessment, which was food safety, and they redesigned the operating model with better processes and new sales channels. The results were delivered by focusing on preparation and world-class implementation, and Mexican food never tasted better. Chipotle has achieved tasty results, with the stock in 2024 up over 120-fold since its IPO 18 years before and strong financials across the board.[225]

Strategic operating model continuum

The continuum of strategic operating models (illustrated in Figure 14) is something I've used extensively over the years. This framework helps organizations determine how they operate to achieve their strategic goals by identifying which one of the four operating models along the continuum best characterizes their business: financial holding, strategic architect, strategic controller, or strategic operator.

Each operating model type, or option, represents a different integration level between the organization's strategy and operations and is influenced by many factors, including the degree of involvement of the corporate head office in the functions and business units, the level of control required, integration, and standardization. I've found that where an organization lands on this continuum, based on the unique combination of elements in its operating model, is almost a philosophy for how a business operates.

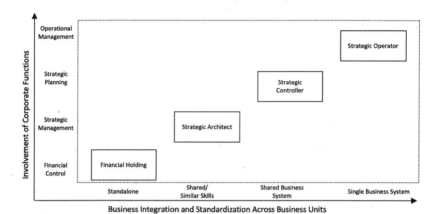

Figure 14: Continuum of strategic operating models

Diving deeper, the four different operating models are described as follows:

- *Financial holding model*: The financial holding model is at the far-left end of the continuum. This model is characterized by high decentralization and independence among business units. Each unit operates as a profit centre, with little coordination or integration with other departments. This model is most commonly used by conglomerates or holding companies that own multiple businesses with little strategic alignment.

- *Strategic architect model*: The strategic architect model is moving toward the middle of the continuum. It involves a higher degree of centralization and coordination across business units. The focus is on creating a common strategy and vision for the organization, with each unit aligning its operations to achieve that vision. Organizations undergoing significant transformation or restructuring often use the strategic architect model.

- *Strategic controller model*: The strategic controller model is closer to the continuum's right end. It involves a higher degree of integration between the organization's strategy and its operations. The focus is on creating a centralized governance structure that enables the organization to monitor and control its operations and achieve its strategic goals. The strategic controller model is commonly used by organizations in highly regulated industries, such as financial services or healthcare.

- *Strategic operator model*: The strategic operator model is at the far-right end of the continuum. This model involves the highest degree of integration between the organization's strategy and operations. The focus is on creating a culture of continuous improvement, with a strong emphasis on operational efficiency and effectiveness. Organizations that most frequently use this model are in highly competitive industries, such as manufacturing or logistics.

It's vital to land on the part of the operating model continuum that is best suited to support the organization's strategy. Nestlé is one firm that managed to hit this sweet spot. In 2014, the company announced it was restructuring its global operations to improve efficiency and competitiveness. As part of this effort, Nestlé redesigned its operating model to simplify its organizational structure and streamline decision-making—aiming for something between strategic architect and strategic controller. The new structure included three central business units focused on food and beverage products, each with profit and loss accounts. Additionally, the company created regional business zones to improve local decision-making and responsiveness to customer needs. Nestlé reported tasty profitability since implementing the new operating model, with higher sales growth and operating margins.[226]

CASE STUDY
Deciding on the operating model spectrum at Ford Motor Company

Ford Motor Company is another example of an organization deliberately deciding where to position itself on the operating model spectrum described in Figure 14. In 2006, Ford needed help. The company's finances were shaky—it had lost about a point of market share in the US every year for the previous 10 years—and its future was uncertain. However, within a few years, Ford rapidly returned to profitability without bailout from the American taxpayer, even after the global financial crisis of 2008.

So, how did Ford achieve the miracle turnaround? The organization moved from regional business units to a global functional operating model, shifting them to a strategic operator on the continuum described in Figure 14 and setting the stage for more efficient and effective operations. For example, creating a global head of product development allowed Ford to reduce the number of vehicle platforms from roughly 40 to 10. But Ford didn't just add a box to the org chart. Each regional unit assumed global responsibilities: North America for large pickups, Europe for compact cars, Australia for small pickups, and so on. This setup drew the business together, eliminating redundant activities and extending the reach of teams with expertise.

Governance and behaviours had to change as well. Alan Mulally, the president and CEO, improved the effectiveness of the weekly business performance reviews, pushing executives for more open debate and honesty about where problems were cropping up. He encouraged his team to simplify their work, eliminating ineffective meetings and liberating thousands of unproductive hours. The company even distributed laminated "One Ford" cards to communicate the new expected behaviours to all employees.[227]

Overall, the strategic operating model continuum provides organizations with a framework to evaluate their current operating model and determine necessary changes in design to align with their strategic goals. As with Nestlé and Ford, the key is balancing centralization and decentralization, governance and flexibility, and alignment and innovation.

The Discipline of Market Leaders: a model for driving differentiation

Various approaches, frameworks, and philosophies offer perspectives on the operating model. For example, *The Discipline of Market Leaders*, by Michael Treacy, is a management book I've used extensively.[228] It proposes that successful companies excel in one of three core business strategies and operating models: operational excellence, product leadership, or customer intimacy. Companies focusing on operational excellence strive for efficiency and cost savings. Those prioritizing product leadership seek to innovate and create superior products. And companies that prioritize customer intimacy focus on building strong customer relationships and delivering customized solutions.

The author argues that companies should choose one of these strategies and fully commit to becoming market leaders. He also suggests that companies should try to excel only in one area and not dilute resources by trying to be good at all three, which causes a lack of focus. Overall, the book provides a framework for companies to develop a clear strategy and operating model in their market.

Here are the details of each discipline:

- *Product leadership*: Organizations that excel in the product leadership discipline focus on creating their industry's most innovative and cutting-edge products or services. These companies prioritize research and development, invest heavily in new technologies, and constantly seek to develop products that will disrupt their industry. They often charge premium prices for their products or services based on the unique value they provide. Companies that excel in the product leadership discipline include Apple, Tesla, and Amazon, which are known for their innovative products, special features, and market-changing technologies. Chapter 18 explores innovation and tactics that support a product leadership–driven operating model.

- *Operational excellence*: Organizations that excel in the operational excellence discipline focus on providing the industry's most efficient and effective processes, systems, and supply chains. They aim to achieve the highest efficiency, quality, and cost control levels. They often have standardized processes and procedures that enable them to consistently deliver high-quality products or services at a lower cost than their competitors. Companies that excel in operational excellence include Walmart, FedEx, and Toyota, which are known for their streamlined operations, standardized processes, and optimized supply chains. Chapter 19 explores cost-management tactics that support an operational excellence–focused operating model.

- *Customer intimacy*: Organizations that excel in the customer intimacy discipline focus on building deep, long-term customer relationships. They prioritize understanding their customers' needs and preferences and work to provide personalized solutions that meet those needs. They often offer a wide range of products or services tailored to individual customers and provide exceptional customer service and support. Companies that excel in the customer intimacy discipline include Nordstrom, Ritz-Carlton, and Zappos, all of which are known for their personalized customer experiences, superior service, and customized offerings.

CASE STUDY
Customer intimacy at Barclays Bank, UK, leads to increased satisfaction and other benefits

Barclays Bank is a great example of focusing on customer intimacy as a strategic choice. In 2013, the global giant announced it was undergoing a significant transformation to improve customer service.

Barclays redesigned its operating model to create a new customer-focused organizational structure as part of this effort. The new structure included four business units focused on specific customer segments: retail banking, corporate banking, wealth management, and investment banking. Each business unit had its own profit and loss account, enabling them to make decisions independently and respond more quickly to changing customer needs.

Since implementing the new operating model, Barclays has reported not only improved customer satisfaction, but also the side benefit of reduced costs in the process of executing this strategy.[229]

I tell my clients that picking the proper discipline is vital. Pets.com is an unfortunate example of focusing on a discipline not closely aligned with your unique strategic advantage. The former San Francisco–based dot-com ignored the competitive positioning of their unique product and experience and instead decided to compete on low prices like its competitors. This mistake led to the sale of merchandise at prices below cost for the duration of its operations, which was fatal given that the online pet market was crowded during the period when Pets.com was alive.[230]

Leveraging the concepts described by Treacy can help organizations to become market leaders. This can be done by boosting their core strengths and focusing on their unique value proposition as part of the development of an operating model. By aligning their strategies and operations with one of the three disciplines, companies can energize themselves compared to their competitors and provide unique value.

Support services activity placement framework

Support services like HR, finance, or IT help the core business succeed. The back-office function in an organization is made up of administration and support personnel who need to be client-centric, but there are options for where these functions are located in relation to the internal and external clients they serve. I've worked with many companies that have chosen to outsource and offshore back-office roles and activities to reduce costs further. Technology has also allowed many companies to enable remote work arrangements, the benefits of which include rent savings and increased productivity. Additionally, remotely employing back-office staff will enable companies to access talent in various geographic areas and attract diverse applicants.

Organizations can use the support services activity placement framework to determine the optimal location for their support services activities based on two dimensions: the complexity of transactions and the need for local control and proximity to customers.

Here's a detailed explanation of the principles of the framework that have helped me support success:

- *The complexity of transactions*: This refers to the complexity of carrying out the specific support services activity. Those involving high levels of complexity require specialized knowledge, skills, and expertise, typically performed by highly trained personnel. Examples of complex activities include financial analysis, research and development, and IT support.

- *Need for local control/proximity to customer*: This refers to the extent to which the support services activity needs to be performed locally to meet the customer's needs. Activities that require proximity to the customer include sales, marketing, and customer support.

Based on these two dimensions, the support services activity placement framework proposes four different placement options:

- *Centralization*: Support services activities are centralized at a single location in this option. It is suitable for activities with low complexity that do not require high local control and proximity to the customer. Centralization helps to achieve economies of scale and reduce costs and duplication of effort.

- *Regionalization*: Support services activities are performed at multiple regional centres closer to the customer. This option suits activities requiring a moderate level of complexity and local control and proximity to the customer. Regionalization helps improve responsiveness to local needs while achieving some economies of scale.

- *Localization*: Support services activities are performed wherever customers are located. This option is suitable for activities that involve a great deal of complexity and a high level of local control and proximity to the customer. Localization helps ensure that the support services are tailored to the customer's local needs. Still, it can be expensive due to duplication of effort.

- *Virtualization*: Support services are performed remotely using video conferencing and cloud-based systems. This option suits activities involving low to moderate complexity and proximity to customers. Virtualization helps to achieve cost savings and improve flexibility, but it may be suitable only for some activities.

Activities where complexity is reduced and proximity to the customer is not critical are great candidates for offshoring and centralizing. For example, IBM has used the global business services (GBS) model for over 20 years. The company has more than 100 GBS centres worldwide and employs over 100,000 people in its GBS division.[231]

Tesla's support services model is perhaps one of the best transformational examples. The direct-to-consumer (DTC) business model sells electric vehicles directly—cutting out intermediaries such as dealerships—and provides its charging station network. This changes the game for buyers, eliminating the inconvenience of haggling prices at dealerships and removing the need for dealerships to stock on their lots 900 cars at a time when buyers themselves prefer to buy online.[232]

In summary, the support services activity placement framework helps organizations determine the optimal location for their activities. Using this framework, organizations can better balance cost savings, responsiveness to customer needs, and the complexity of the support services activities. Support services form a vital and sometimes costly component of running any business, so carefully thinking through the optimal location as part of the operating model design, while still providing a high-quality service, is essential.

♦ ♦ ♦

CONSIDERATIONS

Developing and implementing an operating model takes work. Still, it's worth it to enable strategy execution and gear the organization to achieve its strategic objectives. Consider these critical aspects when undertaking it:

- *Understand the strategy*: Upfront, it's crucial to understand what the business strategy is and how it informs the operating model—effectively understanding whether the current operating model aligns with the organization's strategy. If the operating model does not help bring the strategy to life, then it's not aligned.
- *Assess your current state*: Understanding your current state (process, resources, capabilities, technology, performance management, and governance) is a critical first step to developing

and documenting the optimal operating model. Identify and interview key stakeholders from across your operations with a standard set of questions to capture opportunities, pain points, observations, insights, and overall themes about the current state. In addition, do a solid review of existing documentation to determine if it hangs together and tells the story you want about your why, what, and how.

- *Determine if there is a need to change*: Current state assessments may determine that all that is needed is more robust and compelling documentation of the current state. They may also unearth pain points that, if not solved, will get in the way of achieving strategic goals, hinder growth, or put your organization at risk. If the latter is true, a strong case for change that includes the consequences of not changing must be developed and communicated across the enterprise. Getting employees excited and mobilized around a common need for change or a burning platform is critical to success. Without employee buy-in, an operating model will not be implemented successfully.

- *Get the right people at the table*: Regardless of whether an operating model will simply document the current state or bring about change, getting the right people involved will expedite decisions with representation from across business units and functions. In addition, creating the right working teams and steering committees can bring additional diversity of thought and aid with buy-in, resulting in a suitable approach for your organization.

- *Define your design principles*: Design principles articulate the parameters for the future state, set the context, and are born of an organization's strategic priorities and current state assessment. Usually plotted along a spectrum, design principles result in critical statements to guide the development of the operating model document.

- *Shape your future state*: Developing the future state should happen through workshops, each focused on a different element of your operating model. Each workshop should explain to attendees the purpose of an operating model, the case for change, and a definition of the specific element at hand before diving into facilitated discussions and exercises to help define the future state of that element. Focusing on asking better questions about the current and future state will generate better answers, resulting in more robust documentation of your operating model.

- *Be digital*: The importance of digital transformation cannot be underestimated, so seeking opportunities to transform, internally and externally, how the operating model connects with customers is vital to staying competitive.[233]

- *Get it all down*: Facilitating workshops can be hard work, but capturing all the salient points, decisions, critical questions and answers, and opportunities for change and improvement can be even more challenging. Afterwards, it's time to document the outputs of the workshops into a single coherent and cohesive document that is plainly worded and easily understood.

- *Implement it*: It's critical not to let up on momentum once the operating model is agreed upon. Robust implementation includes identifying initiatives that will help achieve new goals, placing those initiatives in the broader context (asking: What else is going on? How will base operations be impacted?), assigning accountability, and planning and executing those plans.

CHAPTER 16
ORGANIZATION STRUCTURE DEVELOPMENT

"Organizational design is not just about structure,
it is also about people and processes."
—RICHARD BRANSON, FOUNDER OF VIRGIN GROUP

FORM FOLLOWS FUNCTION AT A MIDSTREAM OPERATOR

Growth often acts as a catalyst for structural change. I worked with a large North American midstream pipeline company with significant crude oil supply, trading, and marketing operations. The organization wanted help from me and my team to review, assess, and provide recommendations on how to optimize its structure to deliver on its business strategy. It quickly became evident that a change was required to the company's structural design and hierarchy, which included layering and spans of control. (Spans of control refers to the number of subordinates that report directly to a manager; layers refers to the number of hierarchical levels, or management tiers, within the company.) The company also needed to change the role design, accountabilities, responsibilities, capabilities, and resource or headcount requirements.

Furthermore, the company needed a refresh to help overcome past challenges. The aim of changing the structure was to realign work, build and allocate capacity, increase the clarity of roles, address integration to the rest of the business, address alignment to customer segmentation, and support succession planning.

As the saying goes, "Don't throw the baby out with the bath water," but build on key strengths. Initially, the team assessed the current state through interviews and documentation review (organization structure, accountabilities, role clarity, processes, etc.). Interviews were conducted with the leadership team to understand strengths, weaknesses, and opportunities for improvement.

We needed to be clear on the overarching philosophy. Upfront, we all agreed on some design principles: to provide tangible, high-level boundaries and guides for developing organizational design options so that leadership could keep the "end in mind." Areas of focus related to these principles included clarity of structure, stability, better spans and layers, centralization where it made sense, pushing accountability down, and focus.

Determining the optimal organizational structure was an iterative process. The draft structure was developed by reviewing a series of alternatives and then analyzing what could, and didn't, work to design a final version. The organization structure was developed by reviewing four options and then choosing the best aspects of each to create a new structure.

My team and I evaluated the structure against critical criteria, including alignment to the design principles, ease of implementation, cost, and alignment to leading practice. A responsibility assignment matrix was introduced to the leadership team. This helped to understand, establish, and communicate roles and responsibilities to increase productivity, eliminate duplication, improve cooperation, and enhance motivation. Once roles were defined, we determined the high-level competencies required, starting at the VP and director levels. Work remained to identify the competencies needed for the manager level and below.

Change was necessary despite the fear of unknown consequences. Ultimately, the project was unsuccessful for a few key reasons. Once design efforts were completed, the organization determined that the project was over without considering implementation. The leadership team created a structure that looked like the current state, with unresolved critical issues and pain points. There also needed to be more alignment at the top, where distracted and disengaged leaders resulted in confusion within the organization. Because limited organizational structure changes were implemented, confusion about roles and responsibilities remained, and duplication of work continued. Sometimes, it felt like the structure was designed around keeping people happy rather than the broader organization's needs.

The project team assumed everyone bought into the new design. But change is hard, especially when reporting structures are involved, and it starts with leadership. Those who resist change can channel negativity and rapidly derail efforts to prepare for change. Chapter 16 outlines the deliberate and systematic analysis, design, implementation, and evaluation steps required for a successful organizational redesign while managing the change.

◆ ◆ ◆

WHAT IS ORGANIZATION STRUCTURE DEVELOPMENT?

While the operating model design described in Chapter 15 bridges the *why* of strategy with the *how* of day-to-day operations, the organizational structure outlines the grouping of resources and works to fulfill the operating model requirements and achieve the company's strategy. The organizational structure is just one of the components of the operating model, but its importance warrants separate consideration in this chapter.

Organizational structure and design refer to how leaders arrange the firm's non-financial resources, including people, tasks, and technology, in a logical way to achieve its goals; it's an essential preparation for strategy execution. Some researchers argue that organizational structure if done right should be based on optimal coordination of interactions among activities to drive efficiency and effectiveness. The main idea is that each manager can detect and coordinate interactions only within their limited area of expertise. The optimal design of the organization trades off the costs and benefits of various configurations of managers and direct reports.[234] It involves the formal arrangement of roles, responsibilities, relationships, and communication channels within an organization and describes how the different parts of a company are organized, come together, and relate to each other to drive work outputs. It defines the hierarchy of authority, reporting relationships, span of control, number of layers, and communication channels. Organizational structures can be hierarchical, flat, matrix, or networked, depending on the organization's strategic focus, size, and complexity.

But I often advise clients that it's more than just structure. It involves making decisions about the organization's mission, values, goals, and strategies and designing the roles, responsibilities, and communication channels necessary to implement these strategies. It can involve changes, such as shifting from a hierarchical to a matrix structure or creating new departments or teams. It can also include changes to the processes, policies, and procedures that govern how work is done within an organization. Organizational design is typically achieved through a deliberate and systematic analysis, design, implementation, and evaluation.

The data on structure change efforts are disappointing. McKinsey's research shows that less than a quarter of organizational redesign efforts succeed. However, when the organizational redesign of a company matches its strategic intentions, everyone will be primed to execute and deliver them. Then, the company's structure, processes, and people will all support the most important outcomes and channel the organization's efforts into achieving them.[235] According to the Academy to Innovate HR, organizations with highly mature organizational designs are 30 times more likely to adapt well to change, 5.3 times more likely to be a great workplace, and 2.3 times more likely to exceed financial targets.[236] The returns are dramatic, too. Organizational development affects the bottom line in various ways; through increased innovation and productivity, both efficiency and profits are increased.[237]

CASE STUDY
A novel approach to organizational structure at Zappos.com

For some businesses, the organizational structure is the secret to success. The organizational structure of shoe company Zappos.com is revered as one of America's most innovative and transformative. The unique structure of this company has been so successful that its leaders created a department for business-to-business consultations that assist other companies interested in adopting the model.

From a struggling start-up business to a $1.2 billion merger with Amazon.com in 2009, the company has remained true to its value of "delivering WOW through service" to its customers and employees. Although there are hierarchical levels, there is a sense of transparency that alleviates the stress of authority figures.

An American proverb says, "Before you judge a man, walk a mile in his shoes." Zappos would be considered a flat, decentralized organization. When an issue surfaces, the employee closest to the problem is empowered to decide what action is required. This creates flexibility and preparedness that allows the company to respond promptly to any problems. The integration of the differentiated units within the company is so streamlined that teams can be mixed and reformed from time to time without a hitch.

Former CEO Tony Hsieh wrote a book about delivering happiness and incorporated its practices into the company model. Hsieh established a work environment that prioritizes team-building and family values to create customer loyalty. The lines of authority are far from blurred here. Senior managers' cubicles blend in with the workforce. They are called coaches, and they help solve problems instead of barking out orders.[238]

Business strategy and organizational structure are two critical components of any business. The business strategy defines the direction and goals of the organization while the organizational structure determines how the organization is designed to achieve those goals. I've discovered that these two components must be aligned because they complement each other and work together to accomplish the company's objectives efficiently. A well-designed organizational structure ensures that the right people are in the right roles, with the right skills and resources, to successfully execute the business strategy.

Solid line and dotted line relationships

Through my extensive organizational project experience and leveraging the work of Susan Finerty in her book *Master the Matrix: 7 Essentials for Getting Things Done in Complex Organizations*,[239] I've determined that the boxes on an organizational chart are not enough to represent the structure; the connections between them must also be explained. There are sometimes multiple reporting relationships between roles, including both solid line and dotted line connections.

In an organizational structure, a solid line relationship indicates a direct reporting relationship between two positions or roles. This means one person reports directly to another and is accountable for their performance and results. The solid line relationship shows a transparent chain of command and a hierarchy of authority.

A dotted line relationship indicates a more indirect, or advisory, reporting relationship between two positions or roles. This means that one person provides guidance or support to another person. Although they do not have direct authority over them, this can be an important, though less obvious, point of relationship and influence. The dotted line relationship often shows cross-functional collaboration, where individuals from different departments or teams work together on a project or initiative.

In a matrix organizational structure, employees may have a solid line reporting relationship with their functional manager (who oversees their day-to-day work) and a dotted line reporting relationship with their project manager (who oversees their work on a specific project). This allows the employee to receive guidance and support from both managers while maintaining a transparent chain of command. Philips, a Dutch multinational electronics enterprise, was one of the earliest champions of the matrix structure. After the Second World War, it set up both national organizations and product divisions. As an example, the boss of the washing machine division in Italy would report to the head of Philips in Italy as well as to the washing machine supremo in the Netherlands.[240]

Through various engagements, I've learned that identifying the solid and dotted line relationships is essential to the organizational structure because it clearly defines the reporting structure and communication channels. By understanding the solid and dotted line relationships, employees can easily navigate their roles and responsibilities, communicate more efficiently with their colleagues, and ultimately work together toward achieving organizational goals.

HOW TO APPROACH ORGANIZATION STRUCTURE DEVELOPMENT

Activity analysis model

By understanding what work gets done and by whom, you can begin to organize employees properly. An activity analysis is another tool for the organization design toolbox that I've used to assess the effectiveness of the current state and where improvements can be made. It involves breaking down the work activities performed within an organization into smaller components and examining them in detail to identify inefficiencies, redundancies, and other opportunities for improvement.

I've found that the activity analysis process typically involves the following steps:

1. *Define the scope*: Define the scope of the activity analysis by identifying the business processes, functions, and departments

that will be analyzed. For example, is it enterprise-wide or focused on a particular area of the company.

2. *Map the process*: Map the business process or activity being analyzed, creating a visual representation of the process flow and breaking down the process into smaller components. This step is about understanding the work that gets done at a high level.

3. *Identify the activities*: Break down the process into smaller components and examine each activity in detail. It's about understanding the work at a more detailed level.

4. *Analyze the activities*: Identify inefficiencies, redundancies, and opportunities for improvement by looking at factors such as the time and resources required to perform each activity, the level of complexity, and the potential for automation or reconfiguration of the sequence of steps involved. This is focused on understanding who is spending what time and effort where.

5. *Develop recommendations*: If done right, the activity analysis should uncover insights and opportunities to organize and allocate the work better. Based on the analysis of the activities, recommendations can be developed to improve the efficiency and effectiveness of the process. This may involve streamlining activities, eliminating redundancies, improving communication and collaboration, or introducing new technology or automation.

6. *Implement changes*: Implement the recommended changes and monitor the results. This may involve reorganizing the organization's structure, changing job roles or responsibilities, reducing layers, changing span of control, or introducing new processes or technology.

The repeatability of the activities is also an essential data point for informal structural change. In my experience, activities fall into three main categories: strategic, operational, and transactional. Understanding these is essential because it can help organizations identify inefficiencies and opportunities for improvement.

- *Strategic activities*: These focus on long-term planning and decision-making. Senior executives typically perform these activities, which involve setting goals, developing strategies, and making decisions to guide the organization's direction. Strategic activities are critical to the organization's success but may be performed infrequently.

- *Operational activities*: Operational activities are the day-to-day actions that an organization performs to achieve its goals, typically performed by middle managers and employees. They involve production, customer service, and administrative tasks. Operational activities are essential for the organization's success and are performed frequently.
- *Transactional activities*: Transactional activities are routine tasks to complete a specific transaction. They are typically performed by front-line employees and involve tasks such as data entry, order processing, and invoice processing. Transactional activities are essential for the efficient operation of an organization but are not strategic or highly complex.

The differences between these activities are vital because they require different levels of resources, expertise, and attention. For example, strategic activities may require significant time and resources from senior executives. In contrast, operational and transactional activities may require attention only from front-line employees. By understanding the differences among these activities, organizations can better allocate resources and focus on improving the areas most critical to their success.

In performing the activity analysis, you're looking for clues: Where is the potential for efficiencies? What activities could be combined into one?

Overall, an activity analysis is a valuable tool for assessing the effectiveness of an organizational structure and identifying areas for improvement. By breaking down work activities into smaller components and examining them in detail, organizations can identify inefficiencies and opportunities for improvement that may have gone unnoticed otherwise. I've learned that this can significantly improve productivity, efficiency, and overall organizational performance.

Organization design framework

As illustrated in the model in Figure 15, done right, organizational design is more than just structure. Three additional pillars support it: people's roles, people's capabilities, and available resources. The broader operating model components in the black outside circle (described in Chapter 15) will influence the organization's design. It's essential to consider the broader operating model as well as the overarching strategy and business outcomes.

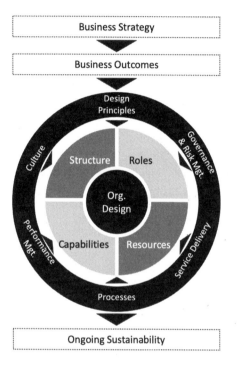

Figure 15: Organization design model

The model is a comprehensive framework that organizations can use to design and optimize their organizational structures and processes. It includes several key elements as follows:

Organization design components

- *Structure*: This element focuses on the overall organizational structure, including how work, tasks, and teams of employees are assembled. It encompasses both formal and informal aspects of the organization.

- *Roles*: Focuses on defining the roles and responsibilities of individual employees, including the skills and competencies required to perform these roles effectively.
- *Capabilities*: Covers the overall capabilities of the organization, including the skills, knowledge, and experience of its employees.
- *Resources*: Addresses the resources required to support the organization's operations, including financial resources, physical assets, and other resources such as technology and infrastructure.

Operating model components

- *Strategy*: The organization's design needs to align with the strategy. This element focuses on the organization's overall strategy, including its vision, mission, goals, strategies, and the tactics used to achieve them.
- *Design principles*: Outlines the principles guiding the overall organizational design process, including simplicity, flexibility, and scalability.
- *Culture*: Focuses on the organizational culture and the values and beliefs that underpin it, including leadership style, communication practices, and employee engagement.
- *Governance and risk management*: Tackles the overall governance structure of the organization, including how decisions are made, how accountability is assigned, and how risks are managed.
- *Service delivery*: Addresses how services are delivered to customers or clients, including the processes and procedures required to ensure high-quality service delivery.
- *Processes*: Covers the overall processes and procedures that underpin the organization's operations, including how work is planned, executed, and monitored.
- *Performance management*: Focuses on the organization overall, including key performance indicators (KPIs) and other metrics used to measure success.
- *Business outcomes*: Includes revenue growth, profitability, customer satisfaction, and other vital metrics.

- *Sustainability*: Includes an organization's overall sustainability, environmental and social impact, and long-term viability and resilience.

CASE STUDY
Organizational harmony at Spotify

Spotify, the music streaming giant, is traded on the New York Stock Exchange through American Depositary Receipts. Offering over 100 million songs and podcasts, Spotify operates on a free-mium model, providing basic features for free with ads and limited control. In contrast, premium subscriptions offer additional perks like offline listening and ad-free experiences. Available in more than 180 countries, Spotify pays royalties based on artists' streaming frequency, distributing approximately 70 percent of its revenue to rights holders.[241, 242]

The company is a marketplace allowing customers to access creators' music and other digital content through a network-like platform. It's music for everyone. The organization required structural flexibility to grow rapidly while competing with digital content distribution efforts from Amazon, Apple, Google, Pandora, and others. As a fundamental element of business development and design, Spotify's corporate structure enabled it to strengthen its competitive advantages over other companies while expanding quickly.

The company's organizational structure, known as an N-shaped design, fosters operational efficiency through knowledge sharing. This structure supports CEO Daniel Ek's vision for rapid global expansion, allowing preparedness and flexibility in adapting to challenges. Employees are organized into "squads" and grouped into "tribes" to maximize knowledge pooling; "guilds," composed of employees from different tribes, share commonalities for operational enhancement.

Recognizing the value of each employee, Spotify's structure encourages horizontal communication and interaction, emphasizing employee contributions to the company's culture. Teams have the freedom to make decisions, experiment, and innovate. This decentralized approach fosters creativity and ownership, leading to better outcomes. Managers are also involved in project-based working groups, promoting equality and collaboration. The structure allows employees to shift roles, contributing to project-based initiatives.

The organizational structure also tightly aligns with Spotify's mission and vision, driving strategic goals of providing profitable opportunities for artists and enjoyable experiences for listeners. Furthermore, it supports an agile culture for software development, aiding in the continuous improvement of the music streaming service. The N-shaped structure facilitates communication channels, aligning with human resource strategies and leveraging core resources in the value chain.

Unlike traditional hierarchical models, Spotify's unique application of the N-form structure showcases its flexibility to meet dynamic business needs in the global digital content market. In essence, Spotify's organizational design combines agility, autonomy, alignment to the mission, cross-functional teams, and a people-centric approach to thrive in the dynamic music streaming industry.

The organization design model provides a comprehensive framework for a company's leaders to design and optimize organizational structures and processes. I've come to understand that by integrating these elements, organizations can create more effective and efficient operating models that drive sustainable business success.

Reorganization approach

A successful reorganization encompasses both strategic design and thoughtful execution, both of which are outlined below in more detail.[243] Here are the steps I've used in designing and executing a new organization design:

1. *Define strategy and prioritize business imperatives*: The team identifies critical business priorities and strategic goals, determines the scope and objectives of the organization's design effort, and establishes clear project goals and success metrics. Researchers argue that structure and strategy are closely related and that structure follows strategy; each is married to the other. The research recommends that top management should ultimately be involved in crafting and formulating the strategy, implementing it, and aligning the structure to follow the strategy.[244]

2. *Review as-is organization*: More broadly explained in Chapter 6, as part of the operating model analysis, this step involves a review of the current organizational structure, roles, and responsibilities.

During the examination, the team needs to assess the strengths and weaknesses of the current organization design, identify areas where it may be hindering business performance, and analyze existing processes, systems, and technologies.

3. *Develop organization design drivers*: This step represents the beginning of thinking about the future. The team defines the key drivers that will shape the new organization design, determines the guiding principles that will govern it, identifies the critical success factors, and conducts a gap analysis between the current organization design and the desired state.

4. *Develop and evaluate organizational options*: The team now generates multiple organization design options based on the drivers and guiding principles, evaluates the pros and cons of each option, conducts a risk analysis of each option, and prioritizes them based on their compatibility with business priorities and strategic goals.

5. *Determine organization sizing*: At this stage, the team determines the appropriate size of the new organization based on the business requirements, develops the optimal span of control for each role, defines the proper levels of hierarchy and reporting lines, and develops job descriptions and responsibilities for each role.

6. *Plan for communication and engagement*: Once the organization's design is selected and sized, the team focuses on developing a communication and engagement plan for it. It's essential to communicate the new design's vision, objectives, alignment to the organization's strategy, and benefits to stakeholders, address any concerns and objections, and obtain support from them.

7. *Implement the selected organization design*: At this stage, it's time to develop an implementation plan and timeline. This is done in a phased manner, developing and implementing training programs for new roles and responsibilities, monitoring and evaluating the new design's performance, and making adjustments as necessary.

My exposure to numerous clients has taught me that these steps provide a structured approach to designing and executing a new organizational design that aligns with business priorities and strategic goals and can improve organizational effectiveness and performance.

CASE STUDY
Organizational design shifts at Coca-Cola demonstrate there is no perfect answer

Making sure that strategy and design drivers are correctly identified is vital to success. It's also essential to review the as-is. Coca-Cola is an infamous example of a big corporation facing disastrous consequences after frequently shifting its organizational design.

In the early 1990s, when globalization seemed like an indispensable business strategy, the then-CEO of Coca-Cola, the late Roberto Goizueta, stated on record that there was no longer a distinction between global and local, ushering in his tagline: Think Global, Act Global. This led to unprecedented globalization and standardization in the company's business functioning. Within a couple of years, Coca-Cola generated a much larger share of its revenues from outside of the US. During this time, it was generally thought that Coca-Cola had finally found a magical formula for success. However, success was short-lived, and with the Asian crisis at the beginning of 1999, Coca-Cola lost more than $70 billion.

When Douglas Daft took over as CEO in 2000, he introduced an aggressive shift in the opposite direction. His mantra was: Think Local, Drink Local. However, a reshuffling and restructuring of the organizational working model failed, as people had adopted an established way of working. This change of strategy resulted in a period during which Coca-Cola saw some of its worst revenues since its inception. One of the biggest reasons behind this global debacle was that the frequent changes in the operational structure affected lines of communication and the working hierarchy. Employees couldn't keep track of the different responsibilities they were handed after every change, and this hampered their overall performance, leading to confusion, cynicism, and job insecurity in employees' minds.[245]

◆ ◆ ◆

CONSIDERATIONS

Form follows function. Organizational design involves creating or modifying an organization's structure and processes to achieve strategic goals and objectives.

When doing organization design work, some key considerations to keep in mind include the following:

- *Remember that structure follows strategy*: The organization's design should align with the company's strategic choices, goals and objectives, and the design should be flexible enough to adapt to changes in the strategy and business environment.
- *Build clear roles and responsibilities*: Clear roles and responsibilities should be defined for each position, including decision-making authority, accountability, and ownership of key business processes. This clarity helps with employee focus on the right things.
- *Define reporting relationships*: The structure should clearly define the reporting relationships, both formal and informal, between positions and teams. It's also essential to define the dotted vs. solid line relationships and how they function within the organization.
- *Consider broader talent management*: The organization design should support the broader talent management processes, including recruiting, onboarding, training, and development, to ensure the organization has the right people in the right roles to achieve its goals.
- *Integrate culture*: The design should consider the organization's culture, including its values, norms, and behaviours. It should also support a positive work environment that fosters collaboration, innovation, and continuous improvement. For example, flat organizational structures can help drive an informal, agile, and flexible culture that supports fast decision-making.
- *Evaluation and feedback*: The design should be evaluated regularly to ensure it still meets the organization's needs and goals, and feedback from employees and stakeholders should be solicited and considered to identify areas for improvement. However, be careful not to constantly change an organization's structure and cause unnecessary employee anxiety about role and job security.
- *Focus on short- and long-term success*: Design new organizational models to help achieve immediate goals, but organizations should

also push themselves so that changes will set them up for long-term success. Anticipating future needs and building a structure to support that is vital to success.

- *Drive structure and rigour*: Apply appropriate rigour to reorganization efforts, including considerable upfront work to understand the current state; align the principles, goals and options; and benchmark against industry norms and leading practices. It's also vital to consider different future options and evaluate the pros and cons.

- *Build organizational capacity to deliver lasting, sustainable results*: This is done by developing leadership experience and intelligence. To support sustainability, organizations need leaders who can redesign the work and understand the core principles of organizational design. These kinds of leaders learn how to evolve the process and operational disciplines to drive cost management and value creation.

- *Don't focus on just structural changes*: Remember that structural changes are only one factor in developing a practical design and strategy. There are some elements that structure can deliver and others where processes, people, culture, strategy, and leadership are necessary to realize change.

- *Include an implementation and communication plan*: The design should include a detailed implementation and communication plan, including timelines, resources, and milestones, to ensure a smooth transition and effective adoption of the new design. It is important to consider the different communication channels within an organization, looking at how they facilitate collaboration and information sharing. Implementation is more than simply rolling out an organization chart.

PART 4

STRATEGY EXECUTION

CHAPTER 17
POST-MERGER INTEGRATION

"Post-merger integration is where the rubber meets the road in terms of realizing the strategic and financial benefits of a merger or acquisition."
—CHRISTOPHER MARQUIS, BUSINESS PROFESSOR AND AUTHOR

REGULATING INTEGRATION THROUGH A STRUCTURED APPROACH

The regulation of energy operations has existed in various forms for more than 100 years. The objectives of a regulator include protecting the environment (including air and water quality), protecting cultural resources, protecting workers' and the public's health and safety, and reducing wasted resources. Proper regulation of the oil and gas industry is critical for everyone, including the industry itself. However, overregulation is counterproductive, stifles development, growth, employment, and economic prosperity and only serves to create shortages and increase costs to the consumer.

New and modified government policy can, over time, drive change in the autonomy of connected organizational bodies like regulators, since they implement policy on behalf of government. In one oil-rich jurisdiction following the passing of a new Energy Act, the legislation catalyzed the need to combine decision-making and oversight related to upstream energy projects under a single regulator. This required transitioning regulatory components from separate government departments into the newly formed single regulator—a merger of sorts. Completing the transition and full integration of the different government departments required the newly created regulator to adhere to the government-set timeline with minimal disruption to ongoing operations. Integrating the various government departments was further complicated by the inability to access and assess the legacy departmental operational capabilities and make the necessary adjustments until after the proclamation date.

It's essential to appoint a team to drive the process of complex mergers. With my help, an integration team was formed to move things forward, ensuring a smooth transition as three government departments were merged into one. A leader within the government was appointed to run the integration, reporting to the CEO.

First, we had to agree on strategic priorities to set a direction for the new combined entity. The integration team translated the strategy into a written report, setting the tone and establishing critical focus areas. This was a priority, given that research by the Institute for Mergers, Acquisitions, and Alliances reports that conflicting goals and strategies are the primary cause of traditional merger failures. Furthermore, stakeholder interviews were held involving industry associations and oil and gas companies that the organization regulated, to understand their perspective correctly. (Similar to the voice-of-the-customer exercise in Chapter 3.) The interviews helped the team understand how the new combined single regulator should be designed and the strengths, weaknesses, and opportunities for improvement in the legacy departments.

Once the strategy was agreed upon, designing a new operating model that defined critical principles of regulation, business processes, stakeholder management, performance management systems, and other features ensured that the new organization's strategy was translated into day-to-day operations. In parallel, an integration management office and workstream lead for each functional department within the organization acted as the engine and air traffic control, driving the integration efforts across the three government departments to help form one merged department. One of the workstreams included the assessment and eventual design of the new organization, including reporting lines, leadership, and departmental roles and responsibilities. Changes in the structure required careful management and communications from a dedicated team of experts.

As mentioned previously, you are what you measure. A critical component of the integration team's efforts was the establishment of key metrics that monitored progress. Performance metrics were designed and tracked to ensure a smooth transition, allowing oil and gas development to continue safely, responsibly, and reliably. Following a disciplined integration process enabled the regulator to meet desired timelines for merging disparate regulatory functions into a single regulator with minimal disruption to operations.

As part of post-merger integration execution success, you need specific people. It's necessary to draw on expert skill sets in various areas, including project management, organizational design, change management, and process redesign. Integration success also requires leaders who understand strategy and operating model design. In this case, these different skills were correctly deployed to successfully meet the government's deadlines.

The team's efforts equipped the regulator with the tools required to continue integration activities and remain operational with no significant impact on operations through the transition periods. The CEO said, "The structure and rigour of methods, tools, and best practices helped us accelerate, track, and manage our transformation efforts . . . In a short period of time we achieved numerous benefits, savings, and tangible outcomes."

This chapter explains the key components of integrating separate organizations, including supporting tools and how they fit into the merger-in-progress. To illustrate, several notable case studies illustrating both success and failure will be unpacked, including the Bank of America and Merrill Lynch, J.P. Morgan and Chase Manhattan Bank, Daimler-Chrysler, and AOL Time Warner. While this chapter focuses on mergers and acquisitions, the principles of the integration approach apply very closely to that of divestment and separation, just in reverse. For simplicity, the remaining sections of this chapter focus on M&A integration.

◆ ◆ ◆

WHAT IS POST-MERGER INTEGRATION?

Following agreement on an M&A or divestment strategy (Chapter 10) and identifying an acquisition target or competitor (Chapter 4), a potential deal is agreed upon and planning for the merger can begin. This chapter explores how you best integrate different entities.

Through trial and error, I've learned that failing to plan is planning to fail. In fact, according to a report by RSM US, a professional services company, 70 percent of post-merger integrations fail to capture planned synergies and value. Why? Because leaders often underestimate the time and effort needed to successfully merge two companies and don't spend enough time planning the integration.[246]

Post-merger integration (PMI) refers to fusing two or more organizations after a merger or acquisition. My involvement in several PMI projects has shown me that thorough planning and execution of activities are needed to integrate various aspects of the merged entities, such as operations, culture, systems, processes, and personnel. PMI aims to achieve the merger's strategic and financial strategy and objectives while minimizing disruptions and maximizing synergies.

My work has uncovered some typical PMI considerations as follows:

- *Planning*: This stage involves developing a detailed integration plan that outlines the goals, timelines, and resources required for a successful integration. The plan should address various areas, including organizational structure, systems and IT integration, cultural alignment, customer and employee retention, and communication strategies.

- *Governance*: Establishing a governance structure is crucial for effective decision-making and coordination during integration; it ensures clear roles, responsibilities, and accountability. This involves forming an integration management office (IMO) or a steering committee comprising key stakeholders from both organizations.

- *Systems and processes integration*: Integrating IT systems, processes, and infrastructure is essential for streamlining operations and realizing synergies. This may involve consolidating or migrating systems, harmonizing business processes, and ensuring data compatibility.

- *Employee integration*: Engaging and retaining employees is critical for maintaining productivity and preserving talent. Effective communication, transparency, and employee support programs are essential. Ensuring a fair and consistent approach to roles, compensation, and career development helps alleviate uncertainties and foster a positive work environment.

- *Customer integration*: It goes without saying that retaining and satisfying customers is necessary to preserve market share and revenue streams. To do so, it's important to communicate the benefits of the merger, maintain service levels, and address any concerns or changes in the customer experience. Identifying cross-selling opportunities and leveraging the combined strengths of the merged entities can enhance the value proposition for customers.

- *Measurement and continuous improvement*: Establishing KPIs and measurement frameworks helps assess the progress and success of the integration efforts. Regular evaluation and monitoring of the integration outcomes enable adjustments and continuous improvement, ensuring the merger's strategic objectives are met.

- *Cultural integration*: Integrating the cultures of the merged organizations is vital for long-term success. This involves aligning values, norms, and behaviours, fostering open communication, and addressing potential cultural clashes. Cultural integration initiatives may include employee workshops, team-building activities, and leadership alignment programs.

CASE STUDY
Integration planning at Daimler and cultural misalignment

Of all the operating components described, organizational culture is the most complex and hard to change. In 1998, German automaker Daimler-Benz purchased US Chrysler for $38 billion. It was one of the most significant cross-border industrial mergers in history, dubbed a "merger of equals." The consolidation of the two automobile giants resulted in a global company with more than $150 billion in sales, making the combined company the fifth largest car manufacturer at the time of the merger. It paved the way for the German auto giant to expand into the United States.

In 2007, after years of losses, Daimler sold the Chrysler Group to Cerberus Capital Management. Two years later, after Cerberus's efforts failed to revive it, Chrysler declared bankruptcy. In 2011, Italian automaker Fiat S.p.A became Chrysler Group's majority owner, clearing the way for a complete company restructuring.

What happened? Daimler-Benz and Chrysler had never fully integrated, and the expected synergies from the deal were unrealized. Daimler-Benz was known for luxury brands and affluent customers, while Chrysler was known for its mass-market brands.[247] So, cultural integration was one of the main challenges faced during the Daimler-Benz and Chrysler merger. The lesson: culture eats strategy for breakfast, and its importance cannot be underestimated when executing M&A strategy in particular.

Effective post-merger integration requires careful planning, strong leadership, clear communication, and effective collaboration. I've found that organizations can achieve operational efficiencies, realize synergies, and create a stronger and more competitive entity by successfully integrating the merged entities.

HOW TO APPROACH POST-MERGER INTEGRATION

Air traffic control through the integration management office

A centralized team directing traffic in such a comprehensive change effort is foundational. Air traffic control, as I like to call it, or an integration management office (IMO), is responsible for keeping the business focused on managing day-to-day operations while creating a dedicated function for managing the integration within an organization.

The IMO typically oversees the overall integration process and ensures it is aligned with the organization's strategic objectives. It is responsible for defining the general integration approach, developing integration plans, coordinating the activities of various stakeholders involved, and monitoring the progress of integration efforts. The office may also be responsible for managing risks and issues related to integration, and ensuring that resources are allocated appropriately and communication channels are open and effective.

Typical IMO activities include the following:

- *Ensuring the program stays on track*: The most important task of the IMO is to drive integration success against agreed-upon milestones. This includes ensuring that steering committees and working teams continually receive updates on progress.

- *Managing workstream dependencies*: Make sure that different teams involved in integration, like human resources, finance, and supply chain, are working together in an integrated way.
- *Tracking and measuring realization of value through synergies*: When bringing organizations together, there can be redundancies in terms of costs, headcount, and supply contracts. Finding opportunities to combine and streamline is a source of value that the IMO must drive.
- *Ensuring day 1/100 has a positive operational outcome*: Everything is geared toward a smooth transition to day one when the organizations officially operate as one. For example, employees receive paycheques from the new entity as of day one. Ensuring business continuity and day-to-day operations continue smoothly, using day 1/100 as the measure, is a critical role of the IMO.
- *Coordinating all change management and communications execution*: When combining organizations (or separating them in a divestment), ongoing management of the change involved and regular communications on decisions related to changes are vital to success. The IMO needs to ensure the change is managed correctly and communications are relevant, regular, and timely.
- *Ensuring accurate functional and leadership team reporting to enable decision-making*: There should be weekly progress reports by the different areas involved in the transaction to help communicate progress to key stakeholders. It's about getting the correct information into the hands of decision-makers.

Success factors for transactions

My exposure to several projects in this space has revealed that integration success in M&A transactions is based on four critical dimensions: deal strategy, synergy, risk mitigation, and speed.

- *Deal strategy*: Upfront, a well-defined deal strategy that aligns with the organization's overall strategic objectives is crucial for a successful merger integration. Conducting thorough due diligence will ensure that all aspects of the deal are evaluated and considered, including potential risks and opportunities. Involving key stakeholders, including senior management from both organizations, during the deal strategy development process can ensure alignment with overall strategy and increase buy-in and support for the integration effort all around.

- *Synergy*: Identifying and quantifying the potential synergies between the two companies in advance of the deal is essential to determine the integration's expected rewards and to set realistic goals. It's also important to develop a detailed integration plan outlining the specific steps required to achieve the identified synergies, including clear timelines and milestones to track progress. Furthermore, forming a dedicated integration team with representatives from both companies is necessary to manage the integration process and drive synergy realization.

- *Risk mitigation*: Conducting a comprehensive risk assessment to identify potential risks associated with the integration is equally important. Develop a risk management plan outlining the steps required to mitigate potential risks and contingency plans to manage unexpected events. Effective communication with all stakeholders, including employees, customers, and shareholders, will help to manage any issues associated with the integration.

- *Speed*: Prioritizing integration efforts based on their potential impact and urgency can help ensure that critical milestones are achieved quickly. Agile project management methodologies focusing on rapid iteration, continuous improvement, and flexibility can help speed up the integration process. Allocating the required resources, including people, technology, and capital, will ensure that the integration efforts progress briskly and efficiently.

CASE STUDY
Integration challenges at AOL and Time Warner

The data suggests that many mergers fail to realize the intended value and hype. One of the largest mergers occurred in 2000 when America Online (AOL, Inc.) merged with Time Warner, Inc., in a staggering $360 billion deal.

At the time, AOL was the largest internet provider in the US. Riding high on its success and massive market share, AOL decided to merge with Time Warner, the mass media and entertainment conglomerate. The vision: the new entity would dominate the news, publishing, music, entertainment, cable, and internet industries.

Over almost a decade, AOL lost value, and the dot-com bubble burst, so the expected successes of the merger failed to materialize. In 2009, Time Warner spun off AOL, and both companies again operated independently. While high-value mergers and acquisitions always make headlines, not all succeed in execution. Most get executed during the growth phase of a particular sector with high anticipation of success. However, failures linked to other factors, like cultural integration, geographical and geopolitical issues, and market dynamics, often mar the expected results.[248]

There is some science behind what drives success in mergers. For example, research on the merger of J.P. Morgan & Co. and Chase Manhattan Bank in 2000 illustrates the drivers of merger success and how to improve the contributions of mergers. Factors that drive success include strategic fit, cultural fit, financial fit, practical communication, strong leadership and integration planning, and execution.[249]

The integration work plan creates the foundation

Without question, integration planning ensures that the right people are focused on the right things. The work plan is a thoroughly researched document listing integration items in the order in which they should occur, along with dates and assigned personnel. The work plan is anticipated to be a "living" data table, and regular amendments will improve the data quality.

CASE STUDY
Integration planning and communication at Atlassian Corporation

Atlassian Corporation is an excellent example of the importance of a solid integration work plan. This Australian software company creates products for developers, project managers, and other software development teams. The global headquarters is in Sydney, Australia, and its US headquarters is in San Francisco.

Mergers and acquisitions are part of Atlassian's strategy for growth; to date, the company has spent approximately $1 billion acquiring more than 20 companies, including recent acquisitions like AgileCraft, Opsgenie, and Trello. Bringing companies together, however, is about more than profits and market share. You're not just combining organizations; you're integrating people and teams, processes, and technology, which can be challenging and emotional for those involved. It's particularly important to handle employees of the acquired company with care from a change-management perspective.

Through experience, Atlassian has learned that companies should have a clear integration plan and communicate that plan to employees. For example, what does getting to day one and day 100 look like? They also suggest that leadership should focus on retaining expert employees that bring differentiated value and work hard at integrating the two companies' cultures. Furthermore, they recommend that companies be transparent about the integration process during execution and communicate regularly with employees to keep them informed on progress, risks, issues, and key decisions. Finally, through the integration process new information can come to light, so Atlassian suggests that companies should be prepared to make changes to their integration plan as needed and be flexible in their approach to integration.[250]

Integration readiness review

Before flipping the switch and operating as one, don't forget to ask if you are ready. While Bank of America Corporation and Merrill Lynch remain united, the 2008 merger initially faced severe readiness challenges. The two companies took a long time to integrate their assets and make key executive announcements. Months after the merger, the two companies still needed to decide which executives would run critical groups within the firms, such as investment banking, and which of the two companies' management models would prevail.

The uncertainty created by this indecision and lack of business readiness led to many Merrill Lynch bankers leaving the company in the months following the merger. Ultimately, these departures all but destroyed the rationale for the merger. This example illustrates how a lack of communication of critical decisions to stakeholders in the company can lead an M&A strategy to failure.[251]

CASE STUDY
Issues management at Volvo and Renault SA

Unresolved issues can get away from you if not properly driven to resolution. The attempted merger of Volvo and Renault SA in 1993 encountered significant problems because the two parties failed to address the ownership structure at the outset. Unlike the Daimler and Chrysler merger, this automotive deal lacked executive and cultural integration.

Think Swedish precision combined with French panache. The two companies began their relationship as joint venture partners, allowing them to acclimate to each other. The merger was expected to save the companies $5 billion. However, the two companies should have considered the issues of combining an investor-owned entity with a government-owned company. The merger would have left Volvo shareholders with a 35 percent stake in the combined company while the French government controlled the remainder of the shares. Many analysts believed that Volvo shareholders and the Swedish public found it unacceptable to sell one of its prized companies to the French government.

◆ ◆ ◆

CONSIDERATIONS

Every deal represents unique integration challenges as well as opportunities, no matter the industry or companies involved. To overcome potential pitfalls, some of the most critical post-merger integration considerations should be factored in.

- *Appoint an integration manager*: There is great value in having an integration manager or director to help set the pace and heartbeat of the integration progress. The goal should be to apply pressure to accelerate the process while providing a climate where people are motivated to work together toward success.[252] It's a critical coordination and oversight role that insures everything related to the integration progresses.

- *Look closely at synergies*: Focusing on synergies is critical to dealing with value and subsequent integration. The effort is often focused on obvious cost synergies rather than a holistic approach to determine untapped hidden upsides from all sources, including tax. Successful companies are now adopting this approach to create more value. However, this requires experience in understanding and identifying where value can be made, what is proven to work, and where the risks lie. It's not easy: often operating with limited information, leadership must identify the value early to give a competitive advantage.

- *Take executive leadership into account*: It's imperative to consider how the combined company's leadership structure will be established and what role key executives from each company will play in the integration process. Questions about balance between the two respective companies in terms of leadership appointments should be considered.

- *Develop a detailed integration plan*: The company should draft a comprehensive plan before deal closing to achieve synergies and fundamental value propositions. The plan should be closely aligned with the most critical components of deal value and synergy realization. In general, the plan should devote the most attention and prioritization to the primary drivers of deal value, whether positive or negative. It is essential to plan getting to day one and day 100.

- *Assign resources and accountability (span of control)*: To realize the fundamental deal value and synergies, a company must deploy the right resources. The right people must be involved at the right time with the proper focus, motivation, and support. When considering who are the right people, organizations need to be honest about their people's capacity and capability. New markets or business issues often require individuals with specific experience that may not exist internally. The integration team should not be a transition role for poor-performing employees.

- *Facilitate collaboration (span of influence)*: Deal teams tend to "own" the investment model; the deal managers will evaluate the cash flows, costs, and other deal components to determine if a transaction meets the necessary financial returns. However, a transaction requires input from several departments with relevant expertise, such as tax, HR, IT, and business units.

- *Prioritize cultural integration*: The cultures of the two companies involved in the merger may be vastly different. The challenge is to find ways to align these cultures to create a cohesive and unified organization. This can include identifying and addressing differences in communication styles, leadership approaches, and corporate values. Typically in a merger one culture will prevail.

- *Build world-class communication*: Research indicates that a communication program is among the most influential factors in a successful M&A.[253] Although often overlooked, it's important to address communication with employees, vendors, and customers.

- *Build a workstream focused on organizational structure*: The organizational structure of the combined company will need to be established during the integration process. This may involve identifying redundancies, overlapping functions and roles, and deciding which organizational structure best supports the company's goals. This effort needs to cut across business units and functions, which is why it needs to be a stand-alone effort.

- *Don't underestimate systems integration*: The systems and processes of the two companies will need to be integrated to ensure smooth operations of the combined entity. This may involve consolidating systems and platforms and establishing new data-sharing and data-management protocols. Some of these changes can be multi-year journeys.

- *Carefully handle workforce management*: The merger may have implications for the combined company's workforce, including redundancies, new roles, and changes in reporting relationships. It is essential to manage these changes effectively to minimize disruption and maintain employee morale.

- *Consider all stakeholders*: The merger may have impacts on a variety of stakeholders, including customers, suppliers, and shareholders. It's vital to leverage the techniques of stakeholder expectation management explained in Chapter 3. Clear communication and engagement strategies are crucial to managing these impacts and ensuring continued support from these groups.

- *Investigate legal and regulatory requirements*: Mergers may have legal and regulatory implications that need to be considered, including antitrust regulations, labour laws, and intellectual property issues. Engaging these stakeholders early is critical.

CHAPTER 18
INNOVATION

*"Innovation is seeing what everybody has seen
and thinking what nobody has thought."*

—DR. ALBERT SZENT-GYÖRGYI, NOBEL PRIZE–WINNING BIOCHEMIST

INNOVATING THE CITIZEN EXPERIENCE

According to the World Economic Forum, there are mixed views on the role of governments in innovation and how ineffective they can be.[254] Internet entrepreneur and academic Kalev Leetaru explains how one of the challenges with government innovation is the need for a real-world understanding of ground conditions and local cultural beliefs and narratives, as well as views worldwide of what works and does not work. For example, the most important lesson is that innovation rarely comes from top-down orders from executive suites. Innovation requires a culture of experimentation and risk-taking; if the government could figure this out, there is hope.[255]

Despite these headwinds, as society evolves and new challenges arise, every level of government must continue to find innovative ways to address emerging issues and meet the changing needs of its citizens. Innovations can help governments improve the delivery of public services and increase efficiency. And governments must remain competitive in a global economy to attract investment, create jobs, and grow their economies.

Additionally, climate change and environmental issues are significant challenges for all governments, and they must address these challenges head-on through new technologies and solutions to reduce carbon emissions, protect natural resources, and promote sustainable development.

Case in point: a provincial government in Canada needed to meet the expectations of a growing and increasingly demanding population without an increase in available resources. Marginal improvement in efficiency was insufficient; the public service needed to fundamentally rethink how services are delivered and how innovative digital solutions are leveraged.

Taxpayers want more for less. To address this challenge, the government needed to explore how to deliver simpler, faster, and better services for people in the digital age. To lead this work, a dedicated innovation office (IO), based in the premier's office, was created to drive work on innovation across the government. The IO would focus on three objectives: improving the experience citizens have with their government, making services more efficient, and creating a more open and participatory government.

So, what were the components of the IO? The team and I provided advice on structural considerations and operational priorities based on analysis, relevant lessons learned from digital offices in other jurisdictions, and experience-based recommendations from our previous work on implementing other innovation offices.

We initially developed a North Star statement, strategy, and principles to guide the design of the operating model. The team also assisted with establishing the process for the IO to identify, prioritize, manage, and, in some cases, deliver on digital innovation initiatives, following the digital innovation process of "create, incubate, and activate." Efforts also included the design of an operating model for the IO to outline how it would be structured, operated, and managed. The operating model was defined through six key dimensions:

- strategy
- governance and leadership alignment
- process
- operations
- people and culture
- performance management

Finally, we helped create a high-level execution plan that outlined key activities to get the office up and running within 180 days.

What was successful about this approach was the disciplined process and stakeholder engagement through various workshops. The broad stakeholder input enabled the government to gain a well-informed vision, a practical model the stakeholders believed would work, and a trusted way forward in standing up an IO to deliver initiatives efficiently.

This chapter uses the same guiding principles of this government example to explore the six tightly integrated building blocks that allow innovation to flourish. It looks at various firms, including Toys"R"Us, 3M, Tesla, Samsung, and Amazon, to analyze why they succeed or fail in this area.

◆ ◆ ◆

WHAT IS INNOVATION?

Innovation is a strategic growth option choice (Chapter 11). According to a recent study published by management consultancy Ayming, around 31 percent of companies failed to innovate during the COVID-19 crisis, with the industrial, automotive, energy, and biotech sectors the most affected. Furthermore, the number of companies with a defined R&D budget decreased from 90 percent to 77 percent, and the number of respondents who feel that their organization undertakes enough innovation fell 14 percentage points, from 85 percent to 71 percent in 2021.[256]

Effective and sustainable innovation is more than simply brainstorming or applying out-of-the-box thinking—it's the force that enables organizations to develop new, viable offerings and create value for their business. Today, against a backdrop of increasingly global competition, rapidly evolving technology, and fiscal, demographic, and social changes, the businesses most likely to thrive are those whose leaders embrace innovation's critical role in their organization's growth strategy.

I always say that innovation is the art of making hard things easy and creating value where it did not previously exist. It is a collaborative, structured process involving different parts of the organization as well as outside partners to contribute, create, and exploit new opportunities and find new ways to solve complex problems. The sole action of generating ideas is not innovating. An idea becomes an innovation only when implemented in a form that creates value.[257]

Some of the most innovative companies are pushing the technological envelope with impressive offerings. According to *Fast Company*, the world's most innovative companies of 2023 included OpenAI, an artificial intelligence research laboratory dedicated to advancing digital intelligence to benefit humanity. OpenAI's new ChatGPT technology is changing the world. A further example is LanzaTech, a biotechnology company that has developed a process to convert carbon waste into valuable products such as ethanol and other chemicals. Another firm on the list, Velo3D, is a 3D printing company that has developed a process for creating lighter, more streamlined parts for aerospace companies. BamCore, a construction technology company, has found a more effective way to build energy-efficient buildings. Finally, the multinational conglomerate Siemens has created a platform for the industrial metaverse.[258]

I've seen many barriers to innovation, but according to a survey of 270 corporate leaders in strategy, innovation, and research and development roles, the most common obstacles in large companies are:

- politics, turf wars, and a failure to align
- cultural issues
- an inability to act on signals crucial to the future of the business
- lack of a sufficient budget
- lack of a proper strategy or vision[259]

Another perspective on thought leadership, published in the blog *Lucidity*, claimed that most organizations and individuals do not achieve their full potential because of fear of failure. There are no guarantees that any new idea will work, so we must accept that failing is integral to learning, development, and progress.[260]

CASE STUDY
Failed innovation at Toys"R"Us leads to bankruptcy

Failing to innovate invariably leads to disaster. A recent example is Toys"R"Us, one of the world's largest toy store chains, which struggled financially and ultimately collapsed because it failed to innovate.

With the benefit of hindsight, one might conclude that Toys"R"Us may have triggered its undoing in 2000 when it signed a 10-year contract to be the exclusive vendor of toys on Amazon.

Despite the deal, Amazon began to allow other toy vendors to sell on its site, and Toys"R"Us sued Amazon to end the agreement in 2004. But in the meantime, Toys"R"Us had missed the opportunity to develop its own e-commerce presence early on.

In May 2017, when it was already far too late, Toys"R"Us announced a plan to revamp its website as part of a $100 million, three-year investment to jumpstart its e-commerce business. By September, it had filed for bankruptcy after struggling to execute under pressure from a US$1 billion debt and fierce online retail competition.[261]

According to business journal *Knowledge at Wharton*, the blame for Toys"R"Us's failure to innovate falls squarely on the company's management. Experts say that Toys"R"Us failed to adapt to changing consumer behaviour, incorporate new technology, or innovate its business model. The company's inability to create and execute compelling reasons for customers to visit, either through a superior store experience or via partnerships to exclusively sell popular brands or products, also contributed to its downfall.[262]

My experience has taught me that a sound foundation for innovation should consist of six tightly integrated components. Here are the critical building blocks of innovation that I've used numerous times and how they contribute to creating a thriving, innovative culture:

- *Strategy*: Innovation begins with a clear vision and a well-defined strategy that outlines an organization's goals, priorities, and resources. With a strong strategy in place, organizations can identify opportunities for growth, set goals, and allocate resources to achieve those goals.
- *Governance*: A robust governance structure ensures that innovation initiatives are aligned with the organization's overall goals and objectives. This structure should provide clear guidelines for decision-making, risk management, and monitoring performance.
- *Culture*: A culture of innovation is necessary to create an environment that fosters creativity and encourages experimentation. It should promote risk-taking, collaboration, and learning from failures.

- *Process*: Innovation processes should be well-defined, efficient, and effective. They should allow organizations to generate visionary ideas, experiment, and iterate quickly and efficiently.

- *People*: Innovation is a team sport that requires diverse teams with complementary skill sets. In an article I wrote with my colleague Kiersten Ermelbauer for *Chief Executive* magazine, we explain the importance and power of diverse teams driving innovation thinking.[263] Organizations should attract, develop, and retain all kinds of talent to contribute to innovation.

- *Ideas*: Innovation requires a steady stream of ideas that can lead to breakthroughs. Organizations should encourage imagination, experimentation, and continuous learning to generate and develop new ideas.

Organizations that can effectively leverage these building blocks are more likely to achieve sustainable innovation and create long-term value.

HOW TO APPROACH INNOVATION

Four approaches to innovation

Although I'm simplifying it, companies can adopt four different approaches to innovation depending on their goals, resources, and capabilities. These approaches can be classified as systematic, marketplace, collaborative, and visionary.

- *Systematic innovation*: Involves a structured approach to generating and implementing ideas by applying proven methods and processes. Companies typically use this approach to improve their existing products or services, aiming to create incremental improvements that will result in significant long-term benefits. For example, 3M Company developed a structured approach to generating ideas and prototyping, which led to the development of the Post-It Note. This product became a global success.

- *Marketplace innovation*: Involves developing new products or services that meet customers' evolving needs and preferences. This approach identifies and responds to market trends and customer feedback to create differentiated and competitive products. Apple's iPhone is a prime example. The company identified the growing demand for smartphones with advanced features and developed a product that transformed the mobile phone industry.

- *Collaborative innovation*: Involves partnering with companies, institutions, or individuals to create new products or services. This approach leverages the strengths and capabilities of many to develop innovative solutions that would not be possible alone. For example, for a decade Nike collaborated with knitting machine manufacturers to build a new manufacturing process that allowed them to create seamless, lightweight Flyknit shoes. Introduced in 2012, they have become a retail sensation and revolutionized the footwear business.

- *Visionary innovation*: Involves creating breakthrough products or services that disrupt the market and create new opportunities. This approach requires a willingness to take risks, experiment, and challenge the status quo. For example, Tesla challenged the traditional automobile industry by developing electric cars offering superior performance and sustainability and by creating innovative energy storage solutions that transformed the industry.

Companies that can effectively adapt and integrate these approaches are more likely to create a sustainable innovation culture and achieve long-term success.

Building a portfolio of innovation

Innovation is not a silver-bullet proposition. The portfolio approach to innovation involves managing multiple initiatives simultaneously to ensure a balanced mix of projects that align with the organization's strategic goals and priorities. It is a structured approach to managing innovation that treats initiatives as a portfolio of investments that can be categorized based on their level of risk and potential impact. Companies that develop and manage a portfolio of three types of innovation (sustaining, adjacent, disruptive) ensure a consistent flow of ideas and can safeguard an organization from becoming stagnant or complacent.

- *Sustaining innovation*: Results in incremental improvements to existing solutions to maintain and protect the core value propositions (e.g., continuous improvement, bottom-up improvement).

- *Adjacent innovations*: Change and expand the core value proposition to potentially alter the competitive environment (e.g., mobile apps in addition to a web presence, process redesign).

- *Disruptive innovation*: Introduces innovative products, services, or business models that can, for example, redefine value propositions to better address customer needs and drive future success (e.g., Amazon drones used for remote delivery of packages).

I've found that by maintaining a balanced mix of sustaining, adjacent, and disruptive innovations, companies can hedge risk and uncertainty and create innovative initiatives that can deliver short-term and long-term benefits.

Creating a culture of innovation

I always tell my clients that culture eats strategy for breakfast. To encourage innovation, organizations must foster a culture that allows people to experiment and work collaboratively in an agile environment with full support from leaders. The operating model (Chapter 15) and the organization structure (Chapter 16) must be set up to support the innovative culture. Creating the right culture involves experimentation, the flexibility to pivot when necessary, leadership focus, and collaborative capability (illustrated in Figure 16).

- *Experimentation*: Jeff Bezos once famously said, "To invent you have to experiment, and if you know in advance that it's going to work, it's not an experiment."[264] You have to take risks to reap the rewards, so supporting experimentation is the first step in creating a culture of innovation. It involves encouraging employees to feel free to try out new ideas, products, and services. Experimentation can take many forms, such as prototyping, testing, and piloting. This step requires leaders to foster an environment in which employees are encouraged to learn from failure and continually tinker with ideas until they find a solution.

- *Pivot to scale*: Unless you commercialize it, an idea is just that. Once an idea has been tested and validated, the organization must pivot to scale. This step involves developing a plan to commercialize and bring the innovation to market. Leaders must identify the resources required to scale the innovation and allocate them accordingly. They must also create a framework for measuring the success of the innovation and make adjustments as needed.

- *Leadership focus*: From what I've seen, buy-in at the top is crucial to creating an effective culture of innovation. Influential leaders provide the necessary support, resources, guidance, and vision to encourage experimentation, pivot to scale, and foster collaborative creativity, ultimately driving innovation and growth within the organization.

- *Collaborative creativity*: More than simply teams working together, this represents how employees share ideas and collaborate on solving problems, inspiring their colleagues to do the same. Leaders must create an environment that promotes diversity of thought and encourages employees to challenge conventional thinking.

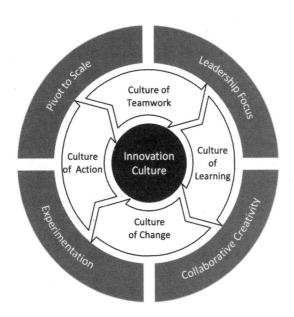

Figure 16: Innovation culture model

CASE STUDY
Customer inspiration at Samsung supercharges innovation

Customers are a source of ideas and inspiration. They can also tell you if you're onto something unique and innovative.

An exciting example of experimentation and seeking customer feedback in the innovation process was demonstrated by Samsung. As one of the world's leading technology companies, Samsung is widely recognized as among the most innovative conglomerates, a tremendous example of open innovation. Its innovation management strategy entails deploying an experienced "creative elite" to lead new projects, ensuring they are primed to incorporate the best practices and yield maximum KPI.

Samsung's creative elite uses open innovation software and corporate tech scouting to achieve its objectives. For example, when new products are released, Samsung utilizes customer feedback to inform their TRIZ problem-solving—which examines contradictions in customers' expressed desires and technological capabilities to establish a clear picture of where innovation efforts should be focused. Once a more precise picture is gained, Samsung then approaches relevant scientific, technological, or corporate bodies that can deliver and execute the expertise and resources needed to make the project happen.[265]

The Samsung approach to innovation has resulted in numerous new patents and millions of dollars in savings. Furthermore, Samsung used the theory of inventive problem solving (TRIZ) method to develop its super AMOLED displays. Super AMOLED is a marketing term created by Samsung for an AMOLED display with an integrated touch screen digitizer: the layer that detects touch is integrated into the display, rather than overlaid on top of it and cannot be separated from the display itself. Furthermore, AMOLED is considered more innovative than OLED for phone displays, because AMOLED builds upon OLED technology by incorporating an active wiring matrix of transistors for individual pixel control instead of using organic materials between conductors of an LED.[266] Innovation realized.

For four years in a row, Samsung has continued to rank as one of the top five most valuable global brands, with a value in 2023 of $91.4 billion, indicating a 4 percent growth from the previous year. They are recognized for promoting an excellent customer experience and leading future technologies such as 6G and AI.[267]

Innovation journey (process)

I'm a process guy, but models that depict innovation as a smooth, well-behaved linear process fail to recognize the nature and direction of the causal factors at work. Innovation is complicated, uncertain, somewhat disorderly, and subject to changes of many sorts. It's also challenging to measure, demanding close coordination of adequate technical knowledge and excellent market judgment to simultaneously satisfy economic, technological, and other constraints. The innovation process must be viewed as a series of changes in a complete system not only of hardware but also of market environment, production facilities and knowledge, and the social contexts of the innovation organization.[268]

The innovation process I've successfully used involves steps organizations can follow to create new ideas, validate their feasibility, and bring them to market. The three primary stages of this process are create, incubate, and activate. Here is a detailed description of each stage:

1. *Create*: The first stage of the innovation process is to create, which involves defining the problem or opportunity an organization wants to address. It must identify customer needs, market trends, and other factors driving innovation. Once the strategic focus and problem/opportunity have been defined, an organization can brainstorm potential solutions. The key to this stage is to encourage creative thinking and generate many ideas that are then filtered and refined. This phase intends to focus innovation strategy and investments on viable opportunities to create and capture economic value.

2. *Incubate*: This stage involves validating the options generated during the create stage. An organization must test the feasibility of each idea and determine whether it is viable. This can include experimenting, prototyping, using market research, and other validation techniques. The goal is to identify the most promising ideas and eliminate those that could be less feasible. This phase aims to validate innovation ideas to manage risk on investments, define operating models, and evaluate partnering opportunities.

3. *Activate*: In this final stage, organizations commercialize the offerings generated during the incubate stage by developing a

plan to bring the innovation to market. This can include product development, marketing, sales, and other activities. The goal is to launch the innovation and generate revenue for the organization.

Metrics to measure innovation

If employees are not incentivized to innovate, they won't do it. In a 2019 article in *Forbes*, Scott Arpajian observed that misaligned incentives could lead to innovation failure.[269] Innovation metrics are essential for measuring the success and effectiveness of initiatives. By tracking KPIs, organizations can evaluate the impact of their innovation efforts and make data-driven decisions to drive continuous improvement as well as shifts in direction.

If innovation is a process, you need to consider the measurement. I've learned that different types of innovation metrics can be used depending on the phase of innovation:

- *Create*: In the ideation phase, the focus is on generating new ideas. The key metrics that can be used to measure success include the number of ideas generated, the number of unique contributors, and the percentage of actionable ideas.
- *Incubate*: The incubation phase focuses on validating ideas and determining their feasibility. The key metrics to measure incubation success include the number of prototypes developed, the percentage of prototypes that meet the defined criteria, and the feedback received from potential customers.
- *Activate*: The activate phase focuses on commercializing the innovation and realizing its benefits. The key metrics that can measure impact include the revenue generated from the innovation, the market share gained, and the effect on customer satisfaction.

The choice of innovation metrics may also vary depending on the innovation being pursued. For example, suppose the focus is on incremental innovation (for example, making minor improvements to existing products or processes). In that case, the metrics may include reduced costs, improved efficiency, or increased customer satisfaction. On the other hand, if the focus is on disruptive innovation (introducing a completely new product or service), the metrics may include revenue growth, market share, or the number of new customers acquired.

My work as an advisor has helped me understand that innovation metrics are essential for measuring the success of these initiatives. The choice of metrics may vary depending on the phase of innovation and the type of innovation being pursued. Still, organizations can drive continuous improvement and achieve innovation goals by tracking key performance indicators.

◆ ◆ ◆

CONSIDERATIONS

An organization needs to manage the current business efficiently while simultaneously exploring future opportunities. An innovation strategy drives success in high-performing organizations by separating the firm's traditional and exploratory units, allowing for different processes, structures, and cultures. Collaboration, diverse leadership, and a balanced portfolio are essential for driving successful innovation and avoiding stagnation. Innovation strategy considerations are as follows:

- *Define the innovation strategy*: Tying innovation to the organization's purpose is vital. Trying to be an innovative company off the side of the desk is impossible. Innovation needs to be long-term and integrated into the corporate strategy and therefore well-understood by the entire organization.
- *Remember that ambidexterity drives success*: High-performing organizations that innovate successfully usually separate their new exploratory units from their traditional exploitative ones, allowing for different decision-making, processes, structures, and cultures. This separation between the current, high-performing organization and the disruptive innovation team is enabled by a tightly integrated senior team that recognizes the need to nurture different types of businesses, combining one adept at exploiting existing capabilities and a second that successfully explores new growth opportunities.

- *Put leadership top of mind*: Having a senior leader responsible for innovation can help a company stay focused on the innovation agenda. It can be important to commercialize ideas that can be embedded in the business units to drive adoption of a single unifying voice at the top. These leaders play a critical role in helping define the strategy, promoting innovation within an organization, where appropriate, and ensuring efforts are coordinated and tightly integrated across the enterprise.

- *Build collaboration mechanisms*: Bringing together different people and business units to innovate and develop ideas often leads to the most successful results and, in the process, generates buy-in from various groups. Diversity of perspective is a significant strength in innovation—different backgrounds, organizational tenure, and even personalities can all lead to more engaged and successful innovation sessions.

- *Manage a portfolio of innovation*: Companies that develop and manage a portfolio of three types of innovation (sustaining, adjacent, and disruptive) ensure a consistent pipeline of ideas and demonstrate that they are creating hospitable environments for innovation to flourish. It's typical to have a large number of sustaining ideas and a small number of large disruptive ideas.

- *Determine the right level of structure and process with innovation*: While a structured innovation process can help organizations focus and manage ideas from creation through incubation to activation, the reality is that structured processes can become overly bureaucratic. Organizations must strike a delicate balance to avoid "process paralysis" in innovation. Based on a two-and-a-half-year study of significant, innovative enterprises by management specialist James Brian Quinn, research suggests how some of the world's most innovative companies interlink careful strategic planning concepts with novel organizational and motivational approaches to achieve their purposes. Neither structured formality nor unstructured chaos works well alone. Innovative companies seem to evolve a sophisticated approach to "managed chaos."[270] Success factors include the right dedicated

people, appropriate funding to support ideas, and measures to
track progress and evaluate success.

- *Develop a culture of innovation*: To be successful, innovation must
be driven through all levels of an organization and promoted at
all levels. Some of the best ideas come from employees lower in
the organizational structure, and broader ideas come from those
higher up. By enabling and promoting innovation company-wide,
organizations can increase the speed of adoption, drive buy-in
and implementation, and reap the rewards sooner.

- *Build the right people capabilities to enable innovation*: It's essential
to have creative thinkers with the right mindset and orientation
to continuously test new ideas. Diversity is vital, and fostering a
network of individuals and teams, both from within and external
to the organization, who are skilled in crucial elements of
innovation will improve the chances of success. An ecosystem of
partnerships and alliances related to innovation can be powerful.

CHAPTER 19
COST MANAGEMENT

"Costs do not exist to be calculated. Costs exist to be reduced."
—TAIICHI OHNO, INDUSTRIAL ENGINEER & BUSINESSMAN

MANAGING COSTS DURING THE COVID-19 CRISIS

Governments at all levels faced a financial apocalypse during COVID-19. As federal governments scrambled to provide massive aid packages, provinces, states, and municipalities made cuts, froze spending and hiring, laid off workers, and drew down rainy-day funds. It was tough, and CNN reported that due to necessary measures to contain the spread of the coronavirus, US states alone faced up to $500 billion in fiscal shock through the fiscal year 2022. For counties, the number comes to $202 billion. And the nation's 19,000 cities, towns, and villages faced a $360 billion loss.[271]

With mounting debts and reduced revenues, one sizable North American city was looking to save millions from its tax-supported operating budget.

A dedicated effort was critical. The municipal government established an internal program with a mandate to meet savings targets but needed additional support to run and manage the initiative. A team was formed to provide a structured approach to finding sustainable savings for the city and to bring leading practice methodologies and tools. The team established an appropriate governance and reporting structure, project management processes, and tools to drive a cost-reduction process.

Any cost-management program starts by looking for appropriate opportunities. One of the first steps was identifying several sources for idea generation, such as interviews, workshops, benchmarking, an employee portal, and past work reviews. The team collected and vetted all ideas through a rigorous approach involving two validation layers and developed opportunity statements for all approved ideas. The team also created a platform for leadership to screen all opportunity statements. Once leadership approved the opportunities, the team made business cases for all approved opportunities, which were then sent back to leadership and eventually to the city council for approval. Following approval, business cases were handed over to the line managers for execution and implementation.

The program team executed successfully by ensuring integration amongst ideas and workstreams, managing stakeholders, and identifying change and communication requirements. Furthermore, reporting and tracking tools and processes helped ensure that leadership had a full view, in real-time, of progress being made against cost-reduction targets, and issues and risks were identified early for resolution.

Cost reduction can be challenging at the best of times, so engagement should be paramount. Given the nature of some of the cost reductions in this case—for example, closing down fire stations, reducing staff training, consolidating call centres, reducing maintenance on city vehicles, and improving financial processes—the CFO rightly said, "Framing conversations with leadership and Council, and developing and implementing a contingency plan, was imperative." The program exceeded its annual savings targets of $25 million in 2021 and an additional $50 million in 2022.

Cost reduction is essential for municipal governments; it helps them to manage their budgets. By reducing costs, municipal governments can free up resources that can be used for other essential purposes such as infrastructure development, social services, and public safety. In addition, cost reduction improves financial stability and reduces reliance on external funding sources. This is particularly important during economic uncertainty when external funding sources may not be reliable. Finally, cost reduction can improve performance by encouraging municipalities to adopt more efficient practices. This can lead to better service delivery and increased citizen satisfaction in a post-pandemic world.

Building on this municipal government example, this chapter outlines how to develop and execute a potent cost-reduction program in any organization, supported by leading practice case studies drawn from IKEA, Ryanair, Deere & Company, Intel, and Starbucks.

◆ ◆ ◆

WHAT IS COST MANAGEMENT?

I've done a lot of cost reduction work, alternatively known as cost management, and have learned over the years that managing costs should be central to any organization's strategy. For many companies, margins are shrinking with increasing competitiveness in the market (for example, oil and gas companies battling a low-price environment). Premier companies must take a strategic look at costs in their businesses, addressing underlying causes and focusing on long-term solutions to bring the most value to their shareholders and remain competitive.

In leading several cost-management projects, I've come to understand that effective cost management has two distinct parts, which must both be successfully completed for an organization to realize the benefits of cost management: brainstorming and implementing initiatives.

First, idea generation and initiative development should be conducted with a view of the value chain in question to help determine areas for improvement and include a review of expenditures. Once identified, these ideas can be developed into initiatives and prioritized according to their value and cost to implement. At this stage, initiatives are selected, and a roadmap is created for rollout.

Secondly, executing cost-reduction projects includes ensuring that effective monitoring, control, and reporting are in place to achieve a successful implementation and address any issues. This part of cost management requires thoroughly determining organizational resource capacity as well as careful change management to ensure initiatives have what they need to get executed, and that any changes caused by the implementation of those initiatives are smoothly managed so as not to cause business disruption.

I define strategic cost management as the process of identifying and implementing cost-reduction strategies that are aligned with an organization's overall business strategy. It involves analyzing and managing costs to support the organization's goals and objectives, such as improving profitability, increasing market share, or reducing risk. Cost management, done well, should address all parts of the business that contain opportunities to improve performance and reduce waste.

Strategic cost management aims to reduce costs and strategically manage them to create long-term value for the organization. Sustaining low-cost performance involves identifying the key drivers of cost in the organization, analyzing how they impact the business, and developing strategies to manage them.

CASE STUDY
Watching the dollars and cents at budget airline Ryanair

Launched 30 years ago, the Irish low-cost carrier Ryanair disrupted the European airline industry and started the low-cost revolution. Ryanair is now Europe's largest airline, with more than 90 million passengers annually and record profits of 875 million euros.

Behind the success of Ryanair is the very effective alignment of its customer value proposition with its low-cost operating model. Ryanair has sustained a low-cost culture by minimizing marketing costs, reducing customer facilities, using a standard fleet, and outsourcing services. This low-cost model was initially copied from the US-based airline Southwest.

A key ingredient of success is the straightforward business model—one that is easy to execute. Ryanair offers cheap air transportation to fare-conscious travellers, specifically targeting customers who might otherwise choose alternative modes of transportation or not to travel at all.[272, 273]

Ryanair's colourful CEO, Michael O'Leary, is relentless in his focus on cost. He once said, "As long as you run around generating noise, it drives people on to our website. And we don't spend hundreds of millions of dollars on marketing to do it. Charging for toilets continues to be the number one story that resurfaces in the press and it's the gift that keeps on giving."[274]

Here are three common strategies for strategic cost management that I've used:

- *Cost reduction*: Involves identifying opportunities to reduce costs through initiatives such as process improvements, outsourcing, or automation.

- *Cost avoidance*: Consists of identifying and mitigating potential costs that may arise in the future, such as risks related to compliance or supply chain disruptions.
- *Cost optimization*: Involves optimizing costs across the organization by analyzing and improving processes, leveraging technology, and reducing waste.

Overall, cost reduction or strategic cost management is a critical component of any organization's overall strategy, as it helps to ensure that resources are used effectively and efficiently in pursuit of the organization's goals.

HOW TO APPROACH COST MANAGEMENT

Cost management principles

The best approach to strategic cost management depends on the specific needs and goals of the organization. I've come to appreciate that no one-size-fits-all method is appropriate for all organizations' cost-management needs. Organizations must determine the right tools and techniques to deploy as part of tailored programs to move from simple cost management to more advanced cost excellence.[275]

However, some fundamental principles I've used include:

- *Align cost management with business strategy*: The first step in strategic cost management is to ensure that cost-management strategies are aligned with the organization's overall strategy. This involves understanding the key drivers of value and identifying the areas where cost management can have the most significant impact.
- *Develop a comprehensive understanding of costs*: To effectively manage costs, it is necessary to have a detailed knowledge of the costs associated with different processes, products, and services. This involves analyzing the cost drivers for each area of an organization and clearly understanding how they impact the business.

- *Focus on continuous improvement*: Strategic cost management is not a one-time event but an ongoing continuous process of improvement. This involves regularly reviewing and analyzing costs, identifying opportunities for improvement, and implementing changes to optimize costs over time.

- *Engage employees in cost management*: Strategic cost management requires the active participation and engagement of employees at all levels of the organization, creating a culture of cost management, providing training and education on cost-management principles, and incentivizing employees to identify and implement cost-saving initiatives.

- *Use technology to support cost management*: Technology can be a powerful tool, providing real-time visibility into costs, automating processes, and identifying opportunities for optimization. I can't recommend highly enough leveraging technology to support the organization's overall cost-management goals.

CASE STUDY
Embedding cost-management principles at Swedish furniture company IKEA

Agreeing on some principles at the outset is fundamental to success. Swedish furniture giant IKEA is an excellent example of a business embedding the philosophy of low-cost operations into everything it does. IKEA is known for its affordable furniture and home goods, mainly due to its commitment to cost management as a critical principle.

When making furniture for the world, you had better have efficient supply chains, and IKEA has developed a highly efficient one that keeps costs low. The company's leaders work directly with manufacturers to produce products at a lower cost and then transport them via IKEA's shipping system to its stores worldwide. IKEA's large size allows it to achieve economies of scale, meaning it can produce and sell goods at a lower cost per unit than smaller competitors. It also uses its size to negotiate lower prices with suppliers.

Furthermore, IKEA strongly focuses on efficiency throughout its organization, constantly looking for ways to streamline its operations and eliminate waste. The founder of IKEA, Ingvar

Kamprad, once said, "Waste of resources is a mortal sin." This is another way the company helps keep costs low while maintaining high productivity levels. Finally, IKEA's furniture is designed to be flat-packed quickly and efficiently for shipping and transport. This reduces shipping costs and is yet another way for the company to offer lower prices to customers. Overall, IKEA's commitment to cost management has been critical to its strategy execution success.[276,277]

To summarize, a practical strategic cost-management approach requires a comprehensive understanding of all costs, a focus on continuous improvement, and the active engagement of employees at all levels of the organization.

Cost-management approach

I've found that a focused, dedicated, and structured approach is crucial to cost management. This is a sample methodology I've often used to deliver part one of cost management (idea generation and initiative development):

1. *Cost-management ideas and hypotheses*: An organization generates theories and hypotheses for cost management. Key activities include thoroughly analyzing the organization's current cost structure, identifying potential areas of waste or inefficiency, brainstorming possible cost-saving ideas and strategies, and developing a business case for each initiative.

2. *Opportunity portfolio prioritization*: The business evaluates each cost-saving initiative's potential impact and feasibility, prioritizes them based on their value to the organization, and develops a portfolio of cost-saving opportunities. This step involves considering financial implications, strategic alignment, resource requirements, and risk.

3. *Initiative selection*: Once the organization has selected the cost-saving initiatives to pursue, define each initiative's scope, objectives, and expected outcomes. This involves assessing resource requirements and constraints for each one and identifying potential risks or barriers to success.

4. *Roadmap and program management*: The objective is to develop a roadmap for implementing the chosen cost-saving initiatives and establish a program management structure to oversee the initiative portfolio.

5. *Change management, culture, and governance*: In this phase, the organization focuses on ensuring that the cost-saving initiatives are successfully implemented and integrated into the organization's culture and governance structures. This involves developing a change management plan for implementing cost-saving initiatives and addressing any potential resistance to change. It also means engaging stakeholders and communicating the benefits of the initiatives, and defining governance structures to ensure ongoing success and sustainability.

CASE STUDY
Supply chain transformation at Deere & Company

Deere & Company is famed for manufacturing and supplying machinery used in agriculture, construction, and forestry, as well as diesel engines and lawn care equipment. Like any manufacturing company, logistics and network planning were a source of cost-reduction opportunities for them.

The company replenished dealers' inventory weekly, using direct shipment and cross-docking operations from source warehouses near Deere & Company's manufacturing facilities. This operation was proving too costly and slow, so the company launched a structured and comprehensive initiative to achieve a 10 percent supply chain cost reduction within four years. It undertook a supply chain network redesign and cost-management program, resulting in the commissioning of intermediate "merge centres" and the optimization of cross-dock terminal locations.

Deere & Company also began executing the consolidation of shipments and using break-bulk terminals during the seasonal peak. Furthermore, the company increased its use of third-party logistics providers and effectively created a network that could be optimized tactically at any given point in time. Deere & Company's supply chain cost-management achievements included an inventory decrease of $1 billion, a significant reduction in customer delivery lead times (from 10 days to five or less), and annual transportation cost savings of around 5 percent.[278]

Success drivers for cost-reduction programs

In my experience, and as I wrote in an article about achieving cost excellence, organizational success in implementing a sustainable cost-reduction program requires building value, pace, and sustainability.[279] For each element, I've developed corresponding objectives, essential questions, and "winning elements," as outlined in Figure 17 below.

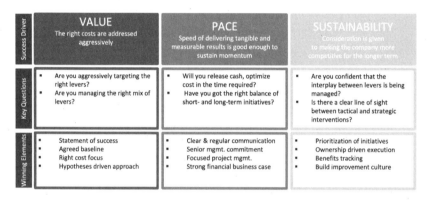

Figure 17: Cost reduction critical success factors

CASE STUDY
Reducing cycle times at Intel leads to lower costs

Intel is one of the world's largest manufacturers of computer chips. However, the company needed to significantly reduce supply chain expenditure after bringing its low-cost Atom chip to market. Supply chain costs of around $5.50 per chip were bearable for units selling for $100, but the new chip was a fraction of that, at about $20. The challenge? To reduce the supply chain costs, Intel had only one area of leverage: inventory.

Intel had already whittled down packaging to a minimum. With a high value-to-weight ratio, the chips' distribution costs could not be pared any further and with each Atom product being a single component, there was also no way to reduce duty payments. If Intel hoped to reduce supply chain costs, the only option would be to reduce inventory levels, which, up to that point, had been kept very high to support a nine-week order cycle. Intel could not afford for the chips not to work, nor could they afford to make any service trade-offs.

To save money, Intel decided to try what was considered an unlikely supply chain strategy for the semiconductor industry: make-to-order. The company began execution with a pilot operation with a manufacturer in Malaysia. They gradually sought out and eliminated supply chain inefficiencies through iteration to incrementally reduce order cycle time. Further improvements included cutting the chip assembly test window from a five-day schedule to a biweekly, two-day-long process.

Intel introduced a formal sales and operation planning process by moving to a vendor-managed inventory model wherever possible. The company eventually drove down the order cycle time for the Atom chip from nine weeks to just two through its incremental approach to cycle time improvement. As a result, the company achieved a supply chain cost reduction to $4 per unit for the $20 Atom chip—a far more palatable rate than the original figure of $5.50 per unit.[280]

Driving outcomes through implementation management

My extensive participation in these kinds of projects has shown me that part two of cost management, implementing cost-reduction initiatives, is the biggest challenge to, and the primary reason for the failure of, transformation projects. Therefore, it is critical to have a properly considered and structured implementation process. Enablers for successful implementation include the following:

- *Coordinated implementation*: Coordination is required across all the different cost-reduction programs selected, in order to mitigate cross-program impacts, manage stakeholders who may be impacted by multiple programs, and coordinate efforts to meet timelines.
- *Adequate change capacity*: Relying on business-as-usual contributes significantly to program failure rates. Investment in change capacity will drive implementation success.
- *Alignment and focus*: Transformations require coordinated, in-depth, and genuine two-way communication with all impacted stakeholders across all the cost reduction programs, considering that stakeholders are likely affected by more than one program. This will drive organizational alignment surrounding the portfolio

of cost-management initiatives and ensure focus remains on the overall transformation vision.

- *Leadership commitment*: Leadership teams are responsible for setting the strategic direction. They must understand the value of a cost-reduction program to drive adoption. Leadership buy-in is critical for building organizational sentiment and will improve a project's success.
- *Proper governance*: Because of the number of cost reduction programs potentially involved, a proper governance structure must be established and followed to ensure all pieces are working toward the common goal of coordination, measurement and monitoring, decision-making, and prioritization.
- *Sufficient sustainment*: It's common for stakeholders to revert to previous behaviours once the fanfare surrounding the launch of an improvement program fades. The benefits realized by a cost-management program must be maintained and integrated into the working processes and culture of the company over the long term.

At both the program and project levels, team leaders must clearly understand why implementation is important, what needs to be accomplished, how it will be completed, and who will be critical to implementation.

CASE STUDY
Discipline and structure at Starbucks yield results

Supply chain management is typically a source of opportunity, and Starbucks is another example of managing costs through a deliberated, structured program. Like many of the most successful worldwide brands, the coffee shop giant has been through periods of supply chain pain. In fact, between 2007 and 2008, Starbucks's leadership began to doubt the company's ability to supply its 16,700 outlets. As in most commercial sectors at that time, sales were falling. At the same time, though, supply chain costs rose by more than $75 million. When the supply chain executive team began investigating the rising costs and performance issues, they found that the service was falling short of expectations.

Starbucks's leadership had three main objectives: to reorganize the supply chain; reduce the service cost; and lay the groundwork for future capability in the supply chain. To meet these objectives, Starbucks divided all its supply chain functions into three main groups, known as "plan," "make," and "deliver." It also opened a new production facility, bringing the total number of US plants to four. Next, the company began terminating partnerships with all but its most effective third-party logistics (3PL) partners. It then began managing the remaining partners via a weekly scorecard system aligned with renewed service level agreements.

According to Peter Gibbons, then executive vice president of global supply chain operations, by the time Starbucks had executed its transformation program, it had saved more than $500 million through 2009 and 2010, of which a large proportion came from supply chain efficiencies.

Business case development

When prioritizing ideas, I've helped organizations use business cases to better understand the resources required to implement the concept. A business case is a detailed document that outlines the rationale, costs, benefits, risks, and potential returns associated with a proposed project or initiative.

By developing a solid business case, organizations can ensure that they are making informed decisions about allocating resources and prioritizing initiatives.

Three-tiered governance model

In my experience, the governance of cost-management programs should be multilayered. The three-tiered governance model is a cost-management framework that helps organizations effectively strategize, steward, and execute their cost-management initiatives.

Each level of governance has a distinct role in the cost-management process, as follows:

- *Strategize*: This level of governance is responsible for developing the overall cost-management strategy for the organization. This involves setting priorities, identifying cost-saving opportunities, and defining the roadmap for implementing the initiatives. The strategizing level is typically led by senior executives or the board of directors, who are responsible for setting the overall direction and goals for the organization.

- *Steward*: This level of governance is responsible for overseeing the implementation of cost-management initiatives and ensuring they align with the organization's strategic objectives. This involves monitoring progress, identifying risks and issues, and adjusting as needed. The steward level is typically led by mid-level managers or cost-management experts who are responsible for implementing the strategy and ensuring it is effectively executed.

- *Execute*: This level of governance is responsible for executing the specific cost-management initiatives identified in the strategy and prioritized by the steward level. It involves identifying cost-saving opportunities, implementing changes to processes or systems, and monitoring results to achieve the desired outcomes. The execution level is typically led by operational managers or project teams responsible for implementing initiatives and delivering the expected cost savings.

Overall, the three-tiered governance model provides a clear and structured approach to cost management. I've discovered that it helps organizations effectively strategize, manage, and implement cost-management initiatives. By having clear roles and responsibilities at each level of governance, organizations can ensure that their cost-management efforts are aligned with their strategic objectives and that they can sustainably and effectively achieve their financial goals. Aligning with strategic priorities and establishing program leadership and accountability are essential to success.[281]

◆ ◆ ◆

CONSIDERATIONS

Maintaining a watchful eye on costs should be part of any company's strategy execution system. Otherwise, they can get away from you quickly. When undertaking a strategic cost-reduction or cost-management program, there are several key considerations that organizations should keep in mind:

- *Embed data and analytics*: The role of data analytics in supporting cost-reduction initiatives, both during the identification of ideas and execution, is critical to success. This involves analyzing financial data, operational metrics, and other relevant information to identify inefficiencies and areas for improvement. Available and quality data does need to exist.
- *Unpack the cost drivers*: It's crucial to explore the key underlying cost drivers for an organization and how they impact the business strategy. This includes understanding the most significant costs in the business and looking for opportunities to reduce or optimize them.
- *Employ benchmarking*: Another fruitful technique is comparing costs to industry benchmarks and exploring opportunities to improve the organization's cost competitiveness. By comparing the organization to others in the competitive field you can truly understand where you stand.
- *Focus on stakeholder buy-in*: A successful cost-management program requires the buy-in and support of critical stakeholders, including senior leaders, employees, and external partners. It is vital to engage these stakeholders early in the process and communicate the program's benefits to gain their support and sustain improvements.
- *Prioritize based on impact*: Organizations should prioritize their cost-management efforts based on the potential impact on the business and focus valuable capacity and effort on the areas where cost management can have the most significant effect, aligning these efforts with the organization's strategic priorities.
- *Combine a centralized and decentralized approach*: When executing sustainable cost-management practices, a key element is centralizing the approach as well as the reporting and enabling processes, while at the same time driving decentralized accountability for owning the cost-management agenda and delivering results to the business units and functions. It is very important to have a proper program management structure

to oversee, help course-correct, monitor, and control the cost-reduction initiatives and the level of execution progress.

- *Keep a long-term vision in mind*: Those companies that merely make short-term, tactical cuts to capital projects and headcount while scaling back growth initiatives and strategic investments take longer to recover from the impact of those cuts. Organizations must manage costs in a strategic, sustainable way, with a focus on addressing the underlying problems, and avoiding across-the-board percentage reductions.

- *Remember, it's a "game of two halves"*: Developing ideas to reduce costs is only half of the effort; success is measured by how well cost-reduction programs are executed. It's important to build the right pace of execution and a continuous push of results and impact.

- *Evaluate the cost-benefit analysis*: It is essential to conduct a cost-benefit analysis of potential cost-reduction initiatives to determine their feasibility and expected returns on investment. This involves considering both the direct costs of the initiative and the possible benefits, such as increased efficiency or improved customer satisfaction.

- *Measure impact*: Consider the best metrics to use to report the progress of execution and implementation of cost-reduction initiatives. Involving finance in the validation of cost-reduction results can help add credibility to stated success.

- *Create a cost culture*: An organization's culture can significantly impact the success of a cost-reduction or cost-management program. The best results are ones that stick, and will come from creating a culture that values cost management, and continuous improvement in general, and encourages employees to identify and implement cost-saving initiatives.

CHAPTER 20
ROADMAP EXECUTION

"The success of a strategy lies not in its formulation,
but in its execution."
—LAWRENCE HREBINIAK, MANAGEMENT EXPERT & AUTHOR

ELECTRIFYING CHANGE THROUGH ROADMAP EXECUTION

Strategy execution is complex and often requires consistent brute determination. A visual roadmap can help keep everyone and everything on track as the organization works through the long and challenging process of implementation. No matter what strategic priorities and programs you decide to focus on in your organization, a roadmap acts as a single reference point to ensure everyone on a team shares the same understanding of the goals they are trying to achieve. Although this overview should be brief and easily understood, it is not simply a task list explaining how to achieve each item; it does, however, show the steps needed to reach a successful outcome.

A roadmap can be created for a single, fairly complex strategic initiative, or it can comprise several different initiatives and programs in one overview document. Because it is an overview, a roadmap will usually show only the critical milestones. This allows an organization to measure progress and helps clarify what the team is working toward in the short and long term. These milestones are organized, and their relationships are defined, to show dependencies, providing a schedule and delivery dates for the entire project. Having a central high-level overview makes it easier to alter or update the priority of tasks and milestones when changes to a strategy and, therefore, an initiative are required. Roadmaps should also include the parties responsible for completing each milestone and the estimated resources allocated. Resources can include budgets, workers, and time required to complete the goal.[282]

In 2019, one of North America's most extensive electricity transmission and distribution providers identified new strategic priorities and supporting initiatives. However, execution stalled. In response, a strategic implementation office was set up with the help of the team and me to provide much-needed assistance to drive execution.

Execution starts with understanding what you need to get done and by when. The collective team and I first qualified, prioritized, and synthesized initiatives onto a roadmap for success, designed a high-level operating model, and built a progress reporting and measurement tracking system to help drive strategy execution.

The pace was essential, too. Initially, the team completed overviews to understand all the strategic initiatives being considered and interviewed owners, sponsors, leaders, and other stakeholders to reduce the number of strategic initiatives to 17 from an original 60. These 17 initiatives were incorporated into a single high-level roadmap to guide the strategy team in overseeing and reporting on the chosen initiatives over five years. The team then updated the one-page overview summaries that had been prepared for each initiative, with current state assessments and necessary next steps for execution. For leadership and board-level reporting, we introduced a tool to capture and report on the health and performance of each initiative represented on the roadmap.

The team and I then designed a prioritization framework based on value/impact, cost/complexity, and impact on lines of business. This assisted in finalizing the prioritization and could be used for future new initiatives as they emerged. To ensure ongoing sustainment of the roadmap, the team built a high-level, target-state operating model that explained who needed to do what and when.

The team used a technology-based project management tool to complement the roadmap and monitor progress while establishing a status reporting approach. Also, the team developed management and board materials that helped the strategy team convey their role, approach, and contribution to achieving the corporate goals. The value of the work was extensive in terms of preparing for execution focus and success.

Alignment needs to be integrated and maintained throughout the implementation process. The roadmaps we helped this power and utility company develop kept team members on the same page regarding each initiative's scope, objectives, and timeline. They also helped those in charge of each program quickly communicate objectives and share status updates. By frequently updating the roadmaps, the organization prevented initiatives from veering off-course and reduced unplanned dependencies that can cause projects to derail. Roadmaps become counterproductive if not used as a living, working document.

This chapter provides a detailed guide to help leaders create efficient and living roadmaps that align with their strategic goals, leveraging examples from Wärtsilä Corporation in Finland and Best Buy.

◆ ◆ ◆

WHAT IS ROADMAP EXECUTION?

Companies need a well-developed and well-executed strategy in today's fast-paced global marketplace. While many organizations have become adept at strategy creation, many of these same organizations get lost in the complexities of executing one. I'm always saying that, too often, companies take the time to develop strategic plans but fail to provide a structure and adequate processes that allow them to follow through.[283]

After initiative prioritization and roadmap development (Chapter 12), the execution process often becomes a significant obstacle. Executives attribute poor execution to a lack of alignment and a weak performance culture. To execute their strategies, companies must foster coordination across units and build the agility to adapt to changing market conditions.[284] Common failures include a lack of commitment on the part of leaders, poor communication, inadequate resources, resistance to change, and ineffective performance measurement systems.[285]

Business initiatives refer to an organization's strategic actions to achieve its objectives and goals. These initiatives are typically specific and measurable and are designed to address a particular challenge or opportunity the organization faces. Business initiatives can take many forms, such as launching a new product, expanding into a new market, improving operational efficiency, or implementing a new technology platform. They are often the result of a detailed planning process and are aligned with the organization's overall strategic objectives.

While resources are always finite, business initiatives require a significant outlay of time and money and are typically managed by a dedicated project team. The success of a business initiative depends on careful planning, effective execution, and ongoing monitoring and evaluation to ensure that the desired outcomes are achieved and resources are successfully allocated.

Effective execution of strategic initiatives allows organizations to be more agile and respond quickly to changes in marketplace or business environments. This explains why effective implementation is so crucial in today's rapidly changing business landscape, where organizations must adapt quickly to remain competitive. A structured approach to strategic initiative execution promotes accountability and ensures that all stakeholders know their roles and responsibilities. This helps to ensure that initiatives are completed on time and within budget.

CASE STUDY
Roadmap execution at Finland's Wärtsilä Corporation

Roadmaps can be applied to all kinds of execution situations. Wärtsilä, based in Finland, is a global leader in innovative technologies and life cycle solutions for the marine and energy markets. They aim to lead the transition toward a 100 percent renewable energy future.

The company needed a bold and unique organizational growth strategy to reach this goal. In July 2021, Wärtsilä executed a significant test program involving carbon-free solutions using hydrogen and ammonia fuels. Wärtsilä's fuel-agnostic approach enables the company to support the energy and marine sectors in shaping sustainable and efficient future fuel strategies in several cost-optimal steps.

Wärtsilä's decarbonization roadmap is based on a company-initiated analysis to identify the critical measures for reaching the carbon neutrality target. The toolbox includes energy savings, green electricity purchases, switching fuels, using more efficient technologies, and using offsets for emissions that are difficult to abate.[286]

Testament to its focus on relentless execution, in 2023 Wärtsilä received recognition from *TIME* as one of the 100 most influential companies in the world. Wärtsilä was praised for its continuous pursuit of, and focus on, innovation and for shaping the decarbonization of the energy and marine sectors.[287]

If you ask me, it's surprising how bad most companies are at execution. About 40 percent of executive leaders say their enterprise accountability and leadership need to be aligned on strategy execution, according to the 2020 Gartner Execution Gap Survey. This isn't a new concern. Gartner's polls of strategy leaders in prior years have shown slow strategy execution to be a top challenge, often because of insufficient visibility and control of the process, a short-term "firefighting" mentality, and employee fatigue.

In summary, it is critical for organizations to execute strategic initiatives to achieve their objectives, remain competitive, and drive innovation. Good execution ensures that resources are allocated efficiently and that all stakeholders are held accountable for the success of the initiatives.

HOW TO APPROACH ROADMAP EXECUTION

Initiative roadmap execution approach

An initiative roadmap visualizes an organization's strategic initiatives over a certain period, typically one to three years. As described in Chapter 12, the roadmap outlines each initiative's timeline, key milestones, and dependencies. It provides a high-level view of how the initiatives fit together to achieve an organization's strategic objectives.

In my experience, when they're done correctly, initiative roadmaps typically include the following elements:

- *Initiative description*: An overview of each initiative, including its purpose, objectives, and expected outcomes.
- *Timeline*: A timeline showing when each initiative starts and ends and critical milestones along the way.
- *Dependencies*: An overview of the dependencies between and within different initiatives, including any dependencies on external factors such as regulatory changes or market conditions.
- *Resource allocation*: A high-level analysis of the resources required for each initiative, including personnel, budget, and technology.
- *Performance metrics*: Metrics to measure the success of each initiative, such as revenue growth, cost savings, and customer satisfaction.

I've learned that during execution, people respond to visuals. An initiative roadmap is a graphic representation of all the initiatives the organization is committing to as a result of the strategic planning process. It provides a clear and concise overview of all these programs, allowing stakeholders to understand how they support the organization's strategic objectives and how they create value.

Also, I'm constantly arguing that roadmap execution should not be static. An initiative roadmap should be a dynamic document that can be regularly updated to reflect changes in the business environment, shifts in priority, or changes in the availability of resources. It is a critical tool for communication, alignment, and accountability, ensuring that all stakeholders know the organization's strategic priorities and progress toward achieving them.

CASE STUDY
Breaking down silos at Best Buy streamlines operations

Best Buy is one company that focuses on enriching lives through technology via relentless execution of strategy initiatives.

But back in 2012, Best Buy struggled with plummeting profits, sales, and stock prices. The company had lost relevance and the ability to compete, so it hired Hubert Joly as its CEO in a last-ditch effort to survive. Joly developed a transformation roadmap called Renew Blue that focused on renewing the customer experience, reducing costs, and increasing revenue. The roadmap included initiatives such as price matching, free shipping, and in-store pickup.

Best Buy also implemented a new governance structure with a cross-functional team responsible for executing the roadmap. The team was made up of senior executives from different departments, such as merchandising, supply chain, and store operations. It was responsible for ensuring that the initiatives in the roadmap were executed effectively and efficiently and had the authority to make decisions and allocate resources across departments. This approach helped break down silos between departments and ensured that everyone was working toward the same goals.

As a result, Best Buy experienced five consecutive years of comparable sales growth, increased its non-GAAP operating income rate, achieved $1.9 billion in cost savings and efficiencies, improved profitability and shareholder returns, increased its net promoter score, and hit record-low employee turnover rates.[288, 289]

During the execution phase, there are different ways to visualize a roadmap. One of the most popular that I've used is the timeline roadmap. Similar to Gantt charts, timeline roadmaps allow you to plan critical activities on your timeline while creating high-level project schedules. They're a fantastic way to align everyone on priorities, key dates, and milestones. Unlike Gantt charts, timeline roadmaps are often high-level, which allows them to communicate project strategy in the simplest possible way.

There are many benefits of using a roadmap for your project. I've found that it helps with quick communication of project plans and goals, given that it's a high-level visual document that is easy to share with stakeholders and other teams. It also helps manage stakeholder expectations by setting early goals, budgets, timelines, and so on and ensuring everyone is on the same page. It assists in decision-making because everyone can refer to the project roadmap and have access to the most important goals and activities, and that helps them prioritize tasks and make quick decisions. And finally, it's an excellent tool for status updates if your roadmap is current with the course.[290]

Linking initiatives to corporate measures

With experience, I've come to understand that to track the success of multiple initiatives during the execution phase, the roadmap must be linked to existing corporate metrics. This makes sense because it helps ensure that the chosen initiatives align with the organization's overall strategy and objectives and are contributing to its success. So, when new strategic business initiatives are linked to corporate measures that are already in place, there is a clear line of sight between the initiatives and the organization's performance, allowing stakeholders to see how the initiatives impact success. This alignment also helps ensure that resources are allocated to the most critical initiatives and that all initiatives contribute to the organization's success. The data can be used to make informed decisions about resource allocation, prioritization, and other critical business decisions.

EasyJet plc, a multinational budget airline, implemented a low-cost culture in its business. The airline's leaders aligned their corporate metrics to their strategic initiatives by measuring cost per seat, load factor (percentage of seats sold per flight), and on-time performance. By tracking these metrics, easyJet could align its corporate goals with its strategic initiatives and ensure they were on track to achieve their objectives.[291] However, as CEO Johan Lundgren said, "Low cost doesn't mean low quality," and the company continues to balance both priorities (cost and quality) through a balanced scorecard measurement system.[292]

In summary, I've learned that linking strategic business initiatives to existing corporate measures makes sense because it helps to ensure alignment with corporate strategy, provides a clear line of sight between the initiatives and the organization's performance, facilitates performance management, promotes focus and prioritization, and enables data-driven decision-making.

Initiative progress dashboard

Anyone who knows me knows that I'm all about visuals. One example I favour as part of the roadmap execution is a strategic initiative progress dashboard, a visual tool used to track and communicate the progress of an organization's strategic initiatives. While the roadmap provides an overview of all initiatives and when they are to start and stop against a timeline, the progress dashboard summarizes the status of the initiatives when they are underway (percentage complete, for example). It allows stakeholders to quickly and easily see how the initiatives are progressing, whether they are on track to meet their objectives, and whether any risks or issues need to be addressed.

The dashboard displays KPIs relevant to the initiatives. These KPIs may include metrics such as revenue growth, cost savings, customer satisfaction, or project completion rate. The dashboard also provides an overview of the status of each initiative, including whether it is on track or at risk of failing to meet its objectives. It also identifies any risks or issues that impede progress and the steps to address them. Furthermore, the dashboard identifies any dependencies among the initiatives and provides an overview of how these dependencies are being managed. It includes a timeline that shows each initiative's planned start and end dates, critical milestones, and an overview of the resources allocated to each initiative, including personnel, budget, and technology.

The dashboard also provides data and insights that can be used to make informed decisions about resource allocation, prioritization, and other critical business decisions. It promotes communication and collaboration among stakeholders by providing a standard view of the progress of the initiatives.

According to a February 2020 Harvard Business School Online article, organizations must constantly monitor, evaluate, and adjust their strategic initiatives to address new challenges and business concerns. When a new strategy needs to be implemented, it's typically up to managers to ensure it rolls out successfully. Whether you're an aspiring, new, or seasoned manager, understanding the strategy implementation process and how it relates to organizational change is critical to ensuring you can be effective throughout your career.[293]

In summary, a strategic initiative roadmap or progress dashboard is essential for tracking and communicating how effectively an organization is executing its strategic initiatives. It provides a high-level overview of the progress of the initiatives, promotes communication and collaboration among stakeholders, and enables informed decision-making and agile management.

♦ ♦ ♦

CONSIDERATIONS

The roadmap is the engine for successful strategy execution, ensuring that things get done to move the organization forward in concert with its vision and strategic priorities. Here are some key considerations to keep in mind when using a roadmap to guide successful strategic initiative execution:

- *Align with strategy*: Ensure the initiatives align with the organization's strategic choices and objectives. Regularly review the roadmap to be sure it continues to align with the organization's strategic priorities as implementation is rolled out. Structure-strategy linkage is the most fundamental task of strategy execution.[294]
- *Assign accountability*: Assign clear accountability for the execution of each initiative, including roles and responsibilities for the team members involved. Furthermore, consider single point accountability, so that there is never any confusion on who needs to ensure the work gets done.
- *Prioritize initiatives*: Prioritize the initiatives based on their potential impact on the organization's success. This may involve deciding which initiatives to pursue and which to postpone or abandon. Too many organizations get caught in the trap of trying to do everything, and then do them poorly, rather than doing a few things well.

- *Measure progress*: Establish clear metrics and milestones to measure the progress of the initiatives and regularly track and report on them. It's important to operate on a no-surprises basis.
- *Communicate progress*: Be sure all stakeholders—including senior leaders, team members, and external partners—are kept up-to-date on the progress of the initiatives. This communication should be transparent, frequent, and timely, and create excitement and momentum.
- *Ensure adaptability*: Be prepared to adjust the roadmap as needed based on changing market conditions, internal priorities, or other factors that may impact the execution of the initiatives. It's also important to challenge leaders to remove initiatives at the same level as adding initiatives, especially when the organizational capacity does not change.
- *Allocate resources*: Ensure the necessary resources are available to execute the initiatives, including personnel, budget, and technology. Consider the potential impact of resource constraints on the timeline and prioritization of initiatives. Also, make sure the same key individuals are not involved in every initiative, otherwise you risk overload and burnout.
- *Embed collaboration*: As I said in a recent article with *Take-It-Personel-ly*, teamwork makes the dream work.[295] Encourage collaboration and teamwork among team members executing the initiatives. Foster a culture of open communication and information sharing to ensure all team members are aligned and working toward the same objectives.

CHAPTER 21
PROGRAM MANAGEMENT AND GOVERNANCE

"Vision without execution is just hallucination."

—HENRY FORD, AMERICAN INDUSTRIALIST AND BUSINESS LEADER

TRANSFORMATION MANAGEMENT ONE BARREL AT A TIME

These days, the energy industry is under pressure to digitize quickly so companies can innovate and compete with new markets and technologies.[296] In 2019, I became involved with a multinational integrated energy organization beginning the journey toward the next phase of its evolution. Earlier that year, the company had discussed the importance of growing its competitive advantage as the world rapidly changes. To do this, it needed to unleash the full potential of its people and work differently, harnessing new technologies to accelerate the journey to world-class status, improve financial performance, generate economic and societal value, and create an inspired and valued workforce.

It was a time of significant change within the company as well as externally. To lead the journey, a transformation management office (TMO) team was assembled to drive, integrate, and accelerate strategic change across the organization. Reporting directly to senior management, the TMO was accountable for creating shared value and competitive advantage by being purpose-driven, people-focused, data-informed, and technology-enabled. The TMO aimed to be the catalyst that accelerated transformational change across the organization.

The organization engaged my team and me to help, as the chief transformation officer said, "To develop a strategic, rapid, and practical approach to standing up the TMO through a governance model." The engagement leveraged leading practices to develop options and recommendations, and the TMO leadership team was engaged in workshops to make decisions.

In transformation, getting the governance right is fundamental. The size and complexity of the company required some careful thinking as the TMO would be responsible for coordinating implementation across three layers: strategic, management, and execution. Upfront work was focused on validating the current governing principles and designing the overall governing structure, as well as those specific to each layer. The three governance layers created within the organization, from high level down to detailed execution, were as follows:

- *Strategic layer*: Included setting direction and guidance to align with the organization's purpose, long-term strategy, and leadership on organizational culture and values.
- *Management layer*: Responsible for oversight of the project portfolio; identification, selection, and prioritization of investments; and realizing the vision (horizontal). Additional duties included the delivery and execution of portfolio planning and stewardship to achieve the transformation.
- *Execution layer*: Included managing and delivering the selected programs and projects and realizing the potential value of each initiative (vertical). It also provided monitoring, controls, and reports on program and project delivery progress—focusing on project performance in terms of quality, schedule, and budget.

Being aware of who was doing what across the enterprise helped the team focus on ensuring the right people were assigned to the right projects. The team then developed a detailed roles and responsibilities matrix, defined principles to measure and track benefits realization and financial performance management, and designed a high-level critical TMO process that included integrated planning, risk management, benefits management, and idea management.

Through the work of the TMO, the organization successfully implemented digital technologies to accelerate operational excellence, achieve world-class performance, generate value (saving hundreds of millions of dollars), enhance its competitive advantage, and create its vision of the future workplace.

Governance is critical to the success of any strategy execution, yet according to McKinsey's research, roughly 70 percent fail when corporations launch transformations. Contributing factors include insufficient aspirations, a lack of organizational engagement, and insufficient investment in building organizational capabilities to sustain the change.[297, 298] This chapter guides readers through a best practice blueprint for achieving program management and governance goals by looking at examples of Verizon, Fujitsu UK and Ireland, and healthcare company Optum Technology.

◆ ◆ ◆

WHAT IS PROGRAM MANAGEMENT AND GOVERNANCE?

Program management is intended to help you structure and manage business programs, whatever they might be. Therefore, it supports post-merger integration (Chapter 17), cost management (Chapter 19), and roadmap execution (Chapter 20). It is designed to be used in conjunction with other service delivery methods that address the technical delivery components of a business program, as well as standard project and portfolio management processes and techniques.

I always say that governance describes how decisions are made and where responsibilities lie within program delivery. Good governance is critical to ensuring that companies select the right projects and successfully execute the strategy. Good program management and governance involve clear accountability and responsibilities amongst team members and a thoughtful management approach to program definition, structuring, planning, and execution.

Project, program, and portfolio management levels

There is a hierarchy in getting the work of strategy execution done. Project, program, and portfolio management are different approaches to managing initiatives within an organization, each with distinct objectives and levels of scope.

- *Project management*: The process of planning, executing, and controlling the work of a team to achieve specific goals and objectives within a defined timeline and budget. A project is a temporary endeavour with a particular scope and funding to deliver a unique product, service, or result. Project management typically involves managing a team of individuals to ensure a specific project is completed on time, within budget, and to the required quality standards.

- *Program management*: The process of managing multiple related projects that are coordinated to achieve broader organizational goals and objectives. It involves overseeing the coordination and integration of various projects, so they are aligned with the organization's strategic objectives.
- *Portfolio management*: Refers to managing the full suite of programs, projects, and other initiatives to achieve an organization's strategic objectives. It involves selecting, prioritizing, and balancing the organization's initiatives to ensure they align with its strategic goals.

Project, program, and portfolio governance requirements

Portfolio, program, and project management each have different levels of responsibility and demand different aspects of governance, as each is responsible for managing various levels of initiatives within an organization.

- *Portfolio management*: Portfolio management ensures that all strategic initiatives executed by an organization are aligned with its strategic goals and resources are allocated effectively and efficiently to achieve the greatest impact and return on investment. Portfolio management also manages risks associated with the initiatives in the portfolio and ensures that the initiatives deliver the organization's expected benefits.
- *Program management*: Program management involves inter-project coordination and integration, which ensures that projects within the program are aligned and that resources are managed across multiple projects and effectively allocated. Program managers oversee project interdependencies, provide consistent project management processes, manage risks associated with

the program, and deliver organizational benefits that individual projects cannot achieve alone. Such benefits include broad strategic alignment of all projects to the strategic goals, resource optimization that is easier to do at the program level, and optimized change management to ensure that the organization is not overwhelmed by too many projects at the same time. It's important to manage integration, pace, impact, and risk at the program level.

- *Project management*: The aspects of governance and responsibility level for project management include scope management, which ensures the project is delivered according to the project plan, within the defined parameters and that resources are effectively allocated to achieve the project objectives. Project managers are responsible for planning, organizing, and directing resources to achieve specific project goals and issues related to the specific project. Finally, project management is expected to manage risks associated with the project, monitor and control progress, and ensure deliverables get done and the project meets the required quality standards and benefits realization.

Figure 18: Governance levels

At its heart, I've discovered that governance helps with managing risk at all implementation levels: project, program, and portfolio. Program management governance, as it is known generally, should be appropriate to the level of work required, as shown in Figure 18. It provides a framework for identifying, assessing, and managing risks associated with the activities of any program. This helps to reduce the likelihood that unexpected issues could derail execution and to ensure that resources are allocated effectively and efficiently to a project or across an entire program or portfolio.

The right governance for the specific level of execution also aligns efforts to communicate with people to get the work done, providing a framework that ensures all stakeholders know a program's objectives, progress, and risks. This helps to maintain stakeholder engagement and buy-in, reduce the likelihood of unwelcome surprises, and improve outcomes. Furthermore, program management governance provides a framework for measuring and monitoring performance against objectives. This helps to identify areas where performance is falling short and provides opportunities for corrective action.

In summary, program management governance is critical to successful strategy execution because it ensures alignment with strategy, effective risk and resource management, improved communication, and robust performance management. By maintaining a solid governance framework, I've learned that programs can operate more efficiently, delivering better outcomes for an organization.

Program governance types

There isn't one approved way to achieve program governance; organizational context is critical. Different governance types can be categorized based on their mode of operation. In a paper I wrote for EY, three governance types are described: advise, orchestrate, and drive.[299]

- *Advise*: In this model, the governing body advises and guides the organization or system but does not have direct control over decision-making. The advisor mode is suitable for organizations or systems that are decentralized and require independent decision-making. This role includes reviewing and analyzing information and providing recommendations, making suggestions to improve the decision-making process, and ensuring compliance with regulations and standards.

- *Orchestrate*: In orchestrator governance, the governing body coordinates and facilitates decision-making among organizational or system stakeholders. It promotes cooperation between stakeholders, manages the allocation of resources, encourages alignment with the organization's strategic objectives, and ensures compliance with regulations and standards. This makes sense in mature organizations where there might be strong accountability in the business to get work done, and there needs to be coordination enterprise wide.

- *Drive*: In this case, the governing body has direct control over decision-making and is responsible for setting the organization's strategic direction. The driver mode suits organizations or systems that require centralized decision-making and strong leadership. The governing body is responsible for the organization's strategic direction, making decisions and setting policies, allocating resources, and ensuring compliance with regulations and standards.

Each governance type has strengths and weaknesses; the choice will depend on the organization's goals, values, and culture. The key to successful governance is to choose the one that offers the most appropriate mode of operation for the organization in question.

HOW TO APPROACH PROGRAM MANAGEMENT AND GOVERNANCE

PMO stand-up approach

The program management office, or PMO (or the TMO in the example that opened the chapter), is the first line of defence for maintaining control over a project, program, or portfolio. It's not especially fun or sexy, but I believe that it's essential to effective strategy execution and good governance. It delegates to the project/program director the responsibility for driving delivery, managing execution risks, and reporting progress.

The PMO is the central nucleus of a successful execution effort, and I'm constantly arguing its importance. Setting up a PMO can help organizations improve their project, program, and portfolio management and increase the success of their strategic initiatives.

Here are the key steps I use to set up a PMO:

1. *Define the PMO's purpose*: Determine why the organization needs a PMO and what it should achieve. This will guide the structure and activities of the PMO.

2. *Establish the PMO's governance structure*: Design the PMO's roles and responsibilities, reporting lines, decision-making authority, and escalation procedures.

3. *Identify the PMO's scope and services*: Outline the services the PMO will offer, such as project management methodologies, tools, templates, and training.

4. *Determine the PMO's staffing needs*: Define the roles and responsibilities of the PMO staff, including the manager and project managers, and identify any necessary training or qualifications.

5. *Define the PMO's processes and procedures*: Develop processes and procedures for the PMO's services, including project initiation, planning, execution, monitoring, control, and closure.

6. *Develop the PMO's toolset*: Identify and implement the appropriate tools to support the PMO's processes and services, such as project management software, collaboration tools, and reporting tools.

7. *Establish the PMO's performance metrics*: Define the metrics that the PMO will use to measure its own performance, such as project completion rates, schedule timelines, and budget performance.

8. *Communicate the PMO's value proposition*: Be clear about the benefits of the PMO to all stakeholders—including senior leadership, project teams, and external partners—and build support for the PMO's services and processes.

9. *Implement the PMO's services and processes*: Roll out the PMO's services and processes to the organization and, to ensure they are adopted, provide training and support to project teams.

10. *Monitor and improve the PMO's performance*: Regularly monitor the PMO's performance against its performance metrics and make improvements to its services and processes as necessary to continuously improve its effectiveness.

I have discovered that by following these key steps, organizations can successfully form a PMO that supports their strategic initiatives and improves project management throughout the enterprise.

An example of strategic alignment of the PMO is telecoms company Verizon. The PMO's push for strategic alignment ensures that projects help the company achieve its business goals. As Verizon's strategies have changed over the years, so have the PMO's. For example, the company's current focus is reducing project cycle times.[300] Thanks to standardized project management processes, they've achieved impressive results. For instance, when the PMO was first established, it took 18 to 24 months to launch a product. Now, they've reduced that cycle time to just 10.3 months.

Healthcare company Optum Technology has a PMO that delivers value by consistently measuring project progress against strategic goals. It is always looking for opportunities to reduce delivery times, so its team focuses on cycle time in each project right from the start—scrutinizing schedules and looking for spots where tasks can be completed more quickly. While the PMO relies on metrics to demonstrate value, it also ensures they don't hinder performance. The metrics help Optum identify what's working and determine where problems are impacting cycle time so they can be addressed. Furthermore, the PMO ensures that all projects align to the company's overall strategic objectives; uses standardized processes and tools for project management; and oversees resource management, risk management, and consistent stakeholder engagement.

CASE STUDY
Multiple PMOs at Fujitsu keep things manageable

If an organization decides to establish a PMO, there's no one-size-fits-all solution. The UK and Ireland division of Fujitsu relies on multiple PMOs to ensure their strategic projects and programs are executed effectively.

The PMO at the senior management level is responsible for setting the organization's project management strategy and focusing on process improvements related to organizational goals, such as growing the business, moving into new markets, and increasing social responsibility. Fujitsu also has PMOs in its central business units to ensure they adhere to governance and standards and that their individual projects meet schedule, budget, and quality goals.

For a large company like Fujitsu, which at any time may have up to 800 projects worth £600 million, a network of PMOs helps keep things manageable.[301]

◆ ◆ ◆

CONSIDERATIONS

Governance of projects, programs, and portfolios ensures that a suitable glue exists around the execution of a strategy. Creating an appropriate governance structure ensures there is leadership and accountability for strategy execution; without it, even the best strategy is likely to fail in the implementation. The PMO structure and function should be closely aligned with the requirements of individual organizations, programs, and cultural and political environments. Some key structural considerations for program management and governance are as follows:

- *Consider the critical governance decisions*: Is the governance structure one-off, short-term, or strategically placed to support several long-term projects and programs? Define the customers of the PMO: Whom will it serve, internal or external? Will there be multiple PMOs, each one standing alone within divisions, or a single PMO to provide a unified approach across all divisions? Also, consider the different levels of governance in terms of strategy, management, and execution.
- *Define location preferences for the team*: Will the staff be on site or operate remotely? It's important to consider the degree of physical collaboration and stakeholder engagement required.

- *Agree on in-house vs. outsourced*: Will the staff be contractors or in-house employees, or will the operation be outsourced? Or a mix of these? The key consideration is where the required skills and capabilities exist and ensuring the right balance of in-house vs. third-party involvement. Skills that are core to how an organization differentiates itself in the market should be retained in-house.

- *Define capacity needs in terms of function and size*: It should be recognized that the function and size of the PMO will change through a project/program life cycle. The initial set of functions may be added to or diminish over time, and the size will increase and decrease to suit the circumstances of different program needs.

- *Create clear roles and responsibilities*: It is crucial to establish how the program will be managed and what roles and responsibilities will be assigned to program managers, project managers, and other team members. Consider what capabilities might cut across the programs like change and communications or risk management.

- *Embed the right organizational culture*: Program management and governance require a strong culture of collaboration, communication, and accountability. Supporting these values ensures that program management and governance processes align with the organization's culture. Researchers have found that the context in which programs operate is critical to program success. Program managers must be able to navigate complex cultural, political, and business environments.[302]

- *Drive the right level of stakeholder engagement*: Effective program management and governance require engagement with various stakeholders, including executives, sponsors, program managers, project managers, team members, customers, and external partners. It is essential to establish clear lines of communication and engagement with stakeholders to ensure they are aware of objectives, progress, and risks.

- *Carefully manage resources*: Effective program management and governance require effective resource management processes that allocate resources based on a program's priorities and constraints.

These processes must be transparent and align with a program's objectives as well as organizational goals.

- *Manage performance from the start*: Effective program management and governance must be well-designed to measure performance against objectives, identify areas for improvement, and facilitate continuous improvement.

- *Drive sustainability through continuous improvement*: Effective program management and governance require a culture of continuous improvement that fosters innovation, encourages experimentation, and facilitates learning. To improve outcomes, it is necessary to establish a continuous improvement culture to make sure that program management and governance processes are continually reviewed and refined.

- *Enable through tools and techniques*: Remember to define which processes and tools will lead to the most effective communication and collaboration across the program.

CONCLUSION

"In a world of constant change, strategy is more important than ever. Only by anticipating and adapting to change can we achieve success in the long term."

—BILL GATES, CO-FOUNDER OF MICROSOFT

WHY IS STRATEGY SO VITAL?

In today's fast-paced business environment, competition is fierce. In its Market Outlook for 2024, J.P. Morgan Research predicts that market volatility is set to remain elevated.[303] Furthermore, J.P. Morgan believes things will worsen, with the volatility index set to trade higher in 2024 compared to 2023.[304] Technological advancements, shifting consumer preferences, climate change, and global geopolitical events are some drivers of rapidly changing market conditions. To stay ahead, companies must have a well-defined and integrated strategy to help them stand out, differentiate, and succeed in this challenging environment.

Volatility is not the only driver at play, highlighting the importance of strategy. According to McKinsey, the world has become deeply interconnected, and trade flows have proven remarkably resilient during the most recent turbulence. The challenge is harnessing the benefits of this interconnection while managing the risks and downsides of dependency—mainly where products are concentrated in their places of origin.[305] A well put together and integrated outside-in, inside-out strategy can help companies expand their operations globally while maintaining competitiveness and sustainability locally.

Digitalization has also disrupted traditional business models, so companies need a digital strategy integrated with the broader outside-in, inside-out strategy to help them leverage technology to improve their operations and customer experiences. A report by major global market intelligence firm International Data Corporation highlights that global spending on services and technologies that will allow digital transformation was estimated at $2.3 trillion in 2023. The value of direct investments in digital transformation between 2020 and 2023 was estimated at $6.8 trillion.[306] These big numbers require a thoughtful strategy to ensure digital spending is allocated to the right places to drive business value.

Climate change is the existential threat of our time and highlights again the importance of a well-integrated outside-in, inside-out strategy. According to the United Nations, climate change is the biggest threat modern humans have ever faced.[307] Climate change increases extreme weather patterns such as hurricanes, floods, wildfires, and droughts. Altered precipitation patterns are leading to water scarcity in some regions and having an impact on the agriculture, manufacturing, and energy production sectors. In response, governments worldwide are implementing new regulations to mitigate the impacts—carbon pricing, emissions standards, renewable energy mandates, increased business compliance costs—and changing market dynamics. Climate change is also modifying consumer preferences toward more environmentally conscious products and services with a smaller carbon footprint, disrupting supply chains through infrastructure damage, and, in some cases, impacting the availability of raw materials.

Finally, business operations have become increasingly complex as well, with more stakeholders involved and frequently changing government policies and regulations.[308] Companies must navigate the complex and rapidly changing business environment to stay ahead of the competition or perish. Sound strategy is a more urgent and imperative than ever.

NOT ALL FRAMEWORKS ARE CREATED EQUAL

I know that throughout this book, I've highlighted the value of various frameworks and their essential role in strategy creation and implementation, including the outside-in, inside-out approach that I've developed, but proceed with caution. Frameworks are everywhere in business. Some have had a lasting impact on strategy and have become game-changers in how we think about strategy development and execution.[309] However, overusing strategic frameworks can be problematic for several reasons.

Many strategic frameworks have been developed based on specific contexts or industries. They're intended to simplify complex issues and provide structured solutions, but applying them indiscriminately in unrelated situations can lead to an exercise that lacks contextual relevance and may limit creative thinking. Classic MBA-type frameworks, when overused, can lead to the adoption of cookie-cutter solutions. Organizations may simply follow the prescribed steps without fully understanding their own underlying issues and tailoring the approach to their specific needs. This can result in generic and superficial strategies that do not address the organization's unique challenges.

Another weakness when adopting generic strategic frameworks is that an organization often fails to rely on internal expertise and knowledge. Trusted employees often deeply understand an organization's strengths and weaknesses as well as industry dynamics. Ignoring their insights and relying solely on external frameworks can undervalue internal capabilities.

Each organization and its unique circumstances will likely require a tailored approach rather than a one-size-fits-all framework. And that's where the holistic outside-in, inside-out strategic planning process comes in. A well-integrated outside-in, inside-out strategy can help companies simplify and align their goals and objectives across all departments and stakeholders, and create a customized roadmap for growth and sustainability that's uniquely suited to their needs, capabilities, and priorities.

THE LEADERSHIP IMPERATIVE

As I explained in an article in *Chief Executive* magazine, "When we reflect on various crises over the last 50 years, we cannot ignore the possibility that history will repeat itself—we seem to enter into one kind of disaster or another approximately every decade."[310] (Although it's hard not to conclude that the pace seems to be accelerating.) In the 21st century, managing economic and political risk and uncertainty has become the most critical leadership challenge. As organizations increasingly look at expanding more quickly and start-ups look at scaling up faster, economic and political uncertainty must be taken into account in any growth strategy.

Against this backdrop, it is critical that leadership achieve a balance between short-term and long-term business objectives to counteract forces with a mid- and long-term impact as well as those that affect the organization in the short term.[311] Organizations are challenging their leaders to deal effectively with a world of disruptive digital business models, augmented workforces, flattened organizations, and an ongoing shift to team-based work practices.[312]

Outside-in, inside-out strategic planning is a game of four quarters—and a game-changer. It requires substantial effort on the outside-in and inside-out analysis itself, in support of strategic choices, but also to develop and execute the strategy. Strategy cannot be seen as a theoretical navel-gazing exercise; for leaders, it may require an equal, if not greater, focus on relentless execution than any other aspect of their job.

For several reasons, leaders in the current business environment need a solid outside-in, inside-out strategy to achieve their goals:

- A thoughtful strategy provides a clear direction for an organization. It outlines the goals, objectives, and priorities an organization needs to focus on, providing a roadmap for success.
- The right strategy also aligns the organization's goals and objectives with its resources, capabilities, and stakeholders. This alignment ensures that all parts of the organization work toward a common goal, maximizing efficiency and effectiveness.
- A comprehensive, coherent process informs the organization's strategic efforts from a wide range of perspectives and, just as importantly, provides a structured approach to execution that will increase the chances of your strategy succeeding.

Furthermore, outside-in, inside-out strategy provides a framework for decision-making based on external and internal information. Leaders can use this holistic strategic planning process to evaluate options and make informed decisions that align with the organization's goals and objectives. It helps leaders prioritize their actions and investments while focusing their efforts and resources on the most critical areas, maximizing their impact, value, and return.

THE STRATEGY SILVER BULLETS

In my experience, effective strategic planning all starts with strong leaders. This book's outside-in, inside-out strategy framework defines the what, why, and how of each component, as well as additional considerations. That may seem easy to follow, but only effective leaders can bring it all together. They act as the glue to ensure the connection points occur, steps are integrated, and a balance between strategy development and execution—and the *outside-in* and *inside-out* framework overall—is achieved.

From what I've learned over the years, everyone in an organization, from the top down, needs to be on the same page. And it is up to leaders to ensure that all objectives align with the strategy and everyone works toward the same goals and priorities. This alignment process also supports feedback, brainstorming, and other forms of collaboration to drive buy-in and engagement. By involving stakeholders, a strategy becomes more inclusive and considers diverse perspectives.

So, this means the responsibility falls to executives to cascade the strategy down to all levels of the organization. This includes specific actions and initiatives (Chapters 12, 20) that each department and team should adopt to support the strategy. Furthermore, monitoring progress against the strategy throughout the implementation is essential. Business performance, performance management, and scorecard management (Chapter 8), and governance (Chapter 21) are critical in monitoring through thoughtful and strategy-aligned KPIs, progress reports, and stakeholder feedback sessions. This helps leaders identify areas of success and areas that need improvement, allowing them to make strategic pivots and new choices (Chapter 11) in real time, as required.

The seamless connection and integration of the different components of the strategy are also vital to ensure people work together and can cross team boundaries easily. It requires close coordination and should be supported by organizational culture and behaviours.

According to a report in the *Harvard Business Review*, most people can't recall the strategy of the organization they work for. Even the executives and managers responsible for strategy struggle, with one study reporting that only 28 percent could list three strategic priorities.[113] The solution, I always say, is to *communicate, communicate,* and *communicate.* As part of strategy development and execution success, leaders must clearly and consistently keep all employees informed. The message should include the strategy's goals, objectives, priorities, and rationale. When communicating a strategy to different stakeholders, it is essential to consider their specific needs, interests, and perspectives.

Over my years of consulting on strategy, I've come to appreciate how vitally important it is to understand your audience. Identify the stakeholders and their level of interest or influence in the organization. This will help you tailor your message and uncover the fact that each stakeholder group will have its own goals and interests about which its members are most concerned.

When communicating the strategy, it is also vital to use appropriate language and anchor the benefits of the strategy. Effective communication is transparent and authentic. When you succeed at this, it will help build trust with employees and other stakeholders and ensure that they are aligned with the strategy and invested in its success.

THE FUTURE OF STRATEGY

Several trends will likely shape the future of strategy in the next several decades. Firstly, the ongoing digital transformation will continue to exert a massive influence on businesses everywhere—including on strategic approaches. Companies must develop digital strategies to help them leverage emerging technologies such as artificial intelligence—including generative AI, quantum computing, blockchain, and the Internet of Things—to improve their operations and customer experiences. According to the AI Index Report 2023, global AI private investment was US$94 billion in 2022, which suggests that businesses already realize they must embrace technology to stay on top.[314]

Second, the increasing focus on sustainability cannot be ignored. Companies must develop strategies that take into account environmental, social, and governance (ESG) considerations and focus on creating sustainable business models. The ongoing disruptions caused by pandemics, climate change, and geopolitical tensions will also influence strategic approaches. For example, companies must develop strategies to help them become more resilient and adaptable to decarbonization, net zero, and ESG-related disruptions.

The world's changing interconnectedness will also play a role in the future. Companies must develop global strategies to help them expand their operations abroad and remain competitive in a global marketplace to gain access to talent, technology, and millions of new consumers.

Austrian American management consultant, educator, and author Peter Drucker famously said, "Innovate or die." The steady pace of innovation will also remain a vital influence as we advance. Companies must develop strategies that foster innovation and creativity and keep them ahead of the competition with new products and services that serve changing and more sophisticated customer needs.

Finally, strategic thinkers must embrace diversity and inclusion in their decision-making processes to succeed in a globalized world. According to research from the Pew Research Center, the "post-millennial" generations entering the workforce will be the most diverse in history.[315] So, managing talent will involve understanding and respecting different cultural perspectives and promoting a diverse range of voices, both in high-level strategic discussions and within organizations at large.

Overall, the future of strategy will likely be shaped by a combination of digitalization, sustainability, resilience, globalization, innovation, diversity, and inclusion. Companies that can carefully balance efforts in the development and execution of strategy, while also considering the outside in and the inside out, will be the ones most likely to succeed in the coming decades.

ACKNOWLEDGEMENTS

As always, this research and writing process has been based on considerable work with clients, and conversation, exploration, and continuous testing of ideas with brilliant people, including family, friends, colleagues, fellow writers, and academics. It's difficult to list and pay homage to all these sources of help and inspiration, so, with advance apologies to those I know I'll miss, I'd like to acknowledge and thank whom I can in these final pages.

Firstly, numerous observations, insights, and recommendations have originated from the outside while the book was underway and have been incorporated into the text. I've tried to do my best with the sources, but sometimes, the influences are too numerous to capture fully.

The book would have never happened without the input and excellent support of my team and colleagues, including Chris Palmer, Karun Gautam, Krista Yates, Kiersten Ermelbauer, Tyson Denhamer, Alexandr Kim, Matthew Anderson, Colton Cuckow, Natalie McVicar, Brett Bradley, Josiah Soliman, Samantha Munk, Armind Cajala, Sean Gunton, Kent Kaufield, Linda Williams, Kerrie Murray, Jad Shimaly, David McQueen, Alycia Calvert, Zahid Fazal, Alasdair Ross, Paul O'Donnell, Karleen Batty, Theo Yameogo, Greg Boone, Daniela Carcasole, Karl Heymann, Terry McKay, Moz Salim, Scott Patrick, Annie Murphy, Matt Mura, Scott Young, Barry Munro, Robert Alexander,

Brett Greenlaw, David Steele, Iain Thompson, Maria Zambakkides, Dean Braunsteiner, Pradeep Karpur, Mark Lindeman, and Brittany Keenan.

I am an insatiable learner, and my ideas have been shaped by the work I've done with my clients and the problems I've helped them solve over the years. This includes Rob Palmer, Dan Collins, Bruno Francoeur, Pramod Jain, Niamh McGrath, Brent Nadeau, Samantha Stuart, John Hill, Mike Burt, Darren Murphy, Rod Graham, Rob Blackadar, Tristan Goodman, Ben Tsui, Glenn McNamara, James Thompson, Megan Hyland, David Milia, Natalie Swann, Peter McNay, Mark Little, Steve Hogan, Oleksiy Osiyevskyy, Harrie Vredenburg, Sean Brosnahan, Mick Fitzpatrick, Mark Chyc-Cies, Chris Lopez, Paul Rollinson, Jason Fitzsimmons, Court Ellingson, Rob Morgan, Andrew Dahlin, Paul Selway, Charity Elder, Kris Smith, Kate Koplovich, Brad Parry, Mark Becker, David Lebeter, John Gracie, Tim Marchant, Davin Kivisto, David Bourgeois, Greg Retzer, Darren Yaworsky, Jana Mosley, Andrew McVie, Graeme Edge, Trevor Carson, Adam Gaffney, Robyn Bews, Alicia Quesnel, Randy Pettipas, Matthew Marshall, Anthony Masleck, Scott Bolton, Ramez Naam, Michael Treacy, Bob Sartor, Karl Moore, Jeff Williams, Mary Moran, Mark Poweska, Jason Rakochy, David Roberts, Chris Stuart, Jim Dewald, Rocky Vermani, Diego Ordonez, Sebastien Gendron, Imad Mohsen, Marcel Teunissen, Grant Fagerheim, Mark Scholz, Kendall Dilling, Claudia D'Orazio, Hugues Jacquemin, Gursh Bal, Greg Twinney, Gary Hart, Scott Balfour, Anne Marie Toutant, Rod Graham, Goldy Hyder, Catherine McLeod-Seltzer, Brad Perry, David Duckworth, and Lisa Sparrow.

A heartfelt thank you to my mum, Jennie Mortlock, and my dad, Richard Mortlock, who instilled in me the combination of curiosity, hard work, discipline, determination, focus, and love that influences all my work and how I approach my life. And to my two brothers and the lifelong friends who champion and support all my crazy ideas and are up for long discussions when I dig excitedly into a new concept, thank you for always being by my side: Kane Mortlock, Tristan Mortlock, Khalid Razak, Sander Sikkema, Sandy Martin, Charlie Malone, Simon Raby, David J Williams, Owen Strode, Scott Gordan, Martin Gagnon, Jaynie Macdonald, and Peter Zoccali.

To David Hayes for his brilliant support throughout the editing and book creation process. He makes me a better writer, storyteller, and thinker. He has always found ways to help me express my thoughts more impactfully. Also, thanks to my agent, Hilary McMahon, and publisher Jennifer Smith, who both believed in my project.

I would also like to thank my mentors, who have shaped the type of leader and person I've tried to be. Howard Blight, who, through numerous business ventures, books, and other transformational activities, has been a source of inspiration, and Scott Garvey, who had faith in bringing me to Canada and unleashing my potential. Also, I want to thank Jay Hutchison, who is my biggest champion professionally at EY and never afraid to tell me what I need to hear, rather than what I want to hear. I have deep gratitude for and appreciation of all three of them.

Finally, a heartfelt thank you to my partner in crime, the love of my life, my best friend and wife, Elisabeth, and my amazing daughters Penelope and Olivianne, whose unconditional love and support allow me to follow my dreams and to be who I am. Thank you.

FIGURE SOURCES

Figure 4: "The Voice of the Customer Meets the Voice of the Expert", by Brian Ward, Affinity Consulting & Training.

Figure 8: "Linking the Balanced Scorecard to Strategy," by Robert S. Kaplan and David P. Norton, California Management Review 39 (1). https://digicoll.lib.berkeley.edu/record/284724/files/991056723509706532_C059236038_39_1.pdf

Figure 9: "Portfolio Management in Oil and Gas—Building and Preserving Optionality," EY. https://www.slideshare.net/slideshow/15011380419-portfolio-management-in-oil-and-gas-tl-final/50221590.

Figure 10: "Ahead of the Curve—Tailoring Integration Strategies to Secure Deal Value," by Erika Schraner and Steven Sellin, Mergers & Aquisitions (May 2021).

Figure 13: "What is Talent Management?" by Josh Bersin, Joshbersin.com, (July 16, 2007).

Figure 17: "A New Energy World: Why Costs Matter in an Era of Resource Abundance," by Lance Mortlock, Barry Munro, and Kent Kaufield, EY Canadian Energy Survey.

NOTES

INTRODUCTION

1.   B. Schroeder (2024). "The Evolution of Business Strategy (1960–1970)." *No Ordinary Strategy*. https://www.bcrschroeder.com/p/evolution-strategy-1960 -70?s=r.

2.   Wikibooks (2019). "Business Strategy/History of Business Management until the 1970s." https://en.wikibooks.org/wiki/Business_Strategy/History _of_Business_Management_until_the_1970s.

3.   M. Koizumi (2017). "Management Theories in the 1980s." In *Inherent Strategies in Library Management*. Elsevier. https://ebrary.net/27289 /management/management_theories_1980s.

4.   J. Kraaijenbrink (September 2019). "20 Reasons Why Strategy Execution Fails." *Forbes*. https://www.forbes.com/sites/jeroenkraaijenbrink/2019/09 /10/20-reasons-why-strategy-execution-fails/?sh=2c3729931ebe.

5.   L. Mortlock and C. Palmer (May 2023). "What Is Strategy, and Why Is It So Important?" *CEOWORLD Magazine*. https://ceoworld.biz/2023/05/18 /what-is-strategy-and-why-is-it-so-important/.

6.   G. L. Neilson et al. (2008). "The Secrets to Successful Strategy Execution." *Harvard Business Review* 86(6). https://hbr.org/2008/06/the-secrets-to -successful-strategy-execution.

7. M. Seidler et al. (June 2022). "How to Make Strategic Trade-Offs." *Harvard Business Review*. https://hbr.org/2022/06/how-to-make-strategic -trade-offs.

8. M. Hay and P. Williamson (1997). "Good Strategy: The View From Below." *Long Range Planning* 30(5): 651–664. https://www.sciencedirect.com/science /article/abs/pii/S0024630197000538.

9. L. Mortlock (2018). "The DNA of the Chief Strategy Officer." Ernst & Young. https://assets.ey.com/content/dam/ey-sites/ey-com/en_ca/topics /performance-improvement/ey-dna-of-the-chief-strategy-officer.pdf.

CHAPTER 1

10. Bureau of Transportation Statistics (2023). "Full Year 2022 U.S. Airline Traffic Data." https://www.bts.gov/newsroom/full-year-2022-us-airline -traffic-data#:~:text=U.S.%20airlines%20carried%20194%20million,and %20388%20million%20in%202020.

11. Statista (2023). "Digitalization of the Travel Industry—Statistics & Facts." https://www.statista.com/topics/7589/digitalization-of-the-travel-industry /#topicOverview.

12. Airlines (November 2018). "Passenger Numbers to Hit 8.2bn by 2037— IATA Report." https://airlines.iata.org/2018/11/26/passenger-numbers-hit -82bn-2037-iata-report.

13. Teachthought (August 2020). "3 Modes of Thinking: Lateral, Divergent & Convergent Thought." https://www.teachthought.com/critical-thinking /3-modes-of-thought-divergent-convergent-thinking/.

14. The Business Development Bank of Canada. "What Is Strategic Planning?" https://www.bdc.ca/en/articles-tools/business-strategy-planning/define -strategy/strategic-planning-demystified.

15. C. Cote (October 2020). "Why Is Strategic Planning Important?" *Business Insights*. https://online.hbs.edu/blog/post/why-is-strategic-planning -important.

16. Gartner. "Build a Better Strategic Plan for Your Function." https://www .gartner.com/smarterwithgartner/9-steps-successful-functional-strategic -planning

17. T. Alonso (November 2022). "How Starbucks Became Everyone's Cup of Coffee." *Strategy Factory.* https://www.cascade.app/studies/how-starbucks -became-everyones-cup-of-coffee.

18. C. Clifford (December 2016). "13 Inspiring Quotes on Leadership and Success from Starbucks CEO Howard Schultz." *CNBC makeit.* https://www.cnbc.com /2016/12/02/13-inspiring-quotes-on-leadership-and-success-from-starbucks -ceo-howard-schultz.html.

19. Starbucks Corporation (May 2024). https://stockanalysis.com/stocks/sbux /revenue/.

20. P. Jarzabkowski and J. Balogun (2009). "The Practice and Process of Delivering Integration Through Strategic Planning." *Journal of Management Studies* 46(8): 1255–1288. https://onlinelibrary.wiley.com/doi/abs/10.1111 /j.1467-6486.2009.00853.x.

21. L. Mortlock (2022). "6 Things I Learned from a Former CIA Director About Success in a Volatile Environment." *Chief Executive.* https:// chiefexecutive.net/6-things-i-learned-from-a-former-cia-director-about -success-in-a-volatile-environment/.

22. J. Vilà and J. I. Canales (2008). "Can Strategic Planning Make the Strategy More Relevant and Build Commitment Over Time? The Case of RACC." *Long Range Planning* 41(3): 273–290. https://www.sciencedirect.com /science/article/abs/pii/S0024630108000253.

23. C. Damon. "13 Notorious Examples of Strategic Planning Failure." *Achieveit.* https://www.achieveit.com/resources/blog/13-notorious-examples-of -strategic-planning-failure/.

24. K. Evens et al. "Warby Parker—Strategy Plans Book." https://static1 .squarespace.com/static/5c0eb2d975f9ee15dd9ed883/t/5d36064b2309e900 01f8ea1c/1563821644626/official-warby-parker-document.pdf.

25. B. Collins (October 2022). "Warby Parker, Once Online-Only Eyeglasses Retailer, Plans Hundreds of More Stores." CNBC. https://www.cnbc.com /2022/10/21/warby-parker-once-online-only-eyewear-sees-hundreds-of-more -stores.html.

26. R. L. Martin (January–February 2014). "The Big Lie of Strategic Planning." *Harvard Business Review.* https://hbr.org/2014/01/the-big-lie-of-strategic -planning.

27. M. J. Eppler and K. W. Platts (2009). "Visual Strategizing: The Systematic

Use of Visualization in the Strategic-Planning Process." *Long Range Planning* 42(1): 42–74. https://www.sciencedirect.com/science/article/abs/pii/S0024630108001180.

28. C. Lynch. "3 Epic Strategy Failures and How to Combat Them." *Chief Executive.* https://chiefexecutive.net/3-epic-strategic-failures-combat/.

29. L. Mortlock and M. Zelaya (April 2023). "New CEO Imperative Calls for Bolder Strategic Plans." *Chief Executive.* https://chiefexecutive.net/new-ceo-imperative-calls-for-bolder-strategic-plans/.

30. C. Dibrell et al. (2014). "Linking the Formal Strategic Planning Process, Planning Flexibility, and Innovativeness to Firm Performance." *Journal of Business Research* 67(9): 2000–2007. https://www.sciencedirect.com/science/article/abs/pii/S0148296313003573.

31. J. Brown (Sept 2006). *The Imperfect Board Member: Discovering the Seven Disciplines of Governance Excellence.* Jossey-Bass.

32. J. M. Bryson (1988). "A Strategic Planning Process for Public and Non-Profit Organizations." *Long Range Planning* 21(1): 73–81. https://www.sciencedirect.com/science/article/abs/pii/0024630188900611.

CHAPTER 2

33. *Global Times* (September 2021). "China Remains the World's Largest Manufacturing Power: MIIT." https://www.globaltimes.cn/page/202109/1234103.shtml?id=11.

34. D. Dahlhoff (January 2015). "Why Target's Canadian Expansion Failed." *Harvard Business Review.* https://hbr.org/2015/01/why-targets-canadian-expansion-failed.

35. S. Ho (January 2015). "In Surprise Move, Target Exits Canada and Takes $5.4 Billion Loss." Reuters. https://www.reuters.com/article/idUSKBN0KO1HQ/.

36. A. Faridani (November 2021). "Why Businesses Can't Afford to Skip Market Research." *Forbes.* https://www.forbes.com/sites/forbesbusinessdevelopmentcouncil/2021/11/04/why-businesses-cant-afford-to-skip-market-research/?sh=7da7175145b1.

37. F. Duarte (April 2023). "Amount of Data Created Daily (2023)." *Exploding Topics.* https://explodingtopics.com/blog/data-generated-per-day.

38. T. Wood (August 2020). "Natural Language Processing Is Changing These 5 Industries." Fast Data Science. https://fastdatascience.com/natural-language-processing-is-changing-these-5-industries/.

39. LinkedIn. "What Are the Best NLP Tools for Sentiment Analysis in Online Reputation Management?" https://www.linkedin.com/advice/0/what-best-nlp-tools-sentiment-analysis-online.

40. Traqline (February 2022). "Top 5 Examples of Market Research Failures." https://www.traqline.com/newsroom/blog/top-5-examples-market-research-failure/.

41. R. Ferdman (October 2015). "How Coca-Cola Has Tricked Everyone Into Drinking So Much of It." The Washington Post. https://www.washingtonpost.com/news/wonk/wp/2015/10/05/how-coca-cola-gets-its-way/.

42. S. Smith (January 2013). "Market Research Example: How Coca-Cola Lost Millions with This Mistake." Qualtrics. https://www.qualtrics.com/blog/coca-cola-market-research/.

43. Traqline (February 2022). "Top 5 Examples of Market Research Failures." https://www.traqline.com/newsroom/blog/top-5-examples-market-research-failure/.

44. G. Collins (April 1995). "Company News; Ten Years Later, Coca-Cola Laughs at 'New Coke.'" The New York Times. https://www.nytimes.com/1995/04/11/business/company-news-ten-years-later-coca-cola-laughs-at-new-coke.html.

45. World Uncertainty Index. "World Uncertainty Index (WUI): Global." https://worlduncertaintyindex.com/.

46. CognitiveScale. "Scalable Enterprise AI." https://www.cognitivescale.com/.

47. U. Lichtenthaler et al. (2010). "Not-Sold-Here: How Attitudes Influence External Knowledge Exploitation." Organization Science 21(5): 1054–1071. https://pubsonline.informs.org/doi/abs/10.1287/orsc.1090.0499.

CHAPTER 3

48. E. Baker (2006). "It's All About ME (Managing Expectations)!" Project Management Institute. https://www.pmi.org/learning/library/managing-stakeholder-expectations-proactively-define-7984.

49. G. Walters and P. Kitchin (October 2009). "Stakeholder Management and Sport Facilities: A Case Study of the Emirates Stadium." Birkbeck University of London. http://sramedia.s3.amazonaws.com/media/documents /Stakeholder%20Management%20and%20Sport%20Facilties(1).pdf.

50. Arsenal in the Community (May 2017). https://www.arsenal.com/community /arsenal-for-everyone/arsenal-in-the-community.

51. Arsenal in the Community's Big Impact (September 2023). https://www .arsenal.com/community/news/impact-survey.

52. Welcome to Arsenal in the Community. https://www.arsenal.com/community /welcome-arsenal-community.

53. L. Mortlock (December 2023). "Racing to Stay Competitive in 2024: Business Resilience." *CEOWORLD Magazine.* https://ceoworld.biz/2023/12/27 /racing-to-stay-competitive-in-2024-business-resilience/#:~:text=The%20 speed%20of%20change%20will,or%20even%20thrive%20in%202024.

54. D. Iacobucci et al. (1995). "Distinguishing Service Quality and Customer Satisfaction: The Voice of the Consumer." *Journal of Consumer Psychology* 4(3): 277–303. https://myscp.onlinelibrary.wiley.com/doi/abs/10.1207/s15327663 jcp0403_04.

55. S. Hyken (July 2018). "Customer Experience Is The New Brand." *Forbes.* https://www.forbes.com/sites/shephyken/2018/07/15/customer-experience -is-the-new-brand/?sh=377d140a7f52.

56. R. Cooper (July 2018). "The Drivers of Success in New-Product Development." *Industrial Marketing Management* 76: 36–47. https://www.sciencedirect.com /science/article/abs/pii/S0019850118300476.

57. A. Griffin and J. R. Hauser (1993). "The Voice of the Customer." *Marketing Science* 12(1): 1–27. https://pubsonline.informs.org/doi/abs/10.1287/mksc .12.1.1.

58. A. Ulwick (August 2005). *What Customers Want: Using Outcome-Driven Innovation to Create Breakthrough Products and Services.* McGraw Hill. Review available: https://www.pdma.org/page/review_what_customer.

59. A. Ulwick (January 2002). "Turn Customer Input into Innovation." *Harvard Business Review.* https://hbr.org/2002/01/turn-customer-input -into-innovation.

60. Tractivity. "Obtaining 100% Response Rate From Stakeholders." https:// www.tractivity.co.uk/blog/edf-energy-case-study.

61. International Atomic Energy Agency. "Stakeholder Engagement: Nuclear Energy." https://www.iaea.org/topics/stakeholder-engagement.

62. S. Ramaswamy and N. DeClerck (2018). "Customer Perception Analysis Using Deep Learning and NLP." *Procedia Computer Science* 140: 170–178. https://www.sciencedirect.com/science/article/pii/S1877050918319999.

63. Expert Panel (March 2023). "16 Ideas to Keep CEOs and Executives Connected to Their Direct Reports." *Forbes.* https://www.forbes.com/sites/forbeshumanresourcescouncil/2023/03/15/16-ideas-to-keep-ceos-and-executives-connected-to-their-direct-reports/?sh=67d244d25a7f.

64. TC Energy (November 2019). "Engaging with our Stakeholders." https://www.tcenergy.com/siteassets/pdfs/commitment/environment/tc-engaging-with-our-stakeholders-fact-sheet.pdf.

65. C. Arthur (June 2010). "Steve Jobs Solves iPhone 4 Reception Problems: 'Don't Hold it that Way'" *The Guardian.* https://www.theguardian.com/technology/blog/2010/jun/25/iphone-reception-problems-solved.

66. C. Cheng (June 2022). "Project Management: A Case Study Analysis of Burj Khalifa." https://www.researchgate.net/publication/362684634_Project_Management_A_Case_Study_Analysis_of_Burj_Khalifa.

67. A. Yadav (January 2019). "Using AI to Get Closer to Your Customer." *Forbes.* https://www.forbes.com/sites/forbestechcouncil/2019/01/29/using-ai-to-get-closer-to-your-customer/?sh=5c2644196477.

CHAPTER 4

68. IBIS World (September 2023). "Caterers in the US—Number of Businesses 2004–2029." https://www.ibisworld.com/industry-statistics/number-of-businesses/caterers-united-states/.

69. Royal Caribbean International. "Royal Caribbean App." https://www.royalcaribbean.com/booked/royal-app.

70. Y. Atsom (June 2017). "To Develop a Winning Strategy, Know Who You Are Fighting." *Strategy and Corporate Finance Blog.* https://www.mckinsey.com/capabilities/strategy-and-corporate-finance/our-insights/the-strategy-and-corporate-finance-blog/to-develop-a-winning-strategy-know-who-you-are-fighting.

71. EduBirdie. "Case Study of Gap: Current Market and Competitive Analysis." https://edubirdie.com/examples/case-study-of-gap-current-market-and -competitive-analysis/.

72. W. Loeb (March 2024). "The Gap Reports Positive Earnings and a Great Outlook." *Forbes.* https://www.forbes.com/sites/walterloeb/2024/03/11 /the-gap-reports-positive-earnings-and-a-great-outlook/?sh=6c19d3a2556e.

73. C. Tompkins (September 2021). "3 Reasons Why a Competitive Analysis Is Essential." *Forbes.* https://www.forbes.com/sites/forbesagencycouncil/2021 /09/03/3-reasons-why-a-competitive-analysis-is-essential/?sh=4e3acaca57 be.

74. Wikipedia. (February 2024). "E. Jerome McCarthy." https://en.wikipedia .org/wiki/E._Jerome_McCarthy.

75. M. Kazim "How to Conduct a Competitive Analysis." BDC. https://www .bdc.ca/en/articles-tools/marketing-sales-export/marketing/how-evaluate -competition.

76. D. Sher (August 2023). "Unleashing the Power of Data: A Statistical Analysis of Nike's Rise to the Top of the Sporting Industry." Investing.com. https://www.investing.com/academy/statistics/nike-facts/.

77. J. Hughes. "Nike Competitors Analysis." *Business Chronicler.* https:// businesschronicler.com/competitors/nike-competitors-analysis/.

78. W. Loeb (October 2021). "Nike's New High-Tech Lab Leads All Sports Developments." *Forbes.* https://www.forbes.com/sites/walterloeb/2021/10 /07/nikes-new-high-tech-lab-leads-all-sports-development/?sh=508095 af5017.

79. L. Thomas (June 2019). "How Nike became No. 1. and How it Plans to Stay There." CNBC. https://www.cnbc.com/2019/06/21/how-nike-became-no -1-and-how-it-plans-to-stay-there.html.

80. B. Fox (July 2016). "Phil Knight Cleared Hurdles to Make Nike a Merchandising Champion." *Investor's Business Daily.* https://www.investors .com/news/management/leaders-and-success/phil-knight-cleared-hurdles -to-make-nike-a-merchandising-champion/.

81. D. Sher (April 2024). "A Statistical Analysis of Nike's Rise to the Top of the Sporting Industry." Investing.com. https://www.investing.com/academy /statistics/nike-facts/#:~:text=In%20fiscal%20year%202023%2C%20Nike's ,a%2010%25%20increase%20in%20revenue.

82. M. Kaput (December 2021). "AI for Competitive Intelligence: What You

Need to Know." Marketing Artificial Intelligence Institute. https://www
.marketingaiinstitute.com/blog/ai-for-competitive-intelligence.

83. N. Sommerford and C. Demichel. "Biopharmaceutical Company Gains
a Comprehensive Competitive Analysis for Their Oncology Products."
IQVIA. https://www.iqvia.com/-/media/iqvia/pdfs/library/case-studies
/asset-intelligence-case-study-042022.pdf.

84. Trevor Carlson (October 2023). "10 Fast Food Restaurants with the Best
Value Menus." Daily Meal. https://www.thedailymeal.com/1408638/fast
-food-restaurants-best-value-menus/.

85. W. Deibel (May 2029). "How to Evaluate a Potential Business Acquisition."
Forbes. https://www.forbes.com/sites/theyec/2019/05/22/how-to-evaluate
-a-potential-business-acquisition/?sh=7e94773d5294.

86. L. Mortlock (2021). "Organizational Learning—The Influencing Dynamics
of Scenario Planning." *Tanveer Naseer Leadership.* https://tanveernaseer
.com/organizational-learning-scenario-planning-lance-mortlock/.

87. E. J. Zajac and M. H. Bazerman (1991). "Blind Spots in Industry and
Competitor Analysis: Implications of Interfirm (Mis) Perceptions for
Strategic Decisions." *Academy of Management Review* 16(1): 37–56. https://
journals.aom.org/doi/abs/10.5465/AMR.1991.4278990.

CHAPTER 5

88. A. Sankaran (July 2019). "Decarbonization, Digitization and Decentralization
Are Accelerating the Countdown to a New Energy World Faster than
Expected." Ernst & Young. https://www.ey.com/en_hu/news/2019/07
/decarbonization-digitization-and-decentralization-are-accelerating-the
-countdown-to-a-new-energy-world-faster-than-expected.

89. Ernst & Young. "An Energy Company's Transformation for the 21st-Century
Customer." https://www.ey.com/en_my/consulting/an-energy-companys
-transformation-for-the-21st-century-customer#:~:text=Energy%20customers
%20are%20demanding%20new,to%20a%20recent%20EY%20survey.

90. L. Mortlock (December 2021). "Scenario Planning vs. Forecasting: 6
Questions to Ask to Prepare for a Post-Pandemic Future." *Leading Blog.*
https://www.leadershipnow.com/leadingblog/2021/05/scenario_planning
_vs_forecasti.html.

91.   P. R. Walsh (2005). "Dealing With the Uncertainties of Environmental Change by Adding Scenario Planning to the Strategy Reformulation Equation." *Management Decision* 43 (1): 113–122. https://www.emerald.com /insight/content/doi/10.1108/00251740510572524/full/html.

92.   T. J. Chermack and L. M. Coons (2015). "Scenario Planning: Pierre Wack's Hidden Messages." *Futures* 73: 187–193. https://www.sciencedirect.com /science/article/pii/S001632871530015X.

93.   L. Mortlock (December 2022). "The Dynamics Behind Using Scenario Planning Enabling Innovation and Organizational Learning." University of Calgary. https://prism.ucalgary.ca/server/api/core/bitstreams/66af6b5b -d819-42c3-bab0-22c98aa98596/content.

94.   L. Mortlock (April 2021). "Disaster Proof—Scenario Planning for a Post Pandemic Future." Barlow Books.

95.   J. Lornic (October 2019). "What Will the Accounting Profession Look Like in 2030?" *Chartered Professional Accountants Canada.* https://dailydividends .cpaalberta.ca/what-will-the-accounting-profession-look-like-in-2030/.

96.   Wikipedia (June 2023). "Business Model Canvas." https://en.wikipedia.org /wiki/Business_Model_Canvas.

97.   J. J. Oliver and E. Parrett (2018). "Managing Future Uncertainty: Reevaluating the Role of Scenario Planning." *Business Horizons* 61(2): 339–352. https://www .sciencedirect.com/science/article/pii/S0007681317301684.

98.   S. Taylor (May 2020). "Air Transport 2035: Four Possible Post-COVID-19 Scenarios for Aviation." APEX. https://apex.aero/articles/air-transport -2035-webinar-results/.

99.   C. Schneider (March 2023). "American Express CFO: Plan on Winning the Recovery." *The Wall Street Journal.* https://deloitte.wsj.com/articles/american -express-cfo-plan-on-winning-the-recovery-deb05685.

CHAPTER 6

100.   Mordor Intelligence. "North America Construction Market Size & Share Analysis—Growth Trends & Forecasts (2024–2029)." https://www .mordorintelligence.com/industry-reports/north-america-construction -market.

101. C. Zott et al. (2011). "The Business Model: Recent Developments and Future Research." *Journal of Management* 37(4): 1019–1042. https://journals.sagepub .com/doi/abs/10.1177/0149206311406265.

102. A. Bollard et al. (March 2017). "The Next-Generation Operating Model for the Digital World." McKinsey & Company. https://www.mckinsey.com /capabilities/mckinsey-digital/our-insights/the-next-generation-operating -model-for-the-digital-world.

103. J. vom Brocke et al. (2021). "A Five-Level Framework for Research on Process Mining." *Business Information Systems Engineering* 63: 483–490. https://link.springer.com/article/10.1007/s12599-021-00718-8.

104. M. de Reuver et al. (2013). "Business Model Road Mapping: A Practical Approach from an Existing to a Desired Business Model." *International Journal of Innovation Management* 17(01). https://www.worldscientific .com/doi/abs/10.1142/S1363919613400069.

105. D. Ibarra et al. (2018). "Business Model Innovation Through Industry 4.0: A Review." *Procedia Manufacturing* 22: 4-10. https://www.sciencedirect.com /science/article/pii/S2351978918302968.

106. M. Blenko and J. Root (April 2015). "Design Principles for a Robust Operating Model." Bain & Company. https://www.bain.com/insights/design -principles-for-a-robust-operating-model/.

107. A. Twin (May 2023). "Key Performance Indicator (KPI): Definition, Types, and Examples." *Investopedia*. https://www.investopedia.com/terms/k/kpi .asp.

108. S. van Kuiken (October 2022). "Tech at the Edge: Trends Reshaping the Future of IT and Business." McKinsey & Company. https://www.mckinsey .com/capabilities/mckinsey-digital/our-insights/tech-at-the-edge-trends -reshaping-the-future-of-it-and-business.

109. M. Reeves et al. (January 2020). "Taming Complexity." *Harvard Business Review*. https://hbr.org/2020/01/taming-complexity.

110. N. Furr et al. (October 2021). "Should Your Global Firm Centralize Digital Operations?" *Harvard Business Review*. https://hbr.org/2021/10/should-your -global-firm-centralize-digital-operations.

111. Servicenow. "Building a Sustainable Flexible Working Model." https://www .servicenow.com/customers/standard-chartered-bank.html.

CHAPTER 7

112.　C. Kostandi (March 2022). "Interactive Map: Crude Oil Pipelines and Refineries of the U.S. and Canada." Elements. https://elements.visualcapitalist.com/mapped-crude-oil-pipelines-and-refineries-of-the-u-s-and-canada/.

113.　C. Vitters and A. Fratta (2017). "Integrating Enterprise Risk Management (ERM) with strategic planning." Deloitte. https://www2.deloitte.com/content/dam/Deloitte/us/Documents/public-sector/us-fed-integrating-erm-with-strategic-planning.pdf.

114.　A. Hines (2012). "Enterprise Risk Management." In *The Definitive Handbook of Business Continuity and Management*, 3rd ed. John Wiley & Sons. https://onlinelibrary.wiley.com/doi/abs/10.1002/9781119205883.ch1.

115.　COSO. "Compliance Risk Management: Applying the COSO Framework." https://www.wlrk.com/docs/Compliance-Risk-Management-Applying-the-COSO-ERM-Framework_(1).pdf.

116.　J. L. West (October 2002). "Integrating Risk Analysis and Prioritization: A Practitioner's Tool." Project Management Institute. https://www.pmi.org/learning/library/integrating-risk-analysis-prioritization-practitioner-tool-8456.

117.　L. Mortlock et al. (September 2021). "Five Essential Strategy Questions Boards Should Be Asking." Harvard Law School Forum on Corporate Performance. https://corpgov.law.harvard.edu/2021/09/26/five-essential-strategy-questions-boards-should-be-asking/.

118.　B. W. Nocco and R. M. Stulz (2006). "Enterprise Risk Management: Theory and Practice." *Journal of Applied Corporate Finance* 18(4): 8–20. https://onlinelibrary.wiley.com/doi/abs/10.1111/j.1745-6622.2006.00106.x.

119.　Nationwide. "2023 Financial Highlights." https://www.nationwide.com/business/insurance/management-liability-specialty/financial/.

120.　Quantivate (April 2019). "Why GRC Matters: 50 Risk & Compliance Statistics." https://quantivate.com/grc-risk-compliance-statistics/.

121.　P. Tehrani (November 2020). "Ongoing Risk Management Failures Bring Major Fines." *Bloomberg Law.* https://news.bloomberglaw.com/bloomberg-law-analysis/analysis-ongoing-risk-management-failures-bring-major-fines.

122.　J. Guerin (October 2023). "Mars, Incorporated Receives Inaugural Family of Brands Recognition in Fast Company's Third Annual List of Brands That Matter." PR Newswire. https://www.prnewswire.com/news-releases/mars

-incorporated-receives-inaugural-family-of-brands-recognition-in-fast
-companys-third-annual-list-of-brands-that-matter-301946347.html#:~:text
=This%20year%2C%20for%20the%20first,BluePearl%E2%84%A2%20and
%20VCA%E2%84%A2.

123. A. Marker (April 2021). "Enterprise Risk Management Case Studies: Heroes
and Zeros." Smartsheet. https://www.smartsheet.com/content/enterprise
-risk-management-examples.

124. J. Walsh. "Business Case Study: Enterprise Risk Management at Toyota."
Study.com. https://study.com/academy/lesson/business-case-study-enterprise
-risk-management-at-toyota.html.

125. Statista (August 2023). "Global Automotive Market Share in 2022, By Brand."
https://www.statista.com/statistics/316786/global-market-share-of-the
-leading-automakers/#:~:text=In%202022%2C%20the%20ranking%20
of,2020%20incumbent%2C%20the%20Volkswagen%20Group.

126. S. Slezak (March 2014). "GM's Risk Management Failures Provide Lessons for
Other Firms." *Global Risk Insights.* https://globalriskinsights.com/2014/03
/gms-risk-management-failures-provide-example-for-other-firms/.

127. M. S. Beasley et al. (2005). "Enterprise Risk Management: An Empirical
Analysis of Factors Associated with the Extent of Implementation." *Journal of
Accounting and Public Policy* 24(6): 521–531. https://www.sciencedirect.com
/science/article/pii/S0278425405000566.

CHAPTER 8

128. J. Drucker (December 2018). "You Are What You Measure." *Forbes.* https://
www.forbes.com/sites/theyec/2018/12/04/you-are-what-you-measure/?sh
=3e5179f82075.

129. intel Retail Edge Program (November 2017). "Impacting Key Performance
Indicators." https://retailedge.intel.com/50/blogs/2017/11/17/Impacting
-Key-Performance-Indicators.

130. *Engineering Blog* (May 2022). "STOMP Out Bad Metrics." https://eng.snap
.com/stomp-out-bad-metrics.

131. C. Kopprasch (November 2012). "Measuring Customer Happiness at
Buffer: October 2012." *Buffer.* https://buffer.com/resources/measuring
-buffer-happiness-october-2012/.

132. Customer Happiness Index (August 2021). https://data.buffer.com/2021 /02/08/customer-happiness-index/.

133. E. Subin (December 2022). "Cautionary Tales: When Tracking KPIs Goes Wrong." *Spider Strategies.* https://www.spiderstrategies.com/blog/kpis-gone -wrong/.

134. R. S. Kaplan and D. P. Norton (September–October 1993). "Putting the Balanced Scorecard to Work." *Harvard Business Review.* https://hbr.org /1993/09/putting-the-balanced-scorecard-to-work.

135. R. S. Kaplan and D. P. Norton (January–February 1992). "The balanced scorecard: measures that drive performance." *Harvard Business Review.* http://home.bi.no/fgl99011/bok2302/MB92.pdf.

136. J. Stables (March 2022). "Fitbit Stress Score Explained: How Stress Tracking and Management Works." Wareable. https://www.wareable.com/fitbit/fitbit -brings-stress-score-to-all-devices-8394.

137. EMBA Pro. "Fitbit Balanced Scorecard Analysis & Solution/ MBA Resources." https://embapro.com/frontpage/balancescorecardanalysis/8266-fitbit-wellness.

138. Statista. (January 2024). "Fitbit—Statistics & Facts." https://www.statista .com/topics/2595/fitbit/#topicOverview.

139. A. Muller et al. (2005). "Metrics for Innovation: Guidelines for Developing a Customized Suite of Innovation Metrics." *Strategy & Leadership* 33(1): 37–45. https://www.emerald.com/insight/content/doi/10.1108/10878570510572590 /full/html.

CHAPTER 9

140. *The New York Times* (August 2020). "Marathon Is Selling Speedway Gas Stations to 7-Eleven's Parent for $21 Billion." https://www.nytimes.com/2020 /08/02/business/marathon-petroleum-speedway-7-11.html.

141. J. Guthrie (February 2023). "How Elliott Became the McDonald's of Activism." *Financial Times.* https://www.ft.com/content/704e2ac3-74ad -41ef-88c1-ddebebe92cbf.

142. L. Baker and B. Ford (January 2023). "Activist Elliott Management Takes Stake in Salesforce." *BNN Bloomberg.* https://www.bnnbloomberg.ca /activist-elliott-management-takes-stake-in-salesforce-1.1873541.

143. P. Strebel and A. V. Ohlsson (January 2006). "The Art of Making Smart Big Moves." *MIT Sloan Management Review*. https://sloanreview.mit.edu/article/the-art-of-making-smart-big-moves/.

144. J. I. Howell and P. A. Tyler (2001). "Using Portfolio Analysis to Develop Corporate Strategy." SPE Hydrocarbon Economics and Evaluation Symposium, OnePetro. https://onepetro.org/SPEHEES/proceedings-abstract/01HEES/All-01HEES/133224.

145. L. Mortlock (October 2023). "No One-Size-Fits-All in Portfolio Management." *Chief Executive*. https://chiefexecutive.net/no-one-size-fits-all-in-portfolio-management/.

146. T. Hansen (April 2023). "Patagonia Shows How Turning a Profit Doesn't Have to Cost the Earth." McKinsey & Company. https://www.mckinsey.com/industries/agriculture/our-insights/patagonia-shows-how-turning-a-profit-doesnt-have-to-cost-the-earth.

147. Strategyzer. "Patagonia Business Model." https://www.strategyzer.com/library/patagonia-business-model.

148. B. J. Bloch (November 2022). "The 4 Key Elements of a Well-Managed Portfolio." *Investopedia*. https://www.investopedia.com/articles/basics/10/4-elements-investment-management.asp.

149. B. Hedley (1977). "Strategy and the 'Business Portfolio.'" *Long Range Planning* 10(1): 9–15. https://www.sciencedirect.com/science/article/pii/0024630177900425.

150. CFA Institute (2023). "Case Study in Portfolio Management: Institutional." https://www.cfainstitute.org/en/membership/professional-development/refresher-readings/case-study-portfolio-management-institutional.

151. F. T. Ionescu (2011). "Boston Consulting Group II–A Business Portfolio Analysis Matrix." *International Journal of Economic Practices and Theories* 1(2): 65–70. https://citeseerx.ist.psu.edu/document?repid=rep1&type=pdf&doi=bc6237028a006c7bd7dbe0546d67d 8ebb7370cf8.

152. M. Reeves and S. Moose. "What Is the Growth Share Matrix?" Boston Consulting Group. https://www.bcg.com/about/overview/our-history/growth-share-matrix.

153. B. Kowitt (December 2017). "Unilever Is Launching a New 'Natural' Line of Shampoos and Soaps to Attract Millennials." *Fortune*. https://fortune.com/2017/12/13/unilever-new-brand-love-beauty-and-planet/.

CHAPTER 10

154. E. B. Picaro (March 2021). "10 Reasons Why Facebook has Been So Successful." Pocket-lint. https://www.pocket-lint.com/apps/news/facebook/126998-10 -reasons-why-facebook-has-lasted/.

155. A. L. Deutsch (March 2022). "WhatsApp: The Best Meta Purchase Ever?" *Investopedia.* https://www.investopedia.com/articles/investing/032515 /whatsapp-best-facebook-purchase-ever.asp.

156. C. Warzel and R. Mac (December 2018). "These Confidential Charts Show Why Facebook Bought WhatsApp." *Buzzfeed News.* https://www .buzzfeednews.com/article/charliewarzel/why-facebook-bought-whatsapp.

157. A. Covert (February 2014). "Facebook Buys WhatsApp for $19 Billion." *CNN Business.* https://money.cnn.com/2014/02/19/technology/social /facebook-whatsapp/index.html.

158. Tech Desk (May 2022). "WhatsApp Has Changed Drastically Since 2014 Facebook Acquisition, Says Former Business Head." News 18. https://www .news18.com/news/tech/whatsapp-has-changed-drastically-since-2014 -facebook-acquisition-says-former-business-head-5115157.html.

159. CISCO. "Acquisitions." https://www.cisco.com/c/en/us/about/corporate -strategy-office/acquisitions.html.

160. H. Singh and C. A. Montgomery (1987). "Corporate Acquisition Strategies and Economic Performance." *Strategic Management Journal* 8(4): 377–386. https://onlinelibrary.wiley.com/doi/abs/10.1002/smj.4250080407.

161. CSP Global. "5 Biggest Mergers of All Time." https://online.csp.edu /resources/article/biggest-mergers/.

162. K. Patel. "Mergers and Acquisitions Examples: The Largest Company M&A Deals List." *DealRoom.* https://dealroom.net/blog/successful-acquisition -examples.

163. PWC. "Transformational M&A." https://www.pwc.com/us/en/services /consulting/deals/library/transformational-mergers-and-acquisitions .html.

164. R. Miller (October 2019). "Microsoft Acquires Mover to Help with Microsoft 365 Cloud Migration." *Techcrunch.* https://techcrunch.com/2019 /10/21/microsoft-acquires-mover-to-help-with-microsoft-365-cloud -migration/?guccounter=1.

165. M. Wohlsen (January 2014). "What Google Really Gets Out of Buying Nest for $3.2 Billion." *Wired*. https://www.wired.com/2014/01/googles -3-billion-nest-buy-finally-make-internet-things-real-us/.

166. K. Patel. "11 Powerful Acquisition Examples (And What We Learned from Them)." *DealRoom*. https://dealroom.net/blog/acquisition-examples.

167. The Strategy Story. "Divestment Strategies: Explained with examples and case study." https://thestrategystory.com/blog/divestment-strategies -explained-with-examples-and-case-study/.

168. S. Goel (October 2022). "Business, Growth & Acquisition Strategy of Salesforce." *The Strategy Story*. https://thestrategystory.com/2022/10/02 /business-growth-acquisition-strategy-salesforce/.

169. Morgan Stanley (October 2020) "Morgan Stanley Closes Acquisition of E*TRADE." https://www.morganstanley.com/press-releases/morgan -stanley-closes-acquisition-of-e-trade.

170. K. Patel (January 2024). "11 Powerful Acquisition Examples (And What We Learned from Them)." *DealRoom*. https://dealroom.net/blog/acquisition -examples.

171. Y. S. Peng and C. P. Fang (2010). "Acquisition Experience, Board Characteristics, and Acquisition Behavior." *Journal of Business Research* 63(5): 502–509. https:// www.sciencedirect.com/science/article/pii/S014829630900112X.

CHAPTER 11

172. T. Wright (April 2023). "The 7 Best Business Strategy Examples I've Ever Seen." *Cascade*. https://www.cascade.app/blog/the-5-best-business-strategies -ive-ever-seen.

173. D. Curry (May 2023). "Airbnb Revenue and Usage Statistics (2023)." *Business of Apps*. https://www.businessofapps.com/data/airbnb-statistics/.

174. N. Li (January 2021). "This Is Why McDonald's Is So Cheap." *Hypebeast*. https://hypebeast.com/2021/1/why-mcdonalds-so-cheap-video-info-profitable.

175. K. Shapiro (May 2020). "From CBD Soda to Street Style, Reccss Releases 'Realitywear' With Three Fresh Flavors." *Forbes*. https://www.forbes.com /sites/katieshapiro/2020/05/19/from-cbd-soda-to-street-style-recess -releases-realitywear-with-three-new-flavors/?sh=2e4867e45b50.

176. M. Gandara (September 2020). "These CBD-Infused Canned Drinks Are a Gift to Sparkling Water Lovers." *Food & Wine*. https://www.foodandwine.com/lifestyle/kitchen/recess-cbd-sparkling-water-review?utm_campaign=foodandwine_foodandwine&utm_content=evergreen&utm_medium=social&utm_source=twitter.com&utm_term=5f91022d64fdb2000172a9ba.

177. T. Wright (April 2023). "The 7 Best Business Strategy Examples I've Ever Seen." *Cascade*. https://www.cascade.app/blog/the-5-best-business-strategies-ive-ever-seen.

178. K. King et al. (October 2014). "When the Growing Gets Tough, the Tough Get Growing." Boston Consulting Group. https://www.bcg.com/publications/2014/corporate-strategy-when-growing-gets-tough.

179. P. Ego (July 2022). "Build, Buy, or Partner? A Systematic Literature Review on the Choice Between Alternative Modes of Growth." *Management Review Quarterly*. https://link.springer.com/article/10.1007/s11301-022-00280-x.

180. C. Damon. "13 Notorious Examples of Strategic Planning Failure." *Achieveit*. https://www.achieveit.com/resources/blog/13-notorious-examples-of-strategic-planning-failure/.

181. J. Adebisi (August 2021). "P&G Case Study: Strategic Choice Cascade in Practice." *Shortform*. https://www.shortform.com/blog/pg-case-study/.

182. *McKinsey Quarterly* (March 2008). "Enduring Ideas: The 7-S Framework." https://www.mckinsey.com/capabilities/strategy-and-corporate-finance/our-insights/enduring-ideas-the-7-s-framework.

183. S. Blount and P. Leinwand (August 2022). "Five Ways to Harness the Power of Purpose." *Strategy+Business*. https://www.strategy-business.com/article/Five-ways-to-harness-the-power-of-purpose.

CHAPTER 12

184. C. Mims (July 2016). "The Lesson of Yahoo: Don't Lose Your Focus." *The Wall Street Journal*. https://www.wsj.com/articles/the-lesson-of-yahoo-focus-1469651219.

185. R. Hollister and M. D. Watkins (September–October 2018). "Too Many Projects—How to Deal With Initiative Overload." *Harvard Business Review*. https://hbr.org/2018/09/too-many-projects.

186. P. J. Whalen (2007). "Strategic and Technology Planning on a Road Mapping Foundation." *Research-Technology Management* 50(3): 40–51. https://www .tandfonline.com/doi/abs/10.1080/08956308.2007.11657440.

187. A. Johnston et al. (October 2017). "Secrets of successful change implementation." McKinsey & Company. https://www.mckinsey.com /capabilities/operations/our-insights/secrets-of-successful-change -implementation.

188. A. Nieto-Rodriguez (December 2016). "How to Prioritize Your Company's Projects." *Harvard Business Review.* https://hbr.org/2016/12/how-to-prioritize -your-companys-projects.

189. Microsoft 365 Team (August 2019). "Project Roadmaps: Tips and Templates That Can Improve Your Skills." Microsoft.

190. G. T. Doran (1981). "There's a SMART Way to Write Management's Goals and Objectives." *Management Review* (70) 11: 35. https://community.mis .temple.edu/mis0855002fall2015/files/2015/10/S.M.A.R.T-Way-Management -Review.pdf

191. L. Mortlock (May 2024). "A Pathway to Elevated Performance With 'SMART+' Goal-Setting." *Take It Personel-ly.* https://takeitpersonelly.com /2024/05/09/a-pathway-to-elevated-performance-with-smart-goal-setting/.

192. T. Leveridge and S. Leith (August 2020). "The Coca-Cola Company Announces Strategic Steps to Reorganize its Business for Future Growth." Businesswire. https://www.businesswire.com/news/home/20200828005054 /en/The-Coca-Cola-Company-Announces-Strategic-Steps-to-Reorganize-its -Business-for-Future-Growth.

193. Stock Analysis (April 2024). "The Coca-Cola Company." https://stockanalysis .com/stocks/ko/revenue/.

194. Mailchimp. "Your Complete Guide to Product Roadmaps." https://mailchimp .com/resources/product-roadmaps/.

195. N. McAllister (April 2024). "The Best Email Marketing Software for 2024." *PC Magazine.* https://www.pcmag.com/picks/the-best-email-marketing -software.

196. S. Fister Gale (June 2016). "Making the Case—Business-Case Templates Give Project Teams the Direction They Need to Deliver the Right Project, Right on Time." Project Management Institute. https://www.pmi.org /learning/library/making-case- business- templates-planning-10113.

CHAPTER 13

197. The Blue Ocean Team. "Strategic Alignment—The Key to Successful Business Strategy." *Blue Ocean Strategy.* https://www.blueoceanstrategy.com /blog/strategic-alignment/#:~:text=Let%E2%80%99s%20look%20at%20 two%20alignment%20examples.%20The% 20first,an%20example%20of%20 strategic%20misalignment%20and%20its% 20consequences.

198. M. Iqbal (March 2024). "Disney Plus Revenue and Usage Statistics (2024)." *Business of Apps.* https://www.businessofapps.com/data/disney-plus-statistics/.

199. Expert Panel (December 2020). "12 Effective Strategies For Aligning Talent And Business Goals." *Forbes.* https://www.forbes.com/sites/forbeshumanre sourcescouncil/2020/12/07/12-effective-strategies-for-aligning-talent-and -business-goals/?sh=6ff703233a66.

200. The Predictive Index. "2024 Report—The State of Talent Optimization." https://www.predictiveindex.com/learn/talent-optimization/resources/ surveys-reports/the-state-of-talent-optimization/.

201. R. Smith (2008). "Harnessing Competencies, Capabilities and Resources." *Research-Technology Management* 51(5): 47–53. https://www.tandfonline .com/doi/abs/10.1080/08956308.2008.11657525.

202. rework with Google.com. "Guide: Create an Employee-to-Employee Learning Program." https://rework.withgoogle.com/guides/learning -development-employee-to-employee/steps/introduction/.

203. Job Assessment Experts. "Accenture Assessment Test Question and Answers Full Practice Guide 2023/24." https://www.graduatesfirst.com/accenture -assessment-tests.

204. Practice Aptitude Tests (2023). "Careers at Accenture Accenture Online Assessment Tests: Practice Questions." https://www.practiceaptitudetests .com/top-employer-profiles/accenture-assessments/.

205. Accenture. "Accenture Fact Sheet Q3 Fiscal 2024." https://newsroom .accenture.com/fact-sheet.

206. ThinkWise. "Using a Competency-Based Approach Linking Core Competencies to Your Business Strategy." https://www.thinkwiseinc.com /linking-competencies-to-business-strategy.html.

207. D. A. Ready et al. (January–February 2014). "Building a Game-Changing Talent Strategy." *Harvard Business Review.* https://hbr.org/2014/01/building -a-game-changing-talent-strategy.

208. Fever-Tree. "Fever-Tree at a Glance." https://fever-tree.com/en_GB/about-us/our-story.

209. Fever Tree. "Investors." https://fever-tree.com/en_GB/investors/reports-and-presentations.

CHAPTER 14

210. G. Dautovic (December 2022). "The 21 Most Important Startup Statistics for 2023." *Fortunly*. https://fortunly.com/statistics/startup-statistics/.

211. K. Hu and A. Chakroborti (March 2023). "Alphabet's CapitalG Appoints Insider Laela Sturdy as Managing Partner." Reuters. https://www.reuters.com/markets/us/alphabets-capitalg-appoints-insider-laela-sturdy-managing-partner-2023-03-01/.

212. CapitalG. "CapitalG is Alphabet's Independent Growth Fund." https://capitalg.com/.

213. Merlon Capital Partners. "A Case Study in Poor Capital Allocation: The Need for Greater Shareholder Protections." https://www.merloncapital.com.au/a-case-study-in-poor-capital-allocationthe-need-for-greater-shareholder-protections/.

214. M. Banholzer (May 2017). "Nine Practices for Better Capital-Investment Management." McKinsey & Company. https://www.mckinsey.com/capabilities/operations/our-insights/nine-practices-for-better-capital-investment-management.

215. P. Ordway (January 2019). "Case Studies of Companies That Do Capital Allocation Right." MOI Global. https://moiglobal.com/phil-ordway-201901/.

216. Macrotrends. "Texas Instruments Revenue 2010–2024 | TXN." https://www.macrotrends.net/stocks/charts/TXN/exas-instruments/revenue.

217. D. Cross (June 2023). "Can the U.S. Keep Up with Asia in the Chip Wars?" American Century Investments. https://www.americancentury.com/insights/can-the-us-keep-up-with-asia-in-the-chip-wars/.

218. N. Clairmont and G. Santayana (July 2013). "Those Who Do Not Study History Are Doomed to Repeat It." EO. https://www.parlia.com/a/learn-past-doomed-repeat.

219. M. J. Mauboussin and D. Callahan (December 2022). "Capital Allocation

Results, Analysis, and Assessment." *Counterpoint Global Insights.* https://www.morganstanley.com/im/publication/insights/articles/article_capitalallocation.pdf.

CHAPTER 15

220. R. Amit and C. Zott (2012). "Creating Value Through Business Model Innovation." *MIT Sloan Management Review.* https://sloanreview.mit.edu/article/creating-value-through-business-model-innovation/.

221. Castus (October 2021). "The Downfall of Sears: 5 Key Reasons Why the Retail Giant Went Under." https://www.castusglobal.com/insights/the-downfall-of-sears-5-key-reasons-why-the-retail-giant-went-under.

222. G. Cuofano (October 2022). "What Happened to Tower Records?" *FourWeekMBA.* https://fourweekmba.com/what-happened-to-tower-records/.

223. *Fortune* (2019). "Chipotle Mexican Grill." https://fortune.com/ranking/fortune500/2019/chipotle-mexican-grill/.

224. Valuer (December 2022). "Examples of Successful Companies Who Embraced New Business Models." https://www.valuer.ai/blog/examples-of-successful-companies-who-embraced-new-business-models.

225. W. Healy (February 2024). "Chipotle Is Up Over 120-Fold Since Its IPO. Here's Why It Will Probably Keep Making Investors Richer." *The Globe and Mail.* https://www.theglobeandmail.com/investing/markets/stocks/CMG-N/pressreleases/23990778/23990778/.

226. J. Revill (October 2021). "Nestle Revamps Geographic Structure, Makes New Board Appointments." Reuters. https://www.reuters.com/business/retail-consumer/nestle-revamps-geographic-structure-makes-new-board-appointments-2021-10-13/.

227. M. Blenko et al. (December 2014). "Winning Operating Models That Convert Strategy to Results." Bain & Company. https://www.bain.com/insights/winning-operating-models-that-convert-strategy-to-results/.

228. M. Treacy and F. Wiersema (1997). *The Discipline of Market Leaders: Choose Your Customers, Narrow Your Focus, Dominate Your Market.* Basic Books.

229. J. Treanor (February 2013). "Barclays' Antony Jenkins: The Man With Transformation on His Mind." *The Guardian.* https://www.theguardian.com /business/2013/feb/13/barclays-antony-jenkins-reputation.

230. Smriti (October 2023). "Pets.com Failure: Learn From One of the Biggest Innovation Failures." *InspireIP.* https://inspireip.com/pets-com-failure/.

231. C. Sagawa (July 2022). "Global Business Services (GBS): What Are They?" Day.IO https://day.io/blog/global-business-services-gbs-what-are-they/.

232. D. Pereira (May 2023). "Tesla Business Model." *The Business Model Analyst.* https://businessmodelanalyst.com/tesla-business-model/.

233. S. J. Berman (2012). "Digital Transformation: Opportunities to Create New Business Models." *Strategy & Leadership* 40(2): 16–24. https://www .emerald.com/insight/content/doi/10.1108/10878571211209314/full/html.

CHAPTER 16

234. M. Harris and A. Raviv (2002). "Organization Design." *Management Science* 48(7): 852–865. https://pubsonline.informs.org/doi/abs/10.1287/mnsc .48.7.852.2821.

235. S. Aronowitz et al. (June 2015). "Getting Organizational Redesign Right." McKinsey & Company. https://www.mckinsey.com/capabilities/people-and -organizational-performance/our-insights/getting-organizational-redesign-right.

236. E. van Vulpen. "Organizational Design: A Complete Guide." AIHR. https://www.aihr.com/blog/organizational-design/.

237. Explorance (June 2023). "5 Key Benefits of Organizational Development." https://explorance.com/blog/5-key-benefits-organizational-development/.

238. S. Cannon (January 2013). "The Organizational Structure of Zappos.com." StudyMode Research. https://www.studymode.com/essays/Organizational -Structure-Zappos-1789834.html.

239. S. Finerty (2012). Master the Matrix: 7 Essentials for Getting Things Done in Complex Organizations. Two Harbors Press.

240. *The Economist* (January 2006). "The Matrix Master." https://www .economist.com/special-report/2006/01/21/the-matrix-master.

241. For the Record. "About Spotify." https://newsroom.spotify.com/company -info/.

242. Business Mavericks (March 2023). "Spotify Organization Structure and Function in a Simplified Way." https://www.corporate-rebels.com/blog/spotify-1.

243. L. Mortlock (December 2016). "Canadian Oil and Gas Reorganizations." Ernst & Young. https://assets.ey.com/content/dam/ey-sites/ey-com/en_ca/topics/oil-and-gas/ey-canadian-oil-gas-reorganizations.pdf.

244. S. Kavale (2012). "The Connection Between Strategy and Structure." *International Journal of Business and Commerce* 1(6): 60–70. https://www.researchgate.net/profile/Dr-Kavale/publication/313444758_THE_CONNECTION_BETWEEN_STRATEGY_AND_STRUCTURE/links/589b017392851c8bb68443e1/THE-CONNECTION-BETWEEN-STRATEGY-AND-STRUCTURE.pdf.

245. Tutorial Point. "How Coca-Cola Fizzled Out on Globalization." https://www.tutorialspoint.com/organizational_design/organizational_design_case_study2.htm.

CHAPTER 17

246. J. Caforio. "Post-Merger Integration: Failing to Plan is Planning to Fail." RSM. https://rsmus.com/insights/industries/private-equity/post-merger-integration-failing-to-plan-is-planning-to-fail.html.

247. B. R. Kumar (2019). "Daimler–Chrysler Merger." In *Wealth Creation in the World's Largest Mergers and Acquisitions*. Management for Professionals. Springer. https://link.springer.com/chapter/10.1007/978-3-030-02363-8_44.

248. S. Seth (May 2021). "The 5 Biggest Mergers in History." *Investopedia*. https://www.investopedia.com/investing/biggest-mergers-in-history/.

249. M. J. Epstein (2005). "The Determinants and Evaluation of Merger Success." *Business Horizons* 48(1): 37–46. https://www.sciencedirect.com/science/article/pii/S0007681304000990.

250. T. Middleton (August 2019). "What 20 Acquisitions Taught Us About Post-Merger Integration." *Atlassian*. https://www.atlassian.com/blog/teamwork/post-merger-integration-tips.

251. L. Pines (July 2021). "4 Cases When M&A Strategy Failed for the Acquirer (EBAY, BAC)." *Investopedia*. https://www.investopedia.com

/articles/insights/061816/4-cases-when-ma-strategy-failed-acquirer-ebay
-bac.asp.

252. S. Maire and P. Collerette (2011). "International Post-Merger Integration: Lessons from an Integration Project in the Private Banking Sector." *International Journal of Project Management* 29(3): 279–294. https://www .sciencedirect.com/science/article/pii/S0263786310000517.

253. V. M. Papadakis (2005). "The Role of Broader Context and the Communication Program in Merger and Acquisition Implementation Success." *Management Decision* 43(2): 236–255. https://www.emerald.com /insight/content/doi/10.1108/00251740510581948/full/html.

CHAPTER 18

254. R. King (March 2022). "Should Government Leave Innovation to the Private Sector?" World Economic Forum. https://www.weforum.org/agenda/2022 /03/should-government-leave-innovation-to-the-private-sector/.

255. K. Leetaru (July 2016). "Why Does the Government Struggle So Much With Innovation?" *Forbes.* https://www.forbes.com/sites/kalevleetaru /2016/07/26/why-does-the-government-struggle-so-much-with-innovation /?sh=39db1dd01648.

256. M. Palmer (October 2021). "31% Of Companies Failed to Innovate During the Pandemic." *Sifted.* https://sifted.eu/articles/innovation-failure-pandemic.

257. L. Mortlock (November 2015). "Innovation: From Ideation to Activation." Ernst & Young. https://www.yumpu.com/en/document/view/55208160 /innovation-from-ideation-to-activation.

258. D. Salazar (February 2023). "The 10 Most Innovative Companies in Manufacturing of 2023." *Fast Company.* https://www.fastcompany.com /90848300/most-innovative-companies-manufacturing-2023.

259. S. Kirsner (July 2018). "The Biggest Obstacles to Innovation in Large Companies." *Harvard Business Review.* https://hbr.org/2018/07/the -biggest-obstacles-to-innovation-in-large-companies.

260. L. Gower (September 2015). "The Ten Barriers to Innovation." *Lucidity.* https://www.lucidity.org.uk/the-ten-barriers-to-innovation/.

261. F. Goh. "10 Companies That Failed to Innovate, Resulting in Business Failure." Collective Campus. https://www.collectivecampus.io/blog

/10-companies-that-were-too-slow-to-respond-to-change#:~:text=10%20
Companies%20That%20Failed%20To%20Innovate%2C%20Resulting%20In,
8%208.%20Compaq%20%281982%20%E2%80%93%202002%29%20More
%20items.

262. A. Basiouny (March 2018). "What Went Wrong: The Demise of Toys R Us."
Knowledge at Wharton. https://knowledge.wharton.upenn.edu/podcast
/knowledge-at-wharton-podcast/the-demise-of-toys-r-us/.

263. L. Mortlock and K. Ermelbauer (February 2024). "Cultivating Creativity:
The Dynamic Duo of Diversity and Innovation." *Chief Executive.* https://
chiefexecutive.net/cultivating-creativity-the-dynamic-duo-of
-diversity-and-innovation/.

264. E. Kim (May 2016). "How Amazon CEO Jeff Bezos Has Inspired People to
Think About the Way They Think About Failure." *Business Insider.* https://
www.businessinsider.com/how-amazon-ceo-jeff-bezos-thinks-about-failure
-2016-5.

265. S. Medley (January 2019). "Five Outstanding Examples of Innovation in
Business." Qmarkets. https://www.qmarkets.net/resources/article/titans-of
-transformation-5-outstanding-examples-of-innovation-in-business/.

266. H. Shaughnessy (May 2013). "What Makes Samsung Such an Innovative
Company?" *Forbes.* https://www.forbes.com/sites/haydnshaughnessy/2013
/03/07/why-is-samsung-such-an-innovative-company/?sh=bdc9eco2ad7e.

267. Samsung Newsroom (November 2023). "Samsung Electronics Ranked as a
Top Five Best Global Brand for the Fourth Consecutive Year." https://news
.samsung.com/global/samsung-electronics-ranked-as-a-top-five-best-global
-brand-for-the-fourth-consecutive-year.

268. S. J. Kline and N. Rosenberg (2010). "An Overview of Innovation." In *Studies
on science and the innovation process Selected works of Nathan Rosenberg*:
173–203. World Scientific. https://www.worldscientific.com/doi/abs/10.1142
/9789814273596_0009.

269. S. Arpajian (June 2019). "Five Reasons Why Innovation Fails." *Forbes.*
https://www.forbes.com/sites/forbestechcouncil/2019/06/04/five-reasons
-why-innovation-fails/?sh=c2ce8b614c6e.

270. J. B. Quinn (1985). "Innovation and Corporate Strategy: Managed Chaos."
Technology in Society 7(2-3): 263–279. https://www.sciencedirect.com
/science/article/pii/0160791X85900296.

CHAPTER 19

271. B. McBride et al. (July 2020). "If State and Local Governments Continue to Struggle, So Will America." CNN. https://www.cnn.com/2020/07/30 /opinions/stimulus-state-local-government-spending-cares-heals-act-big-7 /index.html.

272. UKEssays (January 2015). "Strategy Identification and Implementation of Ryanair." https://www.ukessays.com/essays/management/strategy -identification-and-implementation-of-ryanair-management-essay.php.

273. Harvard Business School (December 2015). "Ryanair: The lowest cost airline in Europe." https://d3.harvard.edu/platform-rctom/submission /ryanair-the-lowest-cost-airline-in-europe/.

274. P. Westberg (March 2024). "How Ryanair's Relentless Cost-Cutting Redefined the Airline Industry." *Quartr.* https://quartr.com/insights /company-research/how-ryanairs-relentless-cost-cutting-redefined-the -airline-industry.

275. L. Mortlock (September 2021). "Weathering Disruption: From Cost Management to Cost Excellence." *CEOWorld Magazine.* https://ceoworld .biz/2021/09/15/weathering-disruption-from-cost-management-to-cost -excellence/.

276. J. Tyler (October 2018). "Here Are IKEA's Secrets to Keeping its Prices So Low." *Business Insider.* https://www.businessinsider.com/why-ikea-is-so-cheap -2018-10.

277. B. Chaundy (July 2000). "Ikea's Self-Assembled Billionaire." *BBC News.* http://news.bbc.co.uk/2/hi/europe/855984.stm.

278. R. O'Byrne (May 2019). "7 Mini Case Studies: Successful Supply Chain Cost Reduction and Management." Logistics Bureau. https://www.logisticsbureau .com/7-mini-case-studies-successful-supply-chain-cost-reduction-and -management/.

279. L. Mortlock (September 2021). "Weathering Disruption: From Cost Management to Cost Excellence." *CEOWORLD Magazine.* https:// ceoworld.biz/2021/09/15/weathering-disruption-from-cost-management-to -cost-excellence/.

280. R. O'Byrne (May 2019). "7 Mini Case Studies: Successful Supply Chain Cost Reduction and Management." Logistics Bureau. https://www

.logisticsbureau.com/7-mini-case-studies-successful-supply-chain-cost
-reduction-and-management/.

281. A. Brown et al. "Cost Reduction: Bridging the Gap—Making Cost Savings Real and Making Them Stick." Deloitte. https://www2.deloitte.com/content /dam/Deloitte/ca/Documents/finance/ca-en-FA-cost-reduction-POV.PDF.

CHAPTER 20

282. Airfocus. "What is a Roadmap." https://airfocus.com/glossary/what-is-a -roadmap/.

283. L. Patten (2015). "The Continued Struggle with Strategy Execution." *International Journal of Business Management & Economic Research* 6(5): 288– 295. http://www.ijbmer.com/docs/volumes/vol6issue5/ijbmer2015060505.pdf.

284. D. Sull et al. (2015). "Why Strategy Execution Unravels—And What to Do About It." *Harvard Business Review* 93(3): 57-66. https://www.prisim.com /wp-content/uploads/2020/01/Why-Strategy-Execution-Unravels.pdf.

285. A. MacLennan (2010). *Strategy Execution: Translating Strategy into Action in Complex Organizations.* Routledge. https://www.taylorfrancis.com/books /mono/10.4324/9780203847336/strategy-execution-andrew-maclennan.

286. Wärtsilä. (October 2021). "Wärtsilä Commits to Carbon Neutrality by 2030." https://www.wartsila.com/media/news/26-10-2021-wartsila-commits-to -carbon-neutrality-by-2030-2995912.

287. J. Binder and V. Keller-Birrer (December 2023). "In the Field with Wärtsilä." IMD. https://www.imd.org/wp-content/uploads/2023/12/IMD-In-the -Field-with-Wartsila-article.pdf.

288. H. Trammell (March 2023). "Strategy Execution: 5 Organizations That Have Done It Well." *ClearPoint Strategy.* https://www.clearpointstrategy .com/blog/strategy-execution-examples.

289. B. Coggins (June 2020). "Transformation and resilience: An Interview with Best Buy's Executive Chairman Hubert Joly." McKinsey & Company. https:// www.mckinsey.com/capabilities/strategy-and-corporate-finance/our-insights /transformation-and-resilience-an-interview-with-best-buys-executive -chairman-hubert-joly.

290. S. Saleh (November 2021). "How to Build a Jira Project Plan and Portfolio

Roadmap." Jexo. https://jexo.io/blog/project-plans-and-jira-portfolio
-roadmaps/.

291.   N. Kumar and B. Rogers (January 2000). "EasyJet: The Web's Favorite
Airline." Harvard Business Publishing. https://hbsp.harvard.edu/produc
t/IMD099-HCB-ENG.

292.   C. Elliot (September 2021). "EasyJet CEO: Low Cost 'Doesn't Mean Low
Quality.'" *Forbes.* https://www.forbes.com/sites/christopherelliott/2021/09
/24/easyjet-ceo-low-cost-doesnt-mean-low-quality/?sh=44042a3a5961.

293.   K. Gibson (2024). "A Manager's Guide to Successful Strategy Implementation."
Business Insights. https://online.hbs.edu/blog/post/strategy-implementation.

294.   A. K. Srivastava (2017). "Alignment: The foundation of Effective Strategy
Execution." *International Journal of Productivity and Performance
Management* 66(8): 1043–1063. https://www.emerald.com/insight/content
/doi/10.1108/IJPPM-11-2015-0172/full/html.

295.   L. Mortlock (August 2023). "Teamwork Makes the Dreamwork—7 Principles
of Success." *Take-It-Personel-ly.* https://takeitpersonelly.com/2023/08/09
/teamwork-makes-the-dreamwork-7-principles-of-success/.

CHAPTER 21

296.   Magenest (June 2022). "Digital Transformation in the Oil and Gas Industry:
Definition, Examples, and Tips." https://magenest.com/en/digital
-transformation-in-the-oil-and-gas-industry/.

297.   H. Robinson (July 2019). "Why Do Most Transformations Fail? A
Conversation with Harry Robinson." McKinsey & Company. https://www
.mckinsey.com/capabilities/transformation/our-insights/why-do-most
-transformations-fail-a-conversation-with-harry-robinson.

298.   McKinsey & Company. "Perspectives on Transformation." https://www
.mckinsey.com/capabilities/transformation/our-insights/perspectives-on
-transformation.

299.   L. Mortlock (January 2020). "How Leadership Can Be Transformed in
the Digital Age." Ernst & Young. https://www.ey.com/en_ca/digital
/transformation/how-leadership-can-be-transformational-in-the-digital
-age.

300. Project Management Institute (April 2014). "The Project Management Office: Aligning Strategy & Implementation." https://www.pmi.org /-/media/pmi/documents/public/pdf/white-papers/pmo-strategy -implement.pdf.

301. Project Management Institute (April 2014). "The Project Management Office: Aligning Strategy & Implementation." https://www.pmi.org/-/media /pmi/documents/public/pdf/white-papers/pmo-strategy-implement.pdf.

302. S. Pellegrinelli et al. (2007). "The Importance of Context in Programme Management: An Empirical Review of Programme Practices." *International Journal of Project Management* 25(1): 41–55. https://www.sciencedirect.com /science/article/pii/S0263786306000998.

CONCLUSION

303. J. P. Morgan (January 2023). "2023 Market Outlook: Stocks Set to Fall Near-Term as Economic Growth Slows." https://www.jpmorgan.com/insights /research/market-outlook.

304. C. Wanna (December 2023). "JPMorgan Expects Stocks Volatility to Climb in 2024." *BNN Bloomberg.* https://www.bnnbloomberg.ca/jpmorgan-expects -stocks-volatility-to-climb-in-2024-1.2009184.

305. J. Seong et al. (November 2022). "Global Flows: The Ties that Bind in an Interconnected World." McKinsey & Company. https://www.mckinsey .com/capabilities/strategy-and-corporate-finance/our-insights/global-flows -the-ties-that-bind-in-an-interconnected-world.

306. A. Eira (April 2023). "72 Vital Digital Transformation Statistics: 2023 Spending, Adoption, Analysis & Data." Finances Online. https:// financesonline.com/digital-transformation-statistics/.

307. United Nations (February 2021). "Climate Change 'Biggest Threat Modern Humans Have Ever Faced', World-Renowned Naturalist Tells Security Council, Calls for Greater Global Cooperation." https://press.un.org/en /2021/sc14445.doc.htm.

308. Vistra (April 2023). "Experts Predict Continued Global Regulatory Complexity: What it Means for Businesses and Investors." https://www.vistra .com/insights/experts-predict-continued-global-regulatory-complexity-what -it-means-businesses-and

309. D. Gray (April 2021). "What Makes Successful Frameworks Rise Above the Rest." *MIT Sloan Management Review.* https://sloanreview.mit.edu/article/what-makes-successful-frameworks-rise-above-the-rest/.

310. L. Mortlock (2021). "Beyond Covid: The 10 Keys to Becoming Future-Ready." *Chief Executive.* https://chiefexecutive.net/beyond-covid-the-10-keys-to-becoming-future-ready/.

311. M. Roll (November 2019). "Leadership in the 21st Century." *Martin Roll.* https://martinroll.com/resources/articles/leadership/leadership-in-the-21st-century/.

312. J. Schwartz et al. (April 2019). "Leadership for the 21st Century: The Intersection of the Traditional and the New." *Deloitte Insights.* https://www2.deloitte.com/us/en/insights/focus/human-capital-trends/2019/21st-century-leadership-challenges-and-development.html.

313. D. Lancefield (November 2022). "How to Communicate Your Company's Strategy Effectively." *Harvard Business Review.* https://hbr.org/2022/11/how-to-communicate-your-companys-strategy-effectively.

314. Stanford University. "The AI Index Report: Measuring Trends in AI." https://aiindex.stanford.edu/report/.

315. R. Fry and K. Parker (November 2018). "Early Benchmarks Show 'Post-Millennials' on Track to Be Most Diverse, Best-Educated Generation Yet." *Pew Research Center.* https://www.pewresearch.org/social-trends/2018/11/15/early-benchmarks-show-post-millennials-on-track-to-be-most-diverse-best-educated-generation-yet/.

INDEX

The letter F following a page number denotes a figure; CS denotes a case study.

ABOUT THE AUTHOR

As the managing partner for the industrials and energy business at global professional services firm EY, Dr. Lance Mortlock's leadership responsibilities include oil and gas, power and utilities, advanced manufacturing and mobility, and mining and metals sectors across Canada. Lance supports the team in driving the growth of key client accounts, quality in delivery, and future services and offerings. Furthermore, Lance coordinates future thinking on industrial- and energy-related business trends, uncertainties, risks, and opportunities.

As a strategy practitioner working with the C-suite, Lance has provided consulting services for over 25 years on 190-plus projects to 80-plus clients in

11 countries. He brings a broad set of strategic skills and experiences, helping clients solve some of their most complex strategic problems. Areas of support and expertise include corporate strategy and planning, strategy execution, market opportunity assessment, merger and transaction integration and carve-outs, cost management, transformation, innovation, business management systems, process improvement, enterprise risk management, organization performance, and design and effectiveness.

Lance has authored more than 40 points of view on various essential business topics and is an expert in Canada's energy trends and market dynamics, with over 160 citations across multiple industry publications, national and international newspapers, and BNN. He is also an opinion columnist, external advisory board member for *CEOWORLD* magazine, and the author of *Disaster Proof: Scenario Planning for a Post-Pandemic Future*, which explores ways scenario planning can help organizations be more resilient, building shock absorbers during great uncertainty and drastic change.

Lance has an undergraduate degree from Exeter University, an MBA from Cardiff Business School, and a doctorate from the University of Calgary, Haskayne School of Business. He is a Certified Management Consultant, a Certified Change Management Professional, a Certified Six Sigma Black Belt, and a Project Management Professional. Lance completed a LEAD certificate in Corporate Innovation at Stanford GSB, advanced strategy at INSEAD, and an AI certificate from MIT. Lance also completed Harvard Business School's high-performance leadership program. Lance is an Adjunct Associate Professor at the University of Calgary, Haskayne School of Business.

Lance is married to Elisabeth, and they have two daughters, Penelope and Olivianne.